"An urgent, necessary, and essential book by one of the most important Christian voices of our time. Christianity is in danger of being hijacked for purposes that would subvert not only the longstanding traditions of Christian social teaching but, more fundamentally, the Gospel itself."
—FR. JAMES MARTIN, SJ, editor at large, *America Media*

"The prophetic voice of Jim Wallis is never more welcome or more needed than it is now; his voice is always reliable, well informed, and emitting great moral passion. . . . Wallis insists simply that the truth be told about our common pathology and about the deep claim of the Gospel. Along the way, his riff on 'woke' in the New Testament is worth the price of the book. This is Wallis at his courageous best; he is the real thing; attention must be paid."
—WALTER BRUEGGEMANN, Columbia Theological Seminary

"I am comforted and inspired by this book. Pastor Wallis calls Christians to their conscience and all people to action: live and breathe ancient wisdom that call us to see the divinity in every human." —RABBI JONAH DOV PESNER, director, Religious Action Center of Reform Judaism

"Jim Wallis is a national treasure. In this powerful new book, he focuses our attention on the pernicious problem of American racism, but more importantly he inspires us to never give up hope on the great promise of American pluralism." —EBOO PATEL, founder and president of Interfaith America; author of *We Need To Build*

"A must-read, eye-opening, high alert for everyone who cares that our precious democracy and increasingly multicultural America lie perilously on the chopping block." —DR. BARBARA WILLIAMS-SKINNER, co-convener, National African American Clergy Network and author of *I Prayed, Now What?*

"A powerful and essential roadmap on how to save the church from the heresy of white Christian nationalism and save our fragile democracy from the real and present danger of racialized fascism by reclaiming the transformational teachings and witness of Jesus." —REV. ADAM RUSSELL TAYLOR, president, Sojourners, author of *A More Perfect Union*

"Insightful books analyzing white Christian nationalism have begun appearing. But Jim Wallis asks the next crucial question—What does this mean for the church? His prophetic answer should galvanize our attention: a 'Remnant Church,' shaped by repentance, return, and restoration. Beyond analysis, this book provides clear answers which offer the hope of real transformation." —WESLEY GRANBERG-MICHAELSON, general secretary emeritus, Reformed Church in America; author of *Without Oars: Casting Off into a Life of Pilgrimage*

"Wallis rightly notes that the need for justice and equity is greater than ever and implores us to reclaim the Jesus of the Gospels in the face of the white Christian nationalism that threatens our democracy, our faith, our common life." —THE MOST REV. MICHAEL B. CURRY, presiding bishop of The Episcopal Church, author of *Love is the Way*

"At this hinge point of American history, this book is an important and urgent call for white Christians to undertake a new discipleship out of whiteness and to unequivocally declare their support for the equality of all." —ROBERT P. JONES, president and founder, Public Religion Research Institute; author of *The Hidden Roots of White Supremacy and the Path to a Shared American Future*

"*The False White Gospel* is an Altar Call. It is an essential book for anyone seeking a deeper understanding of the challenges confronting our society today. It serves as both a sobering reminder and a powerful catalyst for change, urging us to rise above the destructive forces that threaten to erode the foundations of our democracy." —BISHOP VASHTI MURPHY MCKENZIE, president/general secretary, National Council of Churches of Christ in the USA

THE
FALSE
WHITE
GOSPEL

THE
FALSE
WHITE
GOSPEL

Rejecting Christian Nationalism,
Reclaiming True Faith,
and Refounding Democracy

JIM WALLIS

ST. MARTIN'S
ESSENTIALS
NEW YORK

First published in the United States by St. Martin's Essentials, an
imprint of St. Martin's Publishing Group

THE FALSE WHITE GOSPEL. Copyright © 2024 by Jim Wallis.
All rights reserved. Printed in the United States of America. For
information, address St. Martin's Publishing Group, 120 Broadway,
New York, NY 10271.

www.stmartins.com

The Library of Congress Cataloging-in-Publication Data is available
upon request.

ISBN 978-1-250-29189-9 (hardcover)
ISBN 978-1-250-29190-5 (ebook)

Our books may be purchased in bulk for promotional,
educational, or business use. Please contact your local
bookseller or the Macmillan Corporate and Premium Sales
Department at 1-800-221-7945, extension 5442, or by email at
MacmillanSpecialMarkets@macmillan.com.

First Edition: 2024

10 9 8 7 6 5 4 3 2 1

I believe in the next generation and think they are going to change things significantly. Therefore, this book is dedicated to my sons, Luke and Jack; my new daughter-in-law, Anna-Sophia; and to my students who encourage me every day.

If you want Peace, work for Justice.

—Pope Paul VI

January 1, 1972

CONTENTS

FOREWORD

THE LOVE BATTLE TO SAVE
THE SOUL OF AMERICA

WE ARE IN A BATTLE FOR THE SOUL OF AMERICA. BUT IT IS NOT, AND HAS never been, simply a political battle. Ours is a moral struggle over who we take ourselves to be and what kind of country we want to live in. The moral question sits at the heart of our troubles today. It has been a central question since the founding of the Republic and the moment of crisis when it felt as if the entire experiment would fall apart. On the eve of the Civil War, in his first inaugural address, President Lincoln understood the moral gravity of the moment. "I am loath to close," he said:

> We are not enemies, but friends. We must not be enemies. Though passion may have strained it must not break our bonds of affection. The mystic chords of memory, stretching from every battlefield and patriot grave to every living heart and hearthstone all over this broad land, will yet swell the chorus of the Union, when again touched, as surely they will be, by the better angels of our nature.*

---

* Abraham Lincoln's First Inaugural Address, March 4, 1861; https://avalon.law.yale .edu/19th_century/lincoln1.asp.

Lincoln's words were a hopeful and desperate gesture: an appeal to those preparing for war that they would, instead, reach for their better angels and not secede from the union. But at the heart of the American experiment, and Lincoln understood this intimately, rested a distorting and disfiguring view: that some people, because of the color of their skin, ought to be (dare I say must be) valued more than others. This view took shape in the context of a country committed, at once, to the ideals of democracy and to the evil of slavery. And that contradiction threatened to rend the soul of the nation.

But the break had already happened. Before one cannon was fired at Fort Sumter, American Christendom had split over the issue of slavery. The Civil War had already begun over the moral question of holding another human being as chattel. Some Christians found religious justification for their greed and prejudices. Others condemned the practice. Those held in bondage and who bore the brunt of the cruelty of slavery dared, as the theologian Howard Thurman said, to redeem the religion profaned in their midst. This dramatic split would come to characterize the nation's religious landscape as race segregated the idea of the beloved community and many were willing to die and kill to maintain it all. Frederick Douglass would put the point more poignantly: "The slave auctioneer's bell and the church-going bell chime in with each other, and the bitter crises of the heart-broken slave are drowned in the religious shouts of his pious master."

The historian David Wills has insisted that one way to tell the story of American religious history is through this "encounter of black and white," an encounter that "occurred within the context of a slave system"* and the world it created that colors how we see each other and how we imagine being together. And here we are over 160 years after Lincoln's

---

* David Wills, "The Central Themes of American Religious History: Pluralism, Puritanism, and the Encounter of Black and White," in *African-American Religion: Interpretative Essays in History and Culture*, eds. Timothy E. Fulop and Albert J. Raboteau (New York: Routledge, 1997), 15.

first inaugural address still grappling with the moral question of who we take ourselves to be and how a certain distorted view of Christianity sanctifies our hatreds and fears. Will we reach for our better angels?

Jim Wallis has spent a lifetime bearing witness in the face of injustice. He has worked diligently to organize faith communities and leaders to cast away the idolatry of race and to live the gospel. In this powerful book, *The False White Gospel*, he takes on the latest American expression of white Christianity. Without mincing his words, he understands that white Christian nationalists have clothed their hatreds in the garments of their faith. They sacralize power and worship at the altar of autocrats who all too often profane the message of Jesus. These are the descendants of those who so easily reconciled Christianity with slavery and Jim Crow. But Jim Wallis, as he has always done, refuses to sit by silently as these forces hijack his tradition. He understands that this moment is a moral crisis that cries out for courage and conviction and, especially, for Christians to defend their faith by finally leaving behind the idea that some people ought to be valued more than others. And he provides the tools for the fight with Scriptures and commentary that guide our hearts, our minds, and our actions. His is an invitation to us all to engage in the moral battle.

In February 1960, James Baldwin spoke at Kalamazoo College in Michigan. The talk would be published the next year in his book, *Nobody Knows My Name*. It is a fascinating meditation on the idea of America and the so-called problem of minorities. With typical insight and power, Baldwin insisted that "what we really have to do is to create a country in which there are no minorities—for the first time in the history of the world." But, for me, it is how he arrives at this piercing insight—through an interrogation of the role and place of Black people in American life and our view of God—that speaks to the power of *The False White God*. He wrote:

> [T]he role of the Negro in American life has something to with our concept of what God is, and from my point of view, this concept is not big

enough. It has got to be made much bigger because God is, after all, not anybody's toy. To be with God is really to be involved with some enormous, overwhelming desire, and joy, and power which you cannot control, which controls you. I conceived of my own life as a journey toward something I do not understand, which in the going toward, makes me better. I conceive of God, in fact as a means of liberation and not a means to control others. Love does not begin and end the way we seem to think it does. Love is a battle, love is a war; love is growing up.*

God cannot be shackled to the evils of white supremacy nor imprisoned in communities that claim Him as their possession. Baldwin insists that to be with God involves something more expansive and evolving—that it is in "the going towards" that we grow and are made better. Jim Wallis preaches this every day and, in this book, he calls the nation to grow up and he calls us all to fight the love battle to save the soul of America.

—Eddie S. Glaude, Jr.

---

* *James Baldwin: Collected Essays*, ed. Toni Morrison (New York: The Library of America, 1998), 220.

INTRODUCTION

CROSSING THE COLOR LINE

THE ROOM TOLD THE STORY. FACING ONE ANOTHER AROUND THE TABLE WAS a diverse group of young pastors mostly from several southern states. Every Black pastor in the room spoke up, feeling safe in that space to be their authentic selves and offer their voices of deep and urgent concern about what was happening in our country and to their own communities—and congregations.

Several Hispanic and Asian American clergy broadened the conversation. The white pastors, now in a multiracial room, represented both large and smaller Protestant churches—Methodist, Presbyterian, Baptist, Episcopal, and Lutheran. They came from quite different theological backgrounds, from mainline liberal to evangelical, and many places in between. "I am orthodox," some said, "but I don't just go along with the right or the left." There were also Catholic clergy in the room, seeking new relationships with Protestants for their ministries in local communities.

We were in Georgia, and like in many other states represented around this very diverse faith table, voting rights and the real threats of voter suppression fueled the conversation. Efforts currently underway to make it harder—once again—for people of color to vote, and have their votes fairly counted, were discussed with newfound urgency. The late congressman John Lewis, who had been a member of Ebenezer Baptist Church, just down the road from where we were sitting, was remembered for calling votes precious and "almost sacred" because they allowed all of God's children to have their voices heard in public life.

One of the new voting restrictions recently passed by the white-dominated Georgia legislature made it illegal to provide drinks or snacks to people standing in line to vote (and everyone knew that the lines to vote are always longest in communities of color). It didn't take these pastors long to recall Jesus' words in the twenty-fifth chapter of the gospel of Matthew about providing water to the thirsty and food to the hungry. They wondered, engaging the question seriously, would a pastor doing that at Black and brown polling places in the next election get arrested for civil disobedience?

I had spoken at the Chandler School of Theology at Emory University the previous evening at a TheoEd, theological/spiritual TED talk, and was spending the morning with these young pastors to unpack the event. My talk had directly addressed the rise of white Christian nationalism in our country, the false white gospel that was now being preached by many white megachurches, some just blocks away. In many white Evangelical circles, faith was being directly politicized, and congregational members who didn't share a right-wing partisan agenda were being told to leave. The Black pastors around the table expressed their fears about this rise of white Christian nationalism in churches in their own cities and states—and its deliberate embrace by politicians with a racialized autocratic agenda (with some members of Congress wearing T-shirts with "Christian Nationalist" proudly emblazoned on them).

Then we heard from the white pastors in the room. They shared their own fears that now, even in their mainline denominations, truth-telling in our nation about race and American history was increasingly met with aggressive pushback from many white congregants.

They shared stories of pastors under attack for honest and even healing talk about race. Cable news channels, right-wing radio, and conspiratorial webcasts were overwhelming any gospel justice talk. A megachurch pastor had recently said to me, "Jim, I only have my people for two hours a week if I'm lucky, and Fox has them twenty-four seven. I just can't compete." These young clerics knew pastors who had lost their jobs and some who were even getting death threats.

"I need my salary and my parsonage to take care of my family," said a young female pastor. "I'm being told by my senior pastor that we need to respect the demographics of our top donors," lamented a young white male pastor, who was clearly frustrated by what he called a "consumer" approach to church—give the people what they want instead of telling the truth "that will set us free," as Jesus taught.

The Black pastors were challenging and pleading with their white pastor colleagues to tell the truth about our nation's racial history to help equip the country to grow into a genuine multiracial democracy. But the white pastors were all *counting the cost* of doing that. "I feel such a great tension between my professional demands and my prophetic callings," one young pastor told us. Truth, risk, and cost were all issues on the table that day as these pastors took time to be together, look each other in the eyes, and talk and pray with one another.

I suggested that, perhaps, this was a "Bonhoeffer moment" for the American church. They all knew who Dietrich Bonhoeffer was. A young pastor like themselves, he led the "confessing church" movement in opposition to the rise of Nazism in Germany during the 1930s. These were a small minority of churches who dissented from the acquiescence and loyalty of most German churches to Hitler's rise to power. In particular, the confessing church was marked by a younger generation of seminarians whom Bonhoeffer taught and some even lived in community, and whose life together became central to the Christian resistance to the Third Reich. I told them that history doesn't repeat but it often does rhyme, in the words of Mark Twain, and the rise of another racialized authoritarian movement in America—right now—also calls us to a faithful response.

Reflecting on Bonhoeffer and asking together what a confessing church might look like in America now turned into an amazing and insightful conversation—one that I hope to see happening across the country. Where is that Christian resistance emerging now, and where is the true gospel being recovered and reclaimed in response to the false white gospel of Christian nationalism now on the rise? I reminded them that Bonhoeffer failed in his attempt to stop Hitler and was executed in the end—hanged by the Nazis, along with many of his seminarians, in a concentration camp only days before the Allies arrived. But, I asked, how many of the German church pastors who supported Hitler do they remember now? None, of course. The witness of Bonhoeffer later inspired the South African churches as they helped bring down the apartheid regime; and now we were talking about him again.

The truth-telling about racial justice and reconciliation that we now need will, indeed, cost some pastors their jobs and pensions and parsonages; and it will lead to other pastors and leaders of predominantly white churches losing significant numbers of their congregants. A yet unknown number of white Christian leaders will find the courage to stand up while others submit to the "cheap grace" that Bonhoeffer warned against. There will be churches that stay open and faithful to the inclusive and reconciling gospel, despite the loss of some of their members, and new members—especially young people—may *join them* because of their authenticity and courage.

The suffering that comes with the courage to stand against the rise of authoritarian racism cost Bonhoeffer and other resistors to Hitler their very lives. Indeed, one of the pastors in the room that morning recalled a quote by Bonhoeffer, "When Christ calls a man, he bids him come and die." But what it might mean to die to self and live for the gospel truth of Christ is yet to be known in our time, and these young pastors were all wrestling with that.

While we can and must work against such violent outcomes, it is increasingly clear that voting rights, racial equality, civic justice, and democracy itself are now at serious risk in America—and that is becoming an understatement. This is a time of testing—*both* for the future of our democracy and for the integrity of our faith communities.

We are literally in a battle now between false religion and true faith and between racial fascism and multicultural democracy. That fight stems from fear, the motivator of hate, and the threat of violence. Helping to set us free from that fear, hate, racism, and violence is the purpose of this book.

I had said in my talk the previous evening that "crossing the color line" is the pilgrimage that has, and continues to change my life. I believe that crossing the color line to a genuine multiracial democracy will be the path that finally fulfills America's promise. And where the congregations of all faith traditions stand in this battle for the soul of America will define the authenticity of our faith at this critical historical moment. It will also determine whether a new generation will have any interest in embracing any of our faith communities. Like growing numbers of young people around the country, many of my students at Georgetown are not currently practicing any religion and are in the "none of the above" religious affiliation category. But most of these "nones" still believe in God or something beyond themselves, and are looking for authenticity and courage in both leaders and institutions.

Democracy, faith, and the generational future of our faith communities are all at stake. If communities of faith today won't fight for a multiracial democracy in this country, both will fail. My hope in writing this book is that it will help spark some of the deeper conversations and action that we crucially need right now and going forward. It is, finally, *only* the truth that can set us free, as Jesus indeed taught us. Together let us seek the truth for times like this.

PILGRIMAGE TO THE INNER CITY

My first conversion came when a revival preacher spoke at our church one Sunday night and pointed his finger right at me—it felt like—and all the other "unsaved" kids who were made to sit in the front row for the special service. With fire and brimstone, he proclaimed, "If Jesus came back tonight, your mommy and daddy would be taken to heaven, and you would be left all by yourself!"

That got my attention. I was getting up in years—six—and realized that if what the preacher said were to happen, I would have a five-year-old sister to support! My caring mother reassured me Christianity was not about the wrath of God, but that God loved me and wanted me to be his child too. That sounded much better, so I signed up.

My second conversion, and the one which has stayed with me and continues to change my life—as conversions are supposed to do—came when I was a teenager.

I was born and raised in Detroit—the Motor City, Motown. When I was about sixteen, I began to listen to my city—hear the news, read the paper, then some books, and I started to have serious conversations with adults.

Some big questions emerged and I began to feel that something "very big" was very wrong in my city and my country and my church; but I found that people in my white neighborhood, white school, and white church didn't want to talk about it.

I remember the questions I asked:

"Life in white Detroit seems very different from life in Black Detroit. Why is that? I hear about people and families who are poor and even hungry in our city, who don't have enough jobs, or good ones, who live in bad housing and in rough and dangerous places, and many who have family members in jail. I don't know anybody who struggles with these awful things; so how come others do and just a few short miles from where we live?

"I hear there are Black churches. How come we have never been told about them; why haven't we ever visited them or been visited by them?"

The answers from my white church and world were: "You're too young to ask those questions; when you get older you will understand." Or,

"We don't know why things are that way either, but they have always been this way."

The most honest answer I received was: "If you keep asking those kinds of questions you are going to get into a lot of trouble." That was the only answer that later proved to be true.

I realized that I wasn't going to get any real answers to those questions in the world where I lived, so I decided to travel outside my world, to make a personal pilgrimage into another world to find the answers. Now I tell my students to trust their questions and follow them to wherever they lead.

Then, I took my naïve white-boy questions into what we called "the inner city" to try and find out why Black Detroit seemed so different from white Detroit, and why we were so separated, even—and especially—in our churches.

I needed money for college, so I looked for jobs that would place me alongside young Black men in the city of Detroit who might have some answers. In those new jobs I began to listen to their life stories, stories that were very different from mine, stories that would ultimately change my story.

I also went to Black churches—just showed up—and was immediately welcomed in, with patient and generous answers to my many obvious questions. What they said sounded like what I thought Christianity was supposed to be. But I began to realize it was very different to be a Black Christian than a white Christian in Detroit and America.

Perhaps the greatest "epiphany" came when Butch, a new friend, who was a fellow janitor and elevator operator (yes, I am that old!), took me home for dinner one night to meet his family. We discussed the local police, whose treatment of Black people was sparking many confrontations in our city of Detroit. "I tell my children," Butch's mother told me, "if you are ever lost and can't find your way home and you see a white policeman, duck under a stairwell or hide behind a building and wait till he passes before you find your way home on your own."

I was deeply struck by that advice from a mother who wasn't any kind of political militant, but was completely focused on raising and protecting her kids—just like my mother. And at that moment, my own mom's words to her five children just screamed into my head. She told all of us, "If you are ever lost and can't find your way home, *look* for a policeman; policemen are your friends. They will take you by the hand and bring you home safely." Loving mothers who gave completely different advice to their children if they were white or Black. Two mothers. Two cities. Two worlds. Butch and I were born in the same city, but we lived in different countries—and so did our families.

The more I listened across color lines, the more I learned how that different standards applied to everything else too. Across the color line I found a different world, still waiting to be fully, freely, and safely included in America.

JIM CROW IS WEARING A SUIT

Later in life I realized that most of my mentors had also crossed the color line in America—white people making their own pilgrimages into Black communities and churches, and Black leaders venturing into white society and power structures to try and make things better, more just, more human, and more faithful to what our Christian faith calls all of us to be and do. I've learned it is *proximity* that changes us, that teaches us white people the work that we must do in our own communities.

Ironically, and prophetically, Dietrich Bonhoeffer also crossed the color line. During the year he spent at Union Seminary in New York City, he would visit Abyssinian Baptist Church in Harlem every Sunday. This young, white German pastor was likely one of the few white people in that Black congregation from week to week. Scholars, like Reggie Williams, have since shown that Bonhoeffer's encounter with

Black theology, preaching, worship, and music decisively shaped the development and formation of the confessing church in Germany, after he returned to his country, though he knew it might cost him his life.[1]

My own world view has been most shaped by being in places I was never supposed to be, and meeting people I was never supposed to know or listen to or become friends with. Even though I've said the wrong things at times and have made mistakes along the way, this was how I learned that racism was more than personal. It was structural.

Let's compare Butch's family to my family.

My father, James Wallis, Sr., graduated from college, was commissioned in the US Navy, and got married—all on the same day! The military was pushing new troops out to the war in Europe, and to the Pacific where he was sent. When he came home, like all other white World War II veterans, his family was eligible for an FHA loan for a first house and the GI bill to pay for any education they wanted. Every house in our Redford Township neighborhood, next to Detroit, was a three-bedroom ranch headed by a World War II GI like my dad. But no Black sailors on my dad's ship or Black GIs serving anywhere in the military were able to get those huge benefits for housing and education that catapulted white families into the middle class.

That racial exclusion from the biggest affirmative action program in American history was a deliberate racializing of geography. This made my neighborhood, school, and church all white, which was the exact purpose of these racist policies. No racist jokes were allowed in my house, because we were Christians, but the deeper issues were never understood or discussed.

Racism, I learned, shaped everything from voting rights to civil rights, from economic life to educational opportunities, to policing and criminal justice, to health care, to the safety of your kids, and who you go to church with.

So where are we now? Is the incremental progress we have made enough? Many whites I know wish it were, while Black people I talk to don't think so. Slavery is in the past, white people say, and many people want to believe that the Civil Rights Movement fixed everything. So can we finally put the issue of race behind us? And just stop talking about it?

No, we can't.

Now *more than ever* it is time to seek the truth, and understand what's happening in America today. And crossing the color line is what creates the proximity that turns distant groups into people with whom our lives are connected by relationships.

America's original sin of racism with a human hierarchy based on skin color still lingers, and has continued to "evolve" in the words of criminal justice leader Bryan Stevenson.[2] Jim Crow is now wearing a suit, instead of sheets, and is once again making a comeback to prevent a united democratic future.

Here is the new strategy of white supremacy in modern terms—in a single sentence: *to prevent our changing demography from changing our democracy.* It is a commitment to white minority rule by any and all means necessary: covert and overt voter suppression, racial gerrymandering in reshaping representational political districts, restricted immigration, election denial with electoral corruption and manipulation, judicial bias all the way to the Supreme Court, and, when all else fails, the promotion of political violence, as January 6 revealed to us—with the threat of more of all of the above to come.

Today's racism is the resurgence of the old ideology combined with the return of an old heresy. That is the false gospel of white Christian nationalism. Its very name spells its heresy—"white" instead of the diverse human calling the message of the gospel makes; "Christian" but implying domination instead of service; and "nationalism," which is contrary to Jesus' Great Commission, where he tells his followers to go into all the world and make disciples in every nation.

White Christian nationalism doesn't cross lines, it creates them. It seeks to divide us, leading this country down a path that starts with fear, that turns to hate, and ultimately leads to violence. White Christian nationalism defies what Jesus says about loving our neighbor, and even our enemies.

This isn't only important in politics or in Washington, or relegated to the fate of faith communities, but impacts all of us. This is a battle for the soul of the nation and will be fought in all our communities and neighborhoods, in what we teach in our schools, what we preach in our many different congregations, what we vote for in all our elections from top to bottom—from the president, to members of Congress and senators, to our governors and secretaries of state, attorneys general, state legislators, school boards, and even down to our local election officials. And now from our media discussions to our Thanksgiving dinners with family, to our small Bible study and prayer groups—it is time to tell the truth.

Crossing the color line for democracy is the beginning of the journey to repent, repair, and redeem America's original sin for white people, and especially for white Christians.

Crossing the color line is what opens the world for us, letting us find the truth that will set us free—from the bondage and baggage of white supremacy—and creates a network of creative, caring, and bonding relationships that will become the foundation and fabric for the common good; and that will help take us toward the vision of what our nation's civil rights leaders have called the "beloved community."

Faith communities have a key role to play here. If we as people of faith can help a divided and polarized nation cross that color line to democracy, we will be the peacemakers, whom Jesus calls the children of God. And that role must be played alongside people of many religions and no religion at all. What we agree upon is that the deepest issues now in our public life are *moral* and not just *political*; and that all of us, together, will be necessary to save the soul of the nation.

Jesus is a victim of identity theft in America. Instead of wearing a bracelet that says "What Would Jesus Do?" or WWJD, it's time to ask what *did* Jesus *say,* and what did he *do.* And to ask ourselves if we are willing to say and do that too. It's time to invite Jesus to bring his true identity back—especially in the churches. Time to let Jesus do the talking and for us to do the listening—and following.

Let's get started.

1

THE FALSE WHITE GOSPEL

LOOKING BACK ON MY TEENAGE YEARS IN DETROIT, I REMEMBER WHEN A concerned elder in my evangelical church took me aside one night to set me straight. I will never forget what he said: "You need to understand, son, that Christianity has nothing to do with racism—that's political and our faith is personal."

It hit me hard. If the thing that was tearing me up, turning me upside down, and changing me had nothing to do with my faith, then I wanted nothing to do with that kind of religion either. That was the night I left my childhood church and faith—in my head and my heart. Skeptical of the church, I joined the movements of my generation against racism, war, and poverty—but not as a person of faith. I was secular now. If Christianity had nothing to offer the downtrodden and discriminated among us, I wanted nothing to do with it.

I didn't have the words to respond to that elder on that night, but I found them later when I came back to faith in Jesus after years of organizing in social movements: *God is personal, but never private.*

For that elder in the Detroit church of my youth, and for many white Christians today, faith is a private affair—it's only about them and God, only about their own personal sins, only a vertical faith and not a horizontal one that reaches out to the world. They fail to understand the verse I was forced to memorize as a kid, John 3:16:

"For God so loved the world, that he gave his only begotten son, that whosoever believes in him shall not perish but have everlasting life."

We always skipped the first part about God loving the world. We never prayed that God would change us so that we could change the world. Jesus ushered in what he called "the kingdom of God," a whole *new order,* so that we might learn to *love the world,* rather than to just be *saved from the world.*

Without any awareness of the *public discipleship* which Jesus taught, Christians become vulnerable and susceptible to false political religion. And that is what white Christian nationalism is—a *false white gospel.*

White Christians can become tempting or even unconscious targets of ethnocentric religion that is contrary to the gospel of Jesus Christ. Easily politicized by power brokers, this bad religion can infect the body politic by manipulating the body of Christ.

Many won't recognize themselves in the term "white Christian nationalist," but they have become subject to the fears and anger that it promotes. And having only a private faith, they miss the heart of the Lord's prayer that many pray week to week, "Thy kingdom come, thy will be done, *on earth as it is in heaven.*" My hope and prayer is that even some of those who have unwittingly and tacitly adopted white Christian nationalism can be set free from it. Then they can become part of the movement for change and the restoration of both faith and democracy in America.

CALLING OUT FAITH

I am not treating this simply as a political problem and certainly not just as an academic debate about religion, but rather as a faith problem that needs to be solved for both believers and for the sake of the country.

The success of any movement depends on knowing who can be persuaded and who must be defeated—nonviolently, but definitively in the national narrative and at the ballot box. The wealthy and powerful who "win at all costs," the political operatives who are manipulating people for their own autocratic, racist, and economic ends must be fought and defeated in moral debates and in critical elections even now before us. But there are also many people whom I pray we can help set free from their blindness and fear; with an empathetic call to recognize and reclaim their faith and seek to love their neighbors not as "others," but as other children of God. This book is for anyone willing to move into a deeper conversation about faith and willing to take that crucial faith discussion to all those you know and love who may be willing to hear.

This book isn't only for Christians but for our brothers and sisters in other faith traditions, and with no faith at all. When we see a *civic promotion of fear, hate, and violence* as the trajectory of our politics, we need a *civic faith of love, healing, and hope* to defeat it. And that must involve all of us—religious or not. Loving our neighbor, and learning to practice the politics of love, will be central to the future of democracy in America. That will be a *civic discipleship*.

The purpose of this book is to call out faith—specifically the "Christian" in white Christian nationalism—to finally correct and convert the other terms in the phrase—white and nationalism—inviting all who can be persuaded to resist and help dismantle a false gospel that propagates white supremacy and political autocracy. But that can only be done by calling out faith.

My faith has often been called out.

I remember the first time I preached in the Ebenezer Baptist Church in Atlanta, Georgia. Entering that historic pulpit, where Martin Luther King, Jr., and other heroic leaders like John Lewis had been preachers, leaders, and members, felt quite intimidating and overwhelming for me as a young white preacher.

I began timidly. But right away a voice boomed at me from the front row. "C'mon, son, you're supposed to preach!" That perked me up a bit, but he kept going, "Aw, you're not there yet, keep going now!" Slowly, I began to find my voice, in cadence with his "amens," "ahas," "oh yeahs," and "yes, lords!" After I was done, I rushed down to him.

"You just pulled that sermon out of me!" I exclaimed. This very tall man stood up, put his hands on my shoulders, and said, "Son, I have raised up many preachers in my time." He was, of course, the "amen corner" of Ebenezer Baptist Church and he truly had raised up many preachers and others to find their faith and their voice. Indeed, the Black churches in America have often called out genuine faith to their brothers and sisters in white churches—and many of us have recognized that true voice of faith.

We will need many amen corners today to raise up the faith of us all, and to reach out to those who are now oblivious, stuck, conformed, and captive to the ideology and idolatry of white Christian nationalism that is leading us into such great danger.

Together we will examine why white Christian nationalism is such a rising threat and then turn our attention to six basic and iconic biblical texts. These Scriptures are at the heart of what biblical faith means and what Jesus has called us to do. It is time to explicate these Scriptures anew and ask: Do we believe this and act accordingly, or not? These biblical passages, reframed and refreshed for this time of crisis, could call many back to faith—that leads to action.

Can I get an "amen"?

THE MORAL CRISIS WE FACE

We are facing a political and even violent clash of opposite beliefs in either rejecting or accepting a multiracial democracy in America. January 6, 2021, signaled the failure of politics to find a peaceful resolution for our deep cultural polarization around the central conflict of whether human beings from different races, nations, classes, and gender backgrounds can live together peaceably and share equal power in a democratic American future. The answer is either yes or no, and each of us must make a choice. That is true for every American and every Christian.

This crisis is historical, in place since the country's founding—even before—but it now comes to a crescendo as we move from a white majority nation to a country where multiple minorities will soon be the majority—the elephant in the room for almost every political discussion in America today.

This crisis is also a moral and spiritual one with many church communities having been co-opted by, and actively participating in, America's growing polarization. Instead of seeking to build bridges to help navigate a new nation as racially diverse as the global body of Christ, some increasingly vocal Christian leaders are propping up the very segregation that the apostle Paul called on the church to reject. Every pastor can see those critical decisions being lived out among their congregations and parishes, and every preacher with integrity must make these choices clear on the basis of the gospel.

Some national figures, scholars, church leaders, culture watchers, and journalists have been urging us to confront a rising ideology that is rooted in America's original sin: the sin of white supremacy. The armed groups and individuals who are motivated by white supremacy are now judged to be the greatest domestic terrorist threat to our country's security today by many law enforcement authorities. That *old ideology* of white supremacy is now religiously undergirded by an *old heresy*—with a new name: white Christian nationalism. I believe that white Christian nationalism is the single greatest threat to democracy in America and to the integrity of the Christian witness.

These choices that we all must make will have concrete moments and milestones. Election day 2024 will show and perhaps even determine whether democracy will survive or collapse in America due to legal, extra-legal, corrupt, and even violent action amidst racial and social conflict. This is now our clearest and most present danger.

When politics fail, faith communities can offer a way forward because they are founded on the very equality that makes any diverse human community possible—because all human beings are made in the image of God (Genesis 1:26). Do we believe that or not? That is the moral question of our day. Will we practice a politics of the image of God?

WHITE CHRISTIAN NATIONALISM
IS A FAKE CHRISTIANITY

As noted earlier, the strategy of white Christian nationalism is to prevent our changing demography from changing our democracy. And to distort and manipulate religion for those false ends. American demographic changes cannot be halted. But too many white people and their political leaders want to prevent those changes from affecting the outcomes of elections and public policy decisions. And too many of those white power holders consistently fan the flames of white grievances and fears in their constituents in order to hold on to their political power. To put it even more bluntly: the strategy is to ensure white minority rule.

I believe that white Christian nationalism has now become the principal obstruction to achieving multiracial democracy. But it cannot just be defeated politically. It must be addressed at a deeper level, theologically and spiritually. We need a *theology of democracy*.

University of Oklahoma sociology professor Samuel Perry, the co-author of two books on Christian nationalism, writes:

> The fact is, Christian nationalist ideology—particularly when it is held by white Americans—is fundamentally anti-democratic because its goal isn't "government of the people, by the people, and for the people." Its goal is power. Specifically, power for "true Americans like us"— Christians in an almost ethnic sense—who are deemed worthy to belong and govern this country. Stemming from the prior history of "Dominionist" theology, the most salient threat white Christian nationalism poses to democracy is that it seeks to undermine the very foundation of democracy itself: voting.[1]

How did we get here?

HISTORICAL PRECEDENTS

White Christian nationalism is not new. It has been with us since before the founding of the United States, from the first landings of European explorers and settlers to the American continents—the homelands of Indigenous peoples. What is now called the Doctrine of Discovery carried the evil seeds of conquest and slavery, with the violence they required. To not know, or to deny that history, will substantially prevent a new, more just future for America.

In America, Christian nationalism was always white and meant to be, so we will always attach "white" to the term "Christian nationalism" in this book. In European nations today now also experiencing an influx of refugees and immigrants of color, religion has culturally faded. But though the new European nationalism may not be so "Christian" in name, it is still "white" nationalism. "White" is coming back in Europe, uniting different European ethnicities against the arrival of "others" including Africans and Middle Easterners, even in places like Scandinavia, which have prided themselves on being very progressive. That makes this book relevant to European and other English-speaking nations, whose readers are experiencing some of the same right-wing nationalist and autocratic movements as we are here.

From the beginnings of this nation, white nationalism co-opted religion and its preachers. Listen to Cotton Mather, one of the earliest and most celebrated New England Puritan preachers in the late 1600s and early 1700s: "The New Englanders are a people of God settled in those, which were once the devil's territories. And it may easily be supposed that the devil was exceedingly disturbed when he perceived such a people here accomplishing the promise of old made unto our Blessed Jesu—that He should have the utmost parts of the earth for His possession."[2]

Early Protestant settlers believed that America was a land ordained by God for his white people. They sought to justify their possession of the land and the expulsion of its native inhabitants just as the Israelites of the

Old Testament had laid claim to the land promised by God that, at the same time, was occupied by the Amalekites and other nomadic tribes.

Labeling those who must be eradicated, defeated, and destroyed as "satanic" was central to the theology/ideology of conquest. Mather was also involved, not surprisingly, in the Salem witch trials. We will never know exactly what happened at the first "Thanksgiving," but the Indigenous people in America initially showed a willingness to help the new arrivals in their territories and even to share their land with the new immigrants and strangers. Their generosity was repaid with brutal violence that was meant to remove and even extinguish them, their children, and their culture.

The theology of conquest laid the groundwork for another narrative that would become central to white Christian nationalist ideology: the "end times" eschatology, meaning the foretelling of the future—still popular with fundamentalist Christians today. White settlers maintained that at the Second Coming of Christ, America would serve as ground zero for the wars of good and evil. White Americans, of course, would play the role of the good guys. I once pointed out in a television debate, to the chagrin of Reverend Jerry Falwell, Sr., that his religious right pamphlets actually said that God would need the American nuclear arsenal for Armageddon, the final battle between good and evil described in the New Testament! He, of course, denied the charge, until I held up his book and pointed to the page on which he said those very words.

Prior to their migration to America, European settlers were distinguished by ethnicity: they were English, Spanish, French, German, and so on. But upon their arrival, they became bound together as *white* countrymen, distinguishing themselves from the Indigenous natives whom they sought to displace, and the enslaved Africans they exploited. This would establish the character of their newfound society, a nation of white Christian Americans appointed by God. In the antiracism training I helped to lead many years ago, the whites in the room often had real trouble identifying with their European ethnicities—before the profitable ancestry business exploded. I would make jokes to help them understand how different their ancestral cultures were. "I can never tell you Germans from you Irish—exactly the same personalities—or you Italians from you Swedes, hard to tell your cultures apart." That would always get laughs. "I guess you all must be the same, because when you came to America, you all became *white people*." That ended the laughter and a conversation could begin.

Early settlers endorsed the kidnapping and enslavement of Africans on the basis of Old Testament stories depicting the enslavement of "heathens" and prisoners of war. But as second and third generations of enslaved people were born in America, and in many cases converted to Christianity, this ugly rationale was no longer as useful, and enslaved people were forbidden from learning to read the Bible because of what it really said about slavery and freedom.

In fact, the "book" used to justify slavery was eventually read by the enslaved who found that it supported their aspirations to freedom. A slaveholder's bible on display at Fisk University shows how whole portions of the Bible were taken out—including the Exodus story and the Galatians 3:28 text calling for the equality of all believers. The white settlers conspicuously left out the key text in the first chapter of the first book of the Bible saying that we *all* were made in the image and after the likeness of God.

Instead, Christian proponents of slavery claimed that Africans were the descendants of Canaan, the son of Ham, who was condemned to slavery when he saw his father, Noah, drunk and naked and failed to cover him. They reasoned that the Hebrew name of the cursed Ham meant "dark, black, or heat," a translation that has since been discredited by many biblical scholars. Iveson Lewis Brookes (1785–1868), a teacher and Baptist minister, summed up the position of proslavery preachers when he declared, "Negro slavery is an institution of heaven and intended for the mutual benefit of master and slave, as proved by the Bible. . . . God himself authorized Noah to doom the posterity of Ham."[3]

In their treatment of both Native Americans and Africans, white Christian theology deliberately distorted God's word and will to authorize the power of the white European founders of America. And, core to it all, was the tremendous profit supplied by the free labor of the enslaved. Profit and politics prevailed over the Word of God.

Over the years, perceived threats to the established power structure have resulted in the reinforcement and emboldening of white Christian nationalist sentiment and aggression. For example, white Christian nationalism surged in response to the very successful but brief Reconstruction era after the Civil War when the emancipated could vote and many won elective office (which was quickly and violently ended by former white slaveholders when federal troops vacated the South). Again, during the Civil Rights Movement (which was resisted before, during, and after), white Christian nationalism mobilized. White Christian nationalism has also been more prominent during eras when war, heightened immigration, or economic instability threaten the status quo.

Because all these factors are present today, Yale sociologist Philip Gorski calls the modern era a "perfect storm" of white Christian nationalism.[4] The election of our first Black president and the emergence of the Black Lives Matter movement posed new direct challenges to the country's established social, cultural, and political hierarchy. Continued immigration has also led to a more ethnically diverse population and a reduced share of the electorate among white voters.

The status quo is under threat, and the result is the emergence of what Gorski calls "a more full-throated, vulgar kind of Christian nationalism, which will speak not even in subtle ways about racism and will appeal in not very subtle ways to white grievance."

"A VERY PARTICULAR KIND OF CHRISTIANITY"

A foundational element of white Christian nationalism, one rooted in a mythological version of American history authored by its early settlers, is that America is a Christian nation. However, it is a "very particular kind of Christianity," says sociologist Samuel Perry.[5]

He explains that white Christian nationalism "isn't characterized by, say, giving my life to Jesus or wanting to be a good disciple, but is about white Christian ethnoculture, a subculture that characterizes people like us who have been in charge and are the rightful rulers and whose culture should hold sway." In other words, white Christian nationalism is not about true Christian faith, but rather about race and power.

White Christian nationalists are white first and Christians second, and today right-wing Republicans first and Christians second. Selective theology has always provided the justification for upholding racial and political power—from chattel slavery to the continuing evolution of white supremacy.

This, of course, all flies in the face of Jesus' vision of the kingdom of God, which meant to bring diverse and divided people together to be reconciled to Christ. It also contradicts the principles laid out by the founding fathers in the Constitution and Declaration of Independence: "All men are created equal, endowed by their Creator with certain unalienable Rights, that among these are Life, Liberty, and the pursuit of Happiness."

Those founding documents, with all the flaws and hypocrisies of their authors, in principle, still left no easy room for exclusion when they spoke of the "perfect Union" between "we the People," even if few of them at the time would have imagined *all the people* their words would be applied to in future years. White Christian nationalists treat these founding documents with almost the same regard as the Bible, but they pick and choose the passages and interpretations that serve their purposes and maintain their position atop the racial and social hierarchy, and ignore all the rest of Scripture.

Sociologist Andrew Whitehead refers to this as "comfort with authoritarian social control."[6] The rise of strong authoritarian leaders are welcomed as agents of God, appointed to defend against the "evil other" and protect God's chosen land and people by violent means if necessary. Sound familiar?

Conformity to these principles supplies the lifeblood of white Christian nationalism. Political and cultural views that sustain white power, no matter how contrary they are to genuine biblical theology, are legitimized in service of God's sacred will for his chosen people. No dangerous "racial replacement theory" will be allowed; and all this American racial history, that people want to remember or reflect upon, will now be dismissed as the hated critical race theory (CRT), a focused legal instruction about the realities of structural racism generally taught at the university level but now distorted, exploited, and used as a fear tactic to attack and remove honest treatments of American racial history in schools across the country. Jemar Tisby, author of *The Color of Compromise*, puts it succinctly saying CTR is "a junk drawer for anything about race or justice that makes a certain type of person feel uncomfortable." And because of the heightened and inflammatory rhetoric raised about critical race theory, Tisby laments, "much needed conversations about racial justice are being muted in the environments where they are needed most."[7]

There is a white Christian nationalism ideology growing again that results from the espousal of this shared world view, where "real" Christians believe this way and vote this way; and these are the only ways for Christians to be. This is reinforced from the top down, through exhortations from the shepherds, or pastors of megachurches, with the threat of ostracism from the flock for any dissent. For many, this very particular Christianity is all they know, one in which God serves the will of men, white men, and not the other way around. And this is the deep connection between MAGA (Make America Great Again) Republicans and what we can call MEGA churches that have now also become MAGA churches—MEGA/MAGA churches. As Jemar Tisby puts it, "Sin in the form of white nationalism crouches at the door of every congregation."[8]

WHITE CHRISTIAN TRUMPISM

In the MAGA world, the incitement of white grievance is the strategy.
—MICHAEL GERSON, PRESIDENTIAL
SPEECHWRITER AND COLUMNIST[9]

The character of Donald Trump was on full display from the moment he announced he was running for president. In his first speech, he declared Mexican immigrants "rapists" who brought crime and drugs to America. The enthusiasm with which this introduction was received only emboldened him further, giving his crude crassness unbridled expression. He called his political opponents weak and pathetic. He openly mocked others' appearances, even their disabilities. He notoriously and perhaps prophetically declared that he wouldn't lose the votes of his supporters even if he shot someone in the middle of Fifth Avenue.

The *Encyclopedia Britannica* defines a "Faustian bargain" as "a pact whereby a person trades something of supreme moral or spiritual importance, such as personal values or the soul, for some worldly benefit, such as knowledge, power, or riches." That immoral bargain has played out in spectacular and most tragic array by the old religious right who became Trump's religious warriors—to the disastrous detriment of both the church and state. Morality doesn't matter. Character doesn't matter. Values don't matter. The treatment of women or the poor doesn't matter. Only power matters. And faith is trumped.

Trump also projected an image of unapologetic authoritarianism. He bullied and personally attacked his political opponents. He sent paramilitary forces from the Department of Homeland Security to intervene in nonviolent protests. And famously, he actually called out the military to disperse nonviolent protesters with horses and tear gas near Lafayette Park, so that he could make his way to St. John's Episcopal Church right across from the White House to stand in front of the church's closed doors (unannounced and uninvited by the parish priest or local Episcopal bishop, Mariann Budde) for a photo op, holding up a large Bible—ironically but revealingly—upside down. Trump's upside-down Bible became the powerful image sent across the country and around the world of a tyrant turning both true faith and genuine democracy upside down. Trump has never been very comfortable with the Bible; he can't answer media questions about his favorite passages, but he easily used it as a media prop, especially with a group of politically right-wing white evangelical leaders who became his White House chaplains. As white Christian nationalists they were happy to be used for Trump's purposes. He was the strong man who would keep them and their self-interests in power.

And, of course, Trump regularly derided the media, declaring any network or newspaper who criticized his policies as "fake news" and "enemies of the people." Totalitarian leaders always seek to undermine the media because the truth is always their enemy.

Trump eroded trust in the expertise of scientists at the Centers for Disease Control, offering flippant advice that contradicted evidence-based practice. Masses of COVID deaths can be laid at Trump's feet, lives lost because of his incompetence, narcissism, and political calculations. Trump sought to undermine government agencies who interfered with his absolute authority, accusing them of being part of the "deep state." An unprecedented 34 percent of his aides either resigned or were fired during his first year of office.[10] And of course, Trump ultimately sought to usurp the very foundation of our democracy, the electoral system itself, with endless schemes culminating on January 6.

THE POLITICAL TAKEOVER OF EVANGELICALISM

I am often asked the big question, "What does it mean to be an 'evangelical'?" I am even asked, "Are you still an evangelical?" because that was my home church and family tradition, and it has become such a very scary word! David Brooks wrote a piece in *The New York Times* in 2022, "The Dissenters Trying to Save Evangelicalism from Itself," which explains how white evangelicalism has undergone a "Trumpification" and become a racialized partisan force whose values are contrary to the gospel of Jesus Christ.[11] Let's put the issue of white Christian nationalism into a broader evangelical historical context.

I was born and raised an evangelical, by an evangelical family, in an evangelical Christian church in Detroit. The personal nature of faith was and still is deeply embedded in me. But because racism and social justice were not considered matters of Christian faith, I left my home church and childhood faith, as I described in the introduction.

Having departed from evangelicalism, I found myself an outsider from the churches in the student movements of my time. But because of the gospel texts in this book, I came back to the words of Jesus. I went to an evangelical seminary to have an argument—a conversation—with my own tradition. And, in response to the white evangelical heresy of privatizing faith, I have spent my life since then developing a theology of public discipleship.

As David Brooks points out, the evangelical theology that many of us were raised with could indeed be applied to both personal faith *and* social justice—which some of us then did. And that more holistic movement began to successfully impact evangelical churches during the 1970s after my seminary years. Several books about the "young evangelicals" chronicled how many of us were creating a "revolution in orthodoxy."[12] Many people in the older generation, like my own parents, also came around to a more balanced view of the personal and the social gospel. An older generation of evangelical leaders ultimately accepted that more balanced perspective by going back to theology instead of politics. It has always been best when theology drives evangelicalism.

In a pivotal gathering of younger and older evangelical leaders at Chicago's YMCA Wabash Hotel in 1973, we together authored and signed the historic "Declaration of Evangelical Social Concern," which restored the balance between personal and social faith. The statement is relatively short and worth reading again now to see how important that document and movement was, showing what evangelicalism could have become and was beginning to be. In conversation with a young evangelical woman leader of color recently, we both recognized how deeply relevant this now fifty-year-old statement continues to be. As one of the final editors of that declaration, I now lift it back up as something that needs a fresh resurrection.

CHICAGO DECLARATION OF EVANGELICAL SOCIAL CONCERN (1973)

As evangelical Christians committed to the Lord Jesus Christ and the full authority of the Word of God, we affirm that God lays total claim upon the lives of his people. We cannot, therefore, separate our lives from the situation in which God has placed us in the United States and the world.

We confess that we have not acknowledged the complete claim of God on our lives.

We acknowledge that God requires love. But we have not demonstrated the love of God to those suffering social abuses.

We acknowledge that God requires justice. But we have not proclaimed or demonstrated his justice to an unjust American society. Although the Lord calls us to defend the social and economic rights of the poor and oppressed, we have mostly remained silent. We deplore the historic involvement of the church in America with racism and the conspicuous responsibility of the evangelical community for perpetuating the personal attitudes and institutional structures that have divided the body of Christ along color lines. Further, we have failed to condemn the exploitation of racism at home and abroad by our economic system.

We affirm that God abounds in mercy and that he forgives all who repent and turn from their sins. So, we call our fellow evangelical

Christians to demonstrate repentance in a Christian discipleship that confronts the social and political injustice of our nation.

We must attack the materialism of our culture and the maldistribution of the nation's wealth and services. We recognize that as a nation we play a crucial role in the imbalance and injustice of international trade and development. Before God and a billion hungry neighbors, we must rethink our values regarding our present standard of living and promote a more just acquisition and distribution of the world's resources.

We acknowledge our Christian responsibilities of citizenship. Therefore, we must challenge the misplaced trust of the nation in economic and military might—a proud trust that promotes a national pathology of war and violence which victimizes our neighbors at home and abroad. We must resist the temptation to make the nation and its institutions objects of near-religious loyalty.

We acknowledge that we have encouraged men to prideful domination and women to irresponsible passivity. So, we call both men and women to mutual submission and active discipleship.

We proclaim no new gospel, but the Gospel of our Lord Jesus Christ who, through the power of the Holy Spirit, frees people from sin so that they might praise God through works of righteousness.

By this declaration, we endorse no political ideology or party, but call our nation's leaders and people to that righteousness which exalts a nation.

We make this declaration in the biblical hope that Christ is coming to consummate the Kingdom and we accept his claim on our total discipleship until he comes.[13]

The Chicago Declaration, as we called it, would be shocking coming from evangelicals now. It was betrayed by the white evangelical religious right over the last several decades and now in the name of white Christian nationalism. The premier evangelical publication, then and now, *Christianity Today,* wrote back in 1973, "[The authors] represented a wide array of traditions and viewpoints, and they found that they had to confront each other if they were to assure that the declaration they were crafting would be truly comprehensive and speak prophetically. Their manifesto had to address economic justice, peacemaking, racial reconciliation, and gender concerns within a biblical framework, and in ways that honored an evangelical passion for others' salvation in Jesus Christ."[14]

After seminary at Trinity Evangelical Divinity School in the Chicago area in the 1970s, we seminarians began the *Sojourners* magazine and movement. When asked the question "What does it means to be an evangelical?" I would often go back to what I called Jesus' Nazareth manifesto, his first "gig" and the public announcement of his vocation. In his hometown of Nazareth, Jesus quotes from the prophet Isaiah:

> *The Spirit of the Lord is upon me,*
> *because he has anointed me*
> *to bring good news to the poor.*
> *He has sent me to proclaim release to the captives*
> *and recovery of sight to the blind*
> *to let the oppressed go free*
> *to proclaim the year of the Lord's favor.*
>
> (LUKE 4:16–19)

That is what it still means for me to be a genuine evangelical. And, in fact, the Greek word for "good news" in this mission text of Jesus is *evangel,* the foundational word for "evangelical" and "evangelist." Tell me, are the words of Jesus here at his first public appearance the same words that would come to the public mind for describing evangelicalism today? Are today's white evangelicals known for bringing "good news" to the poor?

Jimmy Carter was the first president to call himself "born again," and is likely our most evangelical president. He taught Sunday school every week—even when he was in the White House! The former president will likely be regarded as perhaps the greatest ex-president in American history—for all the remarkable work he has done after leaving the White House; in public health helping to save millions of lives; as a global advocate for democracy including monitoring elections in more than one hundred countries; inspiring the building of legions of Habitat for Humanity houses for poor families around the world; and engaging in endless global peace projects because he believed peacemaking to be the "noblest calling." Carter told me once that "race has shaped and reshaped my whole life," which made racial justice and reconciliation a lifelong mission for him in the religious community and in civil society. And all that work has been motivated and directed by Jimmy Carter's faith. But yet, Jimmy Carter was ultimately rejected by the majority of white evangelicals in favor of Ronald Reagan, a divorced movie actor with no real evangelical bona fides. Carter's Christian faith led him to do justice, seek peace, and fight racism, which did not resonate with most white evangelicals. But if my little home church had followed his exemplar of evangelical faith, I might never have left.

But by 1980, many white evangelicals were following a different and false white gospel. The plan to form a "religious right" was nothing less than a political takeover of evangelicalism by Republican far-right political operatives. I remember my own father saying to me at the time that Jerry Falwell was not a true evangelical but a fundamentalist wanting to take political power.

Those political operatives transformed a faith movement into a steadfast Republican voting bloc. Some of these operatives, like veteran Republican Richard Viguerie, have boasted about that mission and strategy. "We went to people like Jerry Falwell and Pat Robertson," Richard once told me very directly. "We offered to make them household names in America if they would just turn over their mailing lists to us for the massive direct mails that we would use to create the new 'moral majority.'" Richard was the direct-mail guru of that day. It is important to understand how the religious right, which has now morphed into white Christian nationalism, did not come about from theological discernment or religious conferences, but from a political takeover by right-wing operatives in the Republican Party.

The beginnings of the religious right, as Dartmouth religion professor Randall Balmer dramatically demonstrates in his insightful book *Bad Faith*, were anchored in racism. There was great anger and protest by conservative white evangelicals at the federal defunding of segregated Christian schools. Some of that IRS defunding came under Jimmy Carter and he was never forgiven for denying federal funds to Christian schools like the infamous Bob Jones University, a school based on racial discrimination.[15] Abortion, Balmer points out, was an issue that only came later, as it was determined to be a better overt organizing tool than race—but the core of the movement has remained the same, and has continued now into white Christian nationalism. It's worth taking a look at that history as, for example, the Southern Baptist Convention was initially supportive of *Roe v. Wade*.

The new evangelical hero, Ronald Reagan, announced his presidential candidacy in the town of Philadelphia, Mississippi. Why would this new presidential hopeful decide to speak where three young civil rights workers—James Chaney, Michael Schwerner, and Andrew Goodman—had been brutally murdered? Was he suggesting that he was standing with white former Democrats in the South? Reagan even supported the apartheid regime in South Africa, while his chief presidential chaplain, Jerry Falwell, Sr., called South African archbishop Desmond Tutu a "fraud."

Donald Trump is the *culmination* of this religious right political strategy, drawing a majority of white evangelicals while he exemplifies the worst of the immoral, dishonest, unethical, corrupt, and selfish personal and sexual values that would have been anathema in my evangelical home church. Author and political scientist Robert P. Jones sums up what happened:

The one remarkable thing to me is that, since Reagan, if you want a shorthand for understanding the religious landscape in politics, it is that white Christian groups tend to lean toward or strongly support Republican candidates, and everybody else in the country—non-white Christians, non-Christian religious groups, religiously unaffiliated—lean toward or strongly support Democratic candidates. That is the divide we have been living with since Reagan. When the Democratic party became the party of civil rights, whites in the South went to the Republican party.[16]

So, ultimately, the shift to the religious right had nothing to do with theological discourse. It was all politics. Turning around the "white Christian" phrase to describe themselves as Christians first and everything else second should be the calling for a new evangelical movement today.

White Christian nationalism is directly and specifically anti-Christ. Jesus' vision of the kingdom of God, as exemplified by the Galatians text about Christian unity, was deliberately meant to bring diverse and divided people together by being reconciled to Christ. The majority of white evangelicals who have become captivated by white Christian nationalism are standing *against their Black brothers and sisters in the body of Christ,* and even supporting their Republican Party's suppression of their fellow Christians' voting rights, if they are citizens of color. That is an assault on both the image of God (Genesis 1:26), the *imago dei,* and Paul's Galatians vision of a very diverse body of Christ.

How did a man who lacks even the most basic knowledge of the Christian faith go on to win more than 80 percent of white, evangelical votes in 2016 and again in 2020?[17] And why have white evangelicals become Donald Trump's staunchest supporters? That is a question I am always asked.

The reasons are many—the privatizing of faith in our evangelical traditions that have already been addressed, with sin being only personal and never institutional and structural; the focus on only a few single issues like abortion and gay marriage, instead of the broad range of biblical concerns, especially the key issues of how the poor, the marginal, and immigrants are treated; and the transactional political bargain made by evangelical leaders with Trump for power, despite his lack of Christian character. But I believe that central to the answer of why white evangelicals supported Trump, even after seeing what he would do as president, is the core issue of race. A white ethnicity and patriarchal culture—with the power to keep control—is more important to many or even most white evangelicals than any gospel they allege to proclaim.

Kristin Kobes Du Mez, professor of history and gender studies at Calvin University and author of *Jesus and John Wayne* summarizes this Christian captivity well: "For conservative white evangelicals, the 'good news' of the Christian gospel has become inextricably linked to a staunch commitment to patriarchal authority, gender difference, and Christian nationalism, and all of these intertwined with white racial identity. Many Americans who now identify as evangelicals are identifying with this operational theology—one that is Republican in its politics and traditionalist in its values."[18]

I recall a sad lunch with the president of an evangelical seminary who called his job so painfully "abusive" because, he said to me, "Evangelicalism is destroying the *evangel*," which, again, is the Greek word for the "good news" of Jesus Christ.[19] This white evangelical leader cared so deeply about racial justice and reconciliation, but his evangelical culture was using racism to destroy both the church and the country—and deny the good news of the gospel to the poor that Jesus proclaimed as core to his mission in his first sermon at Nazareth in chapter 4 of the book of Luke.

In November 2015, less than a year before he would descend the escalator at Trump Tower to announce his bid for the presidency, Trump submitted an application to the US Patent and Trademark Office for exclusive rights to what would become his political slogan and a trademark of white evangelical Christians more prevalent than the cross of Jesus: Make America Great Again.

The implications were in plain view. Trump was anti-Muslim, calling for a "total and complete shutdown of Muslims entering the United States" on December 7, 2015.[20] He was anti-immigrant, vowing to build a wall that would end the supposedly corrosive effects of Mexicans cross-ing the border in search of a better life. He told elected American con-gressional leaders, who were also women of color, to go back to where they came from. Trump denounced "political correctness," equating sensitivity and equity with cowardice and weakness. At the heart of his slogan, and of his own political identity and presidential campaign, was the implication that he intended to clean up the mess left by Amer-ica's first African American president, whom Trump had repeatedly ac-cused of faking his citizenship. The questioning of Obama's birthright and certificate with the widespread prejudice among white Ameri-cans that he was "unqualified" for the nation's highest office, was the founding campaign of Trump's political career. Donald Trump named the sworn enemies of white Christian nationalism and brought to the surface its most deeply rooted fears. The message was clear. This was "us against them." And the gospel of Jesus Christ be damned.

I still call myself, theologically, an "evangelical" (to the chagrin of my wife and many in my own family), meaning that my faith base is in the Bible and my commitment to Jesus Christ both as savior and Lord. But I do not believe that the white evangelicals who have become white Christian nationalists can any longer honestly call themselves "evan-gelical." This is not just a political debate, but an urgent theological one, that many of us are ready to have with white Christian nationalists. *Please take that as a real invitation to debate and a serious challenge to you, white evangelical MAGA/MEGA church pastors.* It is time to be driven by our theology again. As I always advise my students, "Don't go right. Don't go left. Go deeper."

THE WHITE CHRISTIAN NATIONALIST DOG WHISTLES

According to Philip Gorski, white Christian nationalism is not only an ideology, but also "increasingly a political strategy that is leveraged by people who don't necessarily have to believe the ideology." Trump, who self-identified as a Democrat in 2004, effectively utilized white Christian nationalist rhetoric to sell himself as champion of the causes that most appealed to white group interests. "He was the ultimate fighting champion," says Kristin Kobes Du Mez. Just like John Wayne, instead of Jesus, "he was going to restore Christian America. He was going to do what needed to be done."[21]

This wave of Trumpism was not lost on the Republican Party or the conservative media, who quickly shifted their strategies to capitalize on the fears of white Christian nationalists—for their own political and profitable gain.

Former South Carolina congressman Mark Sanford, who once claimed it was God's will that he remained in office following an extramarital affair, all but named the true spirit of Christian nationalists when he called Republican supporters of Trump "slaves to our ambitions." It took Vice President Mike Pence, who had always been slavishly loyal to Donald Trump, to stand up and put loyalty to the Constitution over the angry demands of a tyrant and his violent mob on January 6. An impressive PBS *Frontline* documentary described the many "blinking red warning lights" along the way that were repeatedly ignored by other Republicans, that made this media celebrity and contemporary fascist political actor succeed; and how the established Republican leadership has ultimately played along with him.[22] The succumbing of the majority of a national political party, along with the faithless religious conformity of white evangelicals, to a narcistic and racist demagogue, has created the most dangerous threat to our democracy in American history.

The consequence of this rallying behind Trump was a shift toward more divisive and fear-based tactics among Republicans, alongside a torrent of what Samuel Perry calls the "dog whistle, or code language" of white Christian nationalism. Taking their cues from Trump's distaste for political correctness, right-wing media and politicians derided "cancel culture." They misappropriated the meaning of "woke" from a commendation of one's awareness of injustice and social consciousness to a bullying tactic and an insult implying pretentiousness, oversensitivity, and discrimination against white people.

Florida governor Ron DeSantis mimics Trump with warnings against the "woke mob" that threatens to take over America. Instead, they want to "own the libs," meaning defeat the political liberals. Do some people who call themselves "woke" attack other social justice advocates who don't fully conform to their words or agendas? Of course. But the excesses of some on the left hardly compare with how divisive and polarizing behavior has become *mainstream* on the right and a regular tactic now of a whole political party.

In that Republican Party we have seen more and more overt support for Christian nationalist ideals. Pennsylvania state senator Doug Mastriano, who then got his party's support to run for governor, declared that America is a Christian nation and that the separation of church and state is a "myth." Representative Marjorie Taylor Greene, from Georgia, suggested, "We need to be the party of nationalism and I'm a Christian, and I say it proudly: We should be Christian nationalists." She calls for a "divorce" between red and blue states. And Representative Lauren Boebert, from Colorado, invoked the "end times story" at the heart of Christian nationalism declaring, "We know that we are in the last of the last days," adding, "It's time for us to position ourselves and rise up and take our place in Christ and influence this nation as we were called to do."

AWAKE AND WOKE

Making "woke" people the enemy, as the Republican Party is now doing, has led me back to the Bible to see how the words "awake" and "woke" are used in the Scriptures. It turns out, the words "awake," "awakened," and "woke" appear many dozens of times in the Hebrew Scriptures and the New Testament—and the references are, of course, all positive. They refer to waking up, being awake, staying awake, becoming awoken from sleeping; and all those awakenings are seen as important spiritual qualities.

Let's look at just a few of the biblical texts, starting with Isaiah 60:1: "Arise, shine, for your light has come, and the glory of the Lord has risen upon you." What a way to start a new day or, better, a new life? Ephesians 5:14 says, "For anything that becomes visible is light. Therefore, awake, oh sleeper, and arise from the dead, and Christ will shine on you." Perhaps many of us as white people have been sleeping far too long in the darkness of racial injustice, and we need to awake by letting the light of Christ shine on us. Luke 21:36 says, "Stay awake at all times," and Matthew 24:42 repeats, "Stay awake, for you do not know on what day your Lord is coming." First Thessalonians 5:6 goes on to say, "So then let us not sleep, as others do, but let us keep awake and be sober." In John 12:35–36, Jesus says, "Walk while you have the light, lest darkness overtake you. The one who walks in the darkness does not know where he is going. While you have the light, believe in the light, that you may become children of light."

These Scriptures about waking up and staying awake go on and on, and could be great biblical resources for reflections about where we are now in our own country. Revelation 3:2 says, "Wake up, and strengthen what remains and is about to die, for I have not found your works complete in the sight of my God." Revelation 3:3 says, "Remember, then, what you received and heard. Keep it, and repent. If you will not wake up, I will come like a thief, and you will not know at what hour I will come against you." Do we remember what Jesus said, what we have heard, as these disciples were here asked to do? Then will we repent of our racial sins by waking up from them? Certainly, our work for a just, fair, compassionate, and democratic country is far from complete—in God's eyes. What would it mean to apply the words of Romans 13:11–12 to our changing situation today: "Besides this you know the time, that the hour has come for you to wake from sleep. For salvation is nearer to us now than when we first believed. The night is far gone; the day is at hand. So then let us cast off the works of darkness and put on the armor of light. Let us walk properly as in the daytime." How do we awake from the works of darkness in America's racial history and put on the armor of light for a new *beloved community*?

Let us throw off the fear-baiting political slogans against "the woke," and apply the Scriptures to the challenging situation we now face in America. We have slept through or turned a blind eye to such injustice for so long.

Pastors and lay church leaders, don't give in to the political attacks on "woke" people! Instead take your fellow congregants back to the Bible to see what it really means to be awake and woke. And call them to do what Peter 1:13–14 says: "Therefore, preparing your minds for action, and being sober-minded, set your hope fully on the grace that will be brought to you at the revelation of Jesus Christ. As obedient children, do not be conformed to the passions of your former ignorance."

What would it mean to *act* in our congregations on Romans 13:11: "Besides this you know the time, that the hour has come for you to wake from sleep. For salvation is nearer to us now than when we first believed." Give the people you love the hope that we can do better than what we have done; and that a better church, better country, and better future are available to us! As 1 Thessalonians 5:5 tells us, "For you are all children of light, children of the day. We are not of the night or of the darkness."

It's time to wake up!

THE SOUL OF THE NATION

Our current battle for the soul of the nation is not just about political divides and clashes, partisan wins and losses, which is how many in politics and the media frame it. Rather, in my view, we are engaged in "spiritual warfare," a term from the apostle Paul in the New Testament.

President Biden first used the word "semi-fascism" to describe the MAGA movement led by Donald Trump in a speech in Maryland on August 22, 2022.

Here is how *Merriam-Webster* defines "fascism": "A political philosophy, movement, or regime (such as that of the Fascisti) that exalts nation and one race above the individual and that stands for a centralized autocratic government headed by a dictatorial leader, severe economic and social regimentation, and forcible suppression of opposition."

Biden delivered another address just over a week later at Independence Hall, which he called the "sacred ground" on which the Declaration of Independence and the Constitution were debated and written more than two hundred years ago. He titled his speech "The Battle for the Soul of the Nation." He was clear and bold about the threat we face: "As I stand here tonight, equality and democracy are under assault. We do ourselves no favors to pretend otherwise."

In this moment of truth telling, Biden said, "There is no question that the Republican Party today is dominated, driven, and intimidated by Donald Trump and the MAGA Republicans, and that is a threat to this country." And he acknowledged, "These are hard things." They are hard indeed.

How exactly do you deal with a movement and political party that has abandoned the rule of law, agreed to violate the Constitution (Trump even once said to "terminate" the Constitution), and tolerates political violence and embraces white supremacy and its supporters with a wink and a nod?

But perhaps the words from the Biden speech that most directly addressed the issue of fascism were: "MAGA Republicans have made their choice. They embrace anger. They thrive on chaos. They live not in the light of truth but in the shadow of lies."

OUR BETTER ANGELS AND WORST DEMONS

Donald Trump has appealed to and unleashed the *worst demons* in our American society. And only the calling forth of the *better angels* of American history will bring us the hope that can carry us forward. America has both the worst demons and better angels, and the vocation of leaders is to call out the angels against the demons.

The results of the midterm elections of 2022 were a sign of that hope with many Americans casting their votes on the basis of saving democracy. The "Big Lie" did suffer a crippling blow as most "election deniers" lost their own elections in 2022. Americans came out to show their support for a constitutional democracy, with all its imperfections and failings. Young people overwhelmingly named democracy as the issue that brought them out to vote, boding well for the future of the country.

But for a final verdict upon which way America will go in the future, the moral jury is still out, in my view.

Democracy won the skirmish of the 2022 midterm elections, but the forces that tried to steal and then overturn the 2020 election are now doubling down for 2024.

Most dangerous is the trajectory of the politics now in place: from fear to hate to violence. Many algorithms in our lives and our social media call us to all three. And whether this country stands up to fear, hate, and violence will indeed be up to all of us.

President Biden said, "History tells us that blind loyalty to a single leader and a willingness to engage in political violence is fatal to democracy." That has always been true.

I participated in a hate summit held at the White House, with Biden and about 150 faith leaders in the fall of 2022, where he said, "We can't allow violence to be normalized in this country. It's wrong. We each have to reject political violence with—with all the moral clarity and conviction this nation can muster. Now. We can't let the integrity of our elections be undermined, for that is a path to chaos . . . [or] the freedom to vote and have your vote counted [could] be taken from you and the American people."

Bono, the lead singer for U2, loves to talk about America as an "idea." He says, "America is not just a country, it's an idea. Ireland is a great country and I'm very proud to be Irish, but it's not an idea. Great Britain is great, but it's not an idea. America is an idea."[23] The spiritual rock star holds politicians to account for the best of the idea of America, which he describes as all of us being "created equal."

FALSE AND TRUE RELIGION: THEN AND NOW

We must distinguish between false and true religion. This chapter has discussed the white slaveholder religion of early America, and connected that false religion with the white Christian nationalism making a comeback today. The parallels between the two are striking. In the *Narrative of the Life of Frederick Douglass: An American Slave*, Douglass writes:

What I have said respecting and against religion, I mean strictly to apply to the slaveholding religion of this land, and with no possible reference to Christianity proper; for, between the Christianity of this land, and the Christianity of Christ, I recognize the widest possible difference—so wide, that to receive the one as good, pure, and holy, is of necessity to reject the other as bad, corrupt, and wicked. To be the friend of the one, is of necessity to be the enemy of the other. I love the pure, peaceable, and impartial Christianity of Christ: I therefore hate the corrupt, slaveholding, women-whipping, cradle-plundering, partial and hypocritical Christianity of this land.[24]

Both then and now, religion that favors white power over all others is not just contrary to the gospel of Jesus, but is opposite to it. A religion that divides us is so different from a faith that purposes to bring us together.

Douglass goes on to say what was real and not real Christianity in his day:

Indeed, I can see no reason, but the most deceitful one, for calling the religion of this land Christianity. I look upon it as the climax of all misnomers, the boldest of all frauds, and the grossest of all libels. Never was there a clearer case of "stealing the livery of the court of heaven to serve the devil in." I am filled with unutterable loathing when I contemplate the religious pomp and show, together with the horrible inconsistencies, which everywhere surround me. We have men-stealers for ministers, women-whippers for missionaries, and cradle-plunderers for church members. The man who wields the blood-clotted cowskin during the week fills the pulpit on Sunday, and claims to be a minister of the meek and lowly Jesus. The man who robs me of my earnings at the end of each week meets me as a class-leader on Sunday morning, to show me the way of life, and the path of salvation. He who sells my sister, for purposes of prostitution, stands forth as the pious advocate of purity. He who proclaims it a religious duty to read the Bible denies me the right of learning to read the name of the God who made me. He who is the religious advocate of marriage robs whole millions of its sacred influence.

THE FALSE WHITE GOSPEL

THE AUCTION BELL AND THE CHURCH BELL

Those brutal inconsistencies go to the heart of the problem of this kind of white Christianity—then and now—which is the *privatizing* of religion; that is the great heresy of American religion, and evangelical Christianity in particular. You can focus on your own relationship to God, to the point where your religion has no relationship to the people around you—especially to people of *color*. It is all about "you and the Lord." Douglass spells out the hypocrisies of that privatization:

> The warm defender of the sacredness of the family relation is the same that scatters whole families—sundering husbands and wives, parents and children, sisters and brothers—leaving the hut vacant, and the hearth desolate. We see the thief preaching against theft, and the adulterer against adultery. We have men sold to build churches, women sold to support the gospel, and babes sold to purchase Bibles for the poor heathen! All for the glory of God and the good of souls! The slave auctioneer's bell and the church-going bell chime in with each other, and the bitter cries of the heartbroken slave are drowned in the religious shouts of his pious master.

It is time for the church bell to ring against everything the auctioneer's bell stood for and modern white supremacy still stands for.

THE CONVERSATION AMERICA ISN'T HAVING

On the last day of our class Faith, Race, and Politics, Ernesto Godinez, one of my Georgetown students, said, "Look around and see how different we all are, and what we have been able to talk about. This conversation isn't happening in America. I want to know if you all are going to stay in this conversation after our class is over." His challenge to his classmates is my challenge to us all.

There is talk about democracy and autocracy, but very little about the role of faith in this struggle. It's time for us to have that conversation. We must be willing to lift up those words of Jesus that fly in the face of any kind of white supremacy or even white preference. It was Jesus, and not Christianity, that called me to faith. And it will be Jesus that can call Christians who have been captivated by white Christian nationalism back to true gospel faith. Those in the pews who have been deceived may not even know the title or language of white Christian nationalism, but have succumbed to it for cultural and political reasons. We must now be the ones to raise the hard questions that will ultimately set people free—both in our churches and outside of them.

It is past time for us to start visioning a new American church.

White Christian pastors, call your white congregants and parishioners back to Jesus—help set them free from their enmeshment with white ideological and idolatrous politics. Will most white Christians come back to the words of Jesus? Perhaps not. But there could be a "remnant" of white Christians who are persuadable, particularly a new generation, who will decisively break away from the idols of white Christianity and come alongside the leadership of Black and brown Christians—for that new American church. This crisis of white Christian nationalism can not only clarify what we are *against,* but also help define what we are *for.* This reconfigured faith community will be a "confessing church" in America, similar to those that emerged in Germany and South Africa—but unique to our own circumstances at this pivotal moment in history. This call will put the word "Christian" ahead of the word "white" and every other word. And this pilgrimage could lead the American churches to look more like the global body of Christ—which is the most diverse human community on the planet. The stakes for that sojourn are very high—for the integrity of faith, the survival and promise of democracy, and the involvement of the next generation in communities of faith in America. Very high indeed. My hope is that this manifesto will be a call to action, and become a teaching tool for that journey.

THE BIBLE TELLS ME SO

While I hail from and am deeply informed by the Christian tradition, the six texts below from the Hebrew Bible and Christian New Testament have at their core a mission and message that are in keeping with the best in all our religious traditions. The *reframing and refreshing* of these ancient texts will help clarify the issues now at stake for all of us, even those who don't profess faith, but are looking for moral guidance. These Scriptures from our holy books will inform the rest of this book.

1. *Luke 10:25–37: "You shall love the Lord your God with all your heart, and with all your strength, and with all your mind, and your neighbor as yourself.... Who is my neighbor?"* The "double love" commandment in all our Abrahamic religious traditions—to love God and love your neighbor, including those neighbors who don't live in our neighborhood—will be a test of both faith and democracy in our time. "Who is my neighbor?" will become the primary question for the future of our democracy.

2. *Genesis 1:26: "Then God said, Let us make humankind in our own image, according to our own likeness."* Will we dehumanize those who are not like us, or will we embrace the image of God, the *imago dei,* in the created equal humanity of all people—all humankind? Are we the *imago dei* movement—or not?

3. *John 8:32: "You will know the truth and the truth will make you free."* Will we be faithless and held captive by deliberate and destructive disinformation and loyalty to the lies of the false prophets of our day, or will we be faithful to the truth that Jesus promises can set us free?

4. *Matthew 25:31–46: "As you have done to the least of these, you have done to me."* Will we care for the marginalized and vulnerable, or will we ignore them? Jesus says how we treat the "least of these" is also how we treat him, and that will be a test of our

discipleship. These are the economics of Jesus and they turn our politics upside down.

5. *Matthew 5:9: "Blessed are the peacemakers, for they shall be called the children of God."* Will we accept the endless escalation of violence, or will we pursue peace in our vocation as "peacemakers" and conflict resolvers? Only those people get the special designation of the "children of God."

6. *Galatians 3:28: "There is no longer Jew or Gentile, there is no longer slave or free, there is no longer male or female, for all of you are one in Christ."* Will we seek the unity and diversity of the kingdom of God, or will we reinforce the social barriers of race, class, gender, and tribalism? Used as the primary text at early church baptisms and one of the first Christian creeds, the apostolic call to overcome those divisions is core to the vocation of the churches, in the United States of America and globally. And the building of new relationships across all boundaries, including religions, will become the foundation for the common good in a multiracial democracy.

May the wisdom and power of these Scriptures offer guidance and support, encourage and sustain us, and assist in the vital work being done by so many: pastors and priests, lay leaders, religious women, community activists, educators, medical and legal practitioners, elected officials and advocates for policy changes; for those seekers, young believers, and everyone looking for something to believe in—as we all try to live up to the integrity of faith and conscience, and the promise of democracy.

2

YOUR NEIGHBOR DOESN'T
LIVE NEXT DOOR

An expert in the law stood up to test Jesus. "Teacher, what must I do to inherit eternal life?"

"What is written in the Law?" Jesus asked.

"How do you read it?" the lawyer answered. "Love the Lord your God with all your heart and with all your soul and with all your strength and with all your mind; and, Love your neighbor as yourself."

"You have answered correctly," Jesus replied. "Do this and you will live."

But he wanted to justify himself, so he asked Jesus, "And who is my neighbor?"

Jesus replied: "A man was going down from Jerusalem to Jericho, when he was attacked by robbers. They stripped him of his clothes, beat him, and went away, leaving him half dead. A priest happened to be going down the same road, and when he saw the man, he passed by on the other side. So too, a Levite, when he came to the place and saw him, passed by on the other side. But a Samaritan, as he traveled, came where the man was; and when he saw him, he took pity on him. He went to him and bandaged his wounds, pouring on oil and wine. Then he put the man on his own donkey, brought him to an inn, and took care of him. The next day he took out two denarii and gave them to the innkeeper. "Look after him," he said, "and when I return, I will reimburse you for any extra expense you may have."

"Which of these three do you think was a neighbor to the man who fell into the hands of robbers?"

The expert in the law replied, "The one who had mercy on him." Jesus told him, "Go and do likewise."

—LUKE 10:25–37

Who is my neighbor? That is the critical question today, as it was in Jesus' time. In fact, it may be the most important moral question, for both the authenticity of our faith communities *and* the future of democracy. But I don't want to just talk *about* the question; I want to direct it to you and ask you to direct it to others around you. "Who is my neighbor?" cannot just be theoretical in a time like this.

A lawyer was the first to ask the crucial question. I suspect he was a Washington lawyer. I can tell by the spirit in which he asked the question, with that critical tone of voice. What he was really asking was, "Who do I need to treat with fairness, and even compassion? And, perhaps most important: Who can I dismiss without getting into trouble?"

The Washington lawyer approached Jesus just after he had welcomed back the seventy-two disciples whom he'd dispatched across the land with a message: "The kingdom of God has come near to you."

The disciples returned emboldened, filled with excitement about how well they had been received by so many people. And the lawyer arrived just as Jesus was having a discussion with his disciples about their new mission in the world. Perhaps feeling skeptical of their enthusiasm, the lawyer decided to put Jesus to the test, not in the spirit of open inquiry, but as a challenge. The man asks, "Teacher, what must I do to inherit eternal life?" It sounds like what many modern people ask today, which is: "What must I do to go to heaven?" But Jews didn't emphasize an individual relationship with God, but rather following

Jewish law. The lawyer knew he could get Jesus into trouble here if he answered wrongly or heretically to Jewish law.

Jesus poses the question back to him, saying: "What is written in the law?" He is in effect saying, "I think you know the answer to the question; and yet, you're asking me?"

The lawyer responds: "Well [you can almost hear him pondering his reply], you shall love the Lord your God with all your heart, with all your soul, and with all your strength and all your mind; and, Love your neighbor as yourself." Like so many of us today, he knows what he is supposed to say. We know *what is written*. But faith always demands more than right answers; faith also insists upon right actions. Jesus responds, "You have answered correctly." In other words, you got it right. Now *do* what you know, and you will *live*.

But then the lawyer gets to the big central question, the real one in his head and heart: "Who, exactly, *is* my neighbor?" He's not asking, "How can I welcome another?" Or, "How can I love better?" And not, "How can I serve my neighbor?" No, the tone and spirit here are very different. The question he's asking, rather, is, "What are the limits of my responsibilities? Do I really need to treat everyone as a 'neighbor'?" He is looking for loopholes—as lawyers and all of us often do. This is not about giving something; it's about getting out of something. As in: "Just exactly *who* are you talking about here, Jesus?" Jesus answers the lawyer's neighbor question with the story of the Good Samaritan.

THE PARABLE OF THE GOOD SAMARITAN

You don't have to be Christian or even particularly religious to know the story of the Good Samaritan. It's a familiar tale ingrained in our common humanity, history, and culture. But few of us, especially we so-called believers, understand the depth and implications of this seemingly simple but transformative parable. This is much more than a popular exhortation to serve others—to volunteer some of your spare time and help out where you can. Rather, if we understand Jesus' radical message about who our neighbor really is, this story will change our lives.

The first thing to point out is that the word "good" never appears in the text. To Jesus' contemporaries—the Judeans—there was no such thing as a *good* Samaritan. The Jews considered Samaritans *foreigners* and *enemies*; *unclean* and *dangerous*. They were thought to be bad people and were treated that way. Samaritans were a mixed race, "halfbreeds," marginal people, and they were not like "us" (that is, Jews, like Jesus, who were certainly the primary audience for this story). Jews stayed away from them, isolated them, and definitely avoided venturing into their communities. The Samaritans were the "others," and the Judeans ensured they remained that way. Yet Jesus chooses a Samaritan to reveal what it means to be a good neighbor. Jesus' designation of the Samaritan "enemy" as the neighbor deliberately overturns all the insider/outsider assumptions of Jesus' time; and does for our time too. To appreciate the power of this parable we need to attend to the details of the story.

A man making his way to Jerusalem on the Jericho road falls into the hands of robbers who take everything he has, beat and strip him, and leave him lying half dead in a ditch, on the side of the road. We all share this fear that suddenly our lives may be violently interrupted, that we may be robbed of our property and potentially our lives. What we have here, along the Jericho road, is a *crime scene*. Right there before us is a victim dying—if not already dead—helpless and in dire need.

The first to encounter the crime scene is a priest making his way down that same road, going about his own business. When he sees the man lying on the ground, he crosses to the other side of the road so as to avoid the scene and its victim altogether. Maybe the man is already dead, and some scholars point to impurity rules in relation to a corpse as the justification for the priest's behavior; others disagree. But, for whatever reasons, the priest decides to ignore the man lying on the road in great need. He cannot be bothered. He has a schedule with perhaps pressing things to do and helping the injured man isn't one of them.

Next comes a Levite, a member of the important Hebrew tribe that assisted the priests with their temple worship. Like the priest, he also chooses to disregard the victim's condition and his needs.

But then along comes this Samaritan, this *other*; *an enemy* of the Jews. The man lying by the side of the road was likely Jewish, as New Testament scholar Amy-Jill Levine and others point out. But when the Samaritan sees the victim, broken and in need of help, he is moved with "pity," meaning with compassion, to come to the injured man's aid. So, the Samaritan, the *other*, decides to help the one who is *other* to him.

TAMING THE PARABLE

Discussions of the Good Samaritan usually *tame* the deeply unsettling universal message at the heart of Jesus' parable. To turn this Good Samaritan into a general exhortation for helping whomever is in need misses, perhaps deliberately, the critical point that Jesus was making. What if the hero of the story were another Jew, like the wounded man in the ditch? Most Jews would have loved the story about someone being a good Jew and doing the right thing, even in contrast to those religious leader types we all get so tired of with their regular pomposities and hypocrisies. But, the fact that the one Jesus chose for his hero was a Samaritan—the foreigner and the enemy—was to be clearly offensive to his Jewish audience.

Referencing Amy-Jill Levine, historian Diana Butler Bass, in a sermon on the parable, notes, "When the lawyer asks, 'Who is my neighbor,' Jesus responds: 'The very worst person you can imagine, your enemy.'"

Ask yourself or your congregation: Who would be the hated Samaritan, the enemy, for you or us today?

Bass goes on, "From the perspective of the man in the ditch, Jewish listeners might balk at the idea of receiving Samaritan aid. They might have thought, 'I'd rather die than acknowledge that one from that group saved me. I do not want to acknowledge that a rapist has a human face or I do not want to recognize that a murderer will be the one to rescue me.' That's what the Jews in Jesus' day thought of Samaritans—that they were descended from rapists and murderers, collaborators with rulers who oppressed God's people and who worshiped at a corrupt Temple. That's who showed up as the hero in the story, the person who administered mercy—their enemy."[1]

This story is not just about volunteering in our extra time. We must not tame the Good Samaritan parable, but listen and learn from what Jesus is deeply saying here—for such a time as this.

REVERSING THE QUESTIONS

The opening of the Good Samaritan story is a crime scene. When you come upon a crime scene and discover what has just happened, there is no guarantee that the perpetrators are not still present, lurking somewhere and even waiting for another victim. You begin to consider: "Maybe this could happen to me. What if I stop and try to help, and the same thing that happened to him happens to me?" You are taking a *risk* by stopping, drawing near to one who is suffering, and making yourself vulnerable to attack by offering to help. And clearly, you're offering your own time, maybe your own money, and seriously interrupting your own schedule.

The priest and Levite were just too busy or perhaps too selfishly inclined. They offered neglect and indifference; but the Good Samaritan stopped and offered himself, his time, and resources in service to one in need.

The story continues. The Samaritan bandages the man's wounds, pours oil and wine on the injuries to aid in their healing, picks the man up and places him on his own donkey. Then he walks the donkey with the wounded man to an inn, a place of safety, rest, and healing.

The Samaritan stays with the injured man overnight to help him heal in this secure location. The next day, before he leaves, he gives two denarii (one was the equivalent of a daily wage for a skilled laborer in those days) to the innkeeper, saying, "Look after him, and when I come back, I will repay you for whatever more you spend."

Having told this story to the lawyer, Jesus asks him, "Which of these three do you think was the neighbor to the man who fell into the hands of the robbers?" The lawyer concedes, "The one who showed mercy on him." Notice that the lawyer doesn't say the hated word "Samaritan" but rather "the one."

Satisfied that he has made his point, Jesus then tells the lawyer, "Go and do likewise."

In Dr. Martin Luther King, Jr.'s, powerful sermon "The Jericho Road,"[2] King reflects on the question he thinks the priest and the Levite asked themselves: "If I stop to help this man, what will happen to me?" Then King imagines a different question being asked by the Samaritan: "If I don't stop to help this man, what will happen to him?"

King calls on us to *reverse the question* and ask what will happen to the one in need, before asking what will happen to us. This powerful reversal is at the heart of what Jesus is saying here. King goes on to suggest that such roads should be fixed by sound public policy to make them less dangerous! Always both the personal and the social for King—as it should also be for us. In King's very controversial 1967 speech at Riverside Church in New York City, "Beyond Vietnam: A Time to Break the Silence," crafted for King by my beloved mentor Dr. Vincent Harding, he goes back to his favorite Good Samaritan parable as he did time and time again:

> We are called to play the Good Samaritan on life's roadside; but that will be only an initial act. One day the whole Jericho Road must be transformed so that men and women will not be beaten and robbed as they make their way through life. True compassion is more than flinging a coin to a beggar; it understands that an edifice which produces beggars needs restructuring.[3]

In his speech in opposition to the war in Vietnam, opposed even by fellow civil rights leaders who feared it would anger their ally President Lyndon Johnson, King identified the "giant triplets" of militarism, racism, and poverty, which are deeply connected and must all be addressed. I often say that churches and charities are generally good at pulling the bodies out of the river, but hesitate to go upstream to confront who or what is throwing them in.

A CHALLENGE PARABLE

The question of who will help the man in the ditch in the Good Samaritan story must go along with the question: Who will help us when we fall into a ditch? The deepest theological issues of grace and love are involved here. New Testament scholar N. T. Wright asks,

> Can you recognize the hated Samaritan in your neighbor? If you can't, you too might be left for dead (literally, relationally, or spiritually). For this parable addresses what is at stake for the people of God, then and now, namely whether we will see it as a call and challenge to extend the love and grace of God to the whole world and all people or not. No church and no Christian can remain content with the easy definitions which allow us to watch most of the world lying half dead in the road of life.[4]

The key to understanding the Good Samaritan—both then and now—is to see it, in the words of New Testament scholar John Dominic Crossan, as a "challenge" parable and thus different from parables that are "examples" or even "riddles."[5] Crossan and others point out that one meaning of the word "Samaritan" is "guardian," or "protector." Our task is to take up the *challenge* that Jesus is clearly offering to all those still morally constricted and controlled by racial and social categories. Perhaps we should look to John Lewis, iconic civil rights leader and then member of Congress, and use the Good Samaritan parable to get into "good trouble." And that might happen in congregations if pastors preached the real meaning of Jesus' story today. There is so much at stake here with the Good Samaritan parable—for faith, for justice, and for democracy—right now.

LET JESUS DO THE TALKING

If the question "Who is my neighbor?" is the *most central to our faith and democracy today,* it must be made personal. Who is in and who is out? Who belongs and who does not? Who is "us" and who is "them"? Does our sense of community and democracy go beyond our ethnicity and geography, beyond our tribe? Do we mean "neighbor" only to apply to those whom we perceive to be like us? How, exactly, do we bring neighbors who are different and even distant from us into our community of faith and also into a multiracial democracy? Do social categories, even oppressive categories, define us? Or do we see worth and dignity in each other as persons—as all made in the image and likeness of God (Genesis 1:26)? That is a faith question that we need to be asking ourselves and that pastors should now be asking of their congregations— week in and week out. It is the gospel question for our time.

In a democracy, citizens agree and disagree, collaborate and compete, but must still be neighbors and not enemies. The core issue is what is our *relationship* to one another, especially when the other is in need. We must bring this message of Jesus back into communities of faith. And those politicians—who are literally debasing our neighbors—must be defeated at the ballot box. "Citizenship" must be much more than just a legal term; Who is our "neighbor?" must extend beyond who receives official documentation. Citizens as neighbors must also be a common moral identity, a relationship between people who are part of the same country and community, despite their differences, and who choose to participate in the debates and decisions about the common good of a nation. Do we all belong in this country, and do we also belong to each other in some foundational way?

We see dangerously expanding ideologies that don't regard "others" as belonging—"Go back to where you came from!" Our neighbors are not seen as fellow citizens, but as enemies to destroy, and even erase from our culture and politics by banning their books and history.

That is the *essence of white Christian nationalism*. In our political landscape, tensions are rising, fears are being stoked, and violence is increasing. But the Good Samaritan parable could teach us at this critical time if we have the courage to listen. In the Christian community, and beyond, *it is time to let Jesus do the talking and for us to do the listening*.

I always glean wisdom from the spiritually creative biblical commentaries of Black contemplative pastor Howard Thurman, whose book *Jesus and the Disinherited* was one that Dr. King reportedly always carried in his briefcase when he was traveling.[6] In another book, *Sermons on the Parables,* Thurman describes how the Good Samaritan parable is able, and indeed intended by Jesus, to break down the barriers that every culture draws to segregate and protect themselves from one another.[7] And Thurman reveals how Jesus' description of who our "neighbor" is transforms how we can "actively relate ourselves to one another."

It's not easy, Thurman says, but we can find new ways to relate to one another, exactly *because* of how God relates to us and how that makes "a new world of possibilities open up." The Good Samaritan, Thurman says, "lived on the other side of the tracks" from the wounded man who he stopped to help. "This is a very simple story. Very simple. Who is my neighbor? according to the story," says Thurman, "any man whose need calls me, and I respond to that need."

Thurman acknowledges that people divide themselves into tribes to defend and even to define themselves. "But Jesus seems to be insisting that we relate ourselves to the person," he says. Jesus' call here is to move beyond "tolerance" of other groups. That movement toward a person gets beyond the "limitations" of our world view where those different from us "become secondary." The primary thing is that "When I say, 'I love,' it means that I'm involved in an encounter that leads from the core of me to the core of you." And that is what changes our core, and can even change the core values of a society. Our experience always teaches us that. The white people who are most against immigrants are those who have never lived anywhere near them, and the American citizens most open to immigrants are those who have "encountered" them in their communities.

But Thurman says we have to work at this. "And Jesus says that's the way God deals with human life. And that's the way we are supposed to deal with human life." And to the degree that we work at it, "It is a reasonable thing to dream about a time when this world will be a decent place for friendly men [and women] underneath a friendly sky. Let's try and see." This is the sermon we need to hear afresh today.

Thurman says, "For states, for cultures, and for civilizations, to build themselves into positions of security and power and domination means seeing to it that a line is drawn between those who are and those who are not." He concludes, "One of the reasons why I think that the goals of religion, certainly the religion about which Jesus was insisting, the goals of religion and the goals of civilization, must, of necessity, be mutually exclusive." That is radical indeed, and points to the prophetic and transformative role that religion is supposed to have in a society.

THE RADICAL COMMANDMENT: LOVE IS NOT "US" AND "THEM"

The great commandment, as the lawyer realized, is central to answering all these questions. "Love the Lord your God with all your heart, your mind, your strength; and love your neighbor as yourself." This *double love* commandment is core to the teaching of all of the Abrahamic religious traditions—Christianity, Judaism, and Islam. Jesus says that this is the summation of the law. "On these two commandments hang all the law and the prophets" (Matthew 22:40). This is what *everything* is about: love God, with all of your heart, mind, soul; and then don't forget to love your neighbor as yourself. And indeed, the second commandment—to love your neighbor as yourself—becomes a test of the first commandment: to love God with your whole self. They go together; you can't have one without the other. We are able to love our neighbors *because* God first loves us—all of us.

Many religious people delight in sharing how much they love God. They want to tell us, and even boast about, their individual relationship with God, how close they are to God, how much they talk to God and pray to God and how much God reveals to them. It's about them and God—but not about their neighbor. But here, Jesus says *no,* it's not just about loving God. Faith begins with our relationship to God, but it extends to our neighbor, so "love your neighbor as yourself" is the outcome of loving God.

Jon Meacham, professor at Vanderbilt University and an Episcopalian, talks publicly about democracy all the time. And the message he repeats again and again is that democracy utterly depends on us treating one another as "neighbors" and not as "enemies." He points out that in a nation of about fifty-fifty voting patterns, democracy depends on "just enough" people treating one another as neighbors. This question, he argues, is core to our democracy.

RUNNING AGAINST THE "OTHER" AS A POLITICAL STRATEGY

When I watched Donald Trump come down the escalator at Trump Tower to announce his White House ambitions, I suspected, and feared, that he would become our next president.

The people around me thought I was crazy. The media didn't think it could happen. Republicans didn't even think it was possible at the time. Certainly, the Democrats didn't think so, either. All my colleagues at *Sojourners* thought I was nuts.

Trump was basing his candidacy on fear of the *other*—and, ultimately, that fear leads to hate. As we saw in the Trump presidency, eventually that hate led to violence, most dramatically on January 6. Donald Trump began his political career by attacking immigrants as *others*. *They* are coming to get us, harm us, rape us, bring drugs and gangs and disease into *our* country. Trump claimed that the first Black president was illegitimate; he was an *other* and not one of "us."

Trump was saying from the outset of his political candidacy: people different from you are *not* your neighbors. You don't have to love them. In fact, you have permission to hate them. And I will protect you from *them.*

Trump was always running against the *other, running literally against those who Jesus said were our neighbors and whom we are called to love.* From the beginning of his political career, and throughout his candidacy for president, he was building his case for us against them. And I knew those demons run deep in America and, in a close election, Trump could win.

Many Americans could not understand, and were astonished, that so many white Christians, and white evangelicals in particular, supported Donald Trump.

Here is what their fellow evangelical Michael Gerson, former speechwriter to George W. Bush and longtime *Washington Post* columnist, had to say about why this was so painfully true. This is from one of his last pieces in the *Post* before his untimely death from cancer at age fifty-four. In my opinion, this timely and prophetic piece was, in effect, part of Gerson's last "will and testament." At his memorial service, which I was blessed to attend, this final essay of Mike's was lifted up several times by those who knew him well. Gerson, a political and theological conservative, wrote:

Leaders in the Republican Party have fed, justified, and exploited conservative Christians' defensiveness in service to an aggressive, reaction-
ary politics. This has included deadly mask and vaccine resistance, the
discrediting of fair elections, baseless accusations of gay "grooming"
in schools, the silencing of teaching about the United States' history
of racism, and (for some) a patently false belief that Godless conspir-
acies have taken hold of political institutions.[8]

Conservative white evangelicals' play for political power was a Faustian bargain, he thought:

The credibility of religious conservatives is undermined by the friends
they have chosen to keep. Their political alignment with MAGA activists has given exposure and greater legitimacy to once-fringe ideas,
including Confederate nostalgia, white nationalism, antisemitism, replacement theory, and QAnon accusations of satanic child sacrifice
by liberal politicians.

[. . .] Christ's revolt against the elites could hardly be more different
from the one we see today. Conservative evangelicalism has, in many
ways, become the kind of religious tradition against which followers
of Jesus were initially called to rebel.

The best way to respond to bad religion is with true religion. Preach
this parable, pastors. Bring out your Bibles, believers. And you, nonreligious people of conscience, you can say to the white Christian nationalists, "Wait a minute! That's not what your story of the Good Samaritan
says. You better read that one again!"

Excluding and attacking those who are different, rejecting the
outcasts and the outsiders, in particular, literally puts you at odds
with Jesus. You have sold out your discipleship for political power.
And seeing his fellow evangelicals on the wrong side of Jesus broke
Gerson's heart:

Woe to evangelical exclusion. In their overwhelming, uncritical support of Trump and other nationalist Republicans—leaders who could never win elections without evangelical votes—White religious conservatives have joined a political movement defined by an attitude of "us" vs. "them," and dedicated to the rejection and humiliation of social outsiders and outcasts. From the start, the Trump-led GOP dehumanized migrants as diseased and violent. It attacked Muslims as suspect and dangerous. Even when evangelical Christians refuse to mouth the words of racism, they have allied themselves with the promoters of prejudice and white grievance. How can it be that believers called to radical inclusion are the most hostile to refugees of any group in the United States? How can anyone who serves God's boundless kingdom of love and generosity ever rally to the political banner "America First"?

In another article, Gerson apologized for previously underestimating the ugly force of racism in American history and public life.

[. . .] This is among the worst errors of moral judgment I have made as a columnist. I tended to view bigotry as one of America's defects or failures. The historical works I read often tried to defend the best elements of the American ideal as dramatically outweighing the worst moments of its application.

But no: the country was soiled by the sin of slavery from its birth. Many White people became wealthy by systematically stealing the wages and wealth of their Black neighbors. White Americans established a social and religious system designed to grant themselves dominance, often while trying to convince African Americans of God's lower regard for their souls. Such systemic abuse could be found in North and South (though it was more heavy-handed in the South). Slaves were raped with impunity and murdered without consequence. And if someone in the North promulgated abolitionist ideas with too much effect, they could be targeted for bounties, beaten in the street, or killed.[9]

Gerson, at the end of his life, strongly acknowledged America's original sin and spoke prophetically to both a dangerous political situation and a religious failure, connecting the two. I am from the same evangelical tradition as Mike was, and we both have witnessed a literal betrayal of the good news of the gospel of Jesus with the bad news of white Christian nationalism.

So if you still believe in the words of Jesus, speak up! We need everyone to challenge those old generation leaders who have sold out the gospel for their politics.

OUTSIDE YOUR NEIGHBORHOOD

The key teaching from Jesus in the Good Samaritan parable is that your neighbors, as Jesus defines them, most likely live outside of your neighborhood. The great commandment, to love God and to love your neighbor as yourself, is, again, in all of our Abrahamic religious traditions. And it is at the center of the best ethics around the world. Religious and nonreligious people hold up this notion of "the golden rule," of treating others the way you would like to be treated.

When our political leaders and media platforms deny the neighbor ethic and even reverse it to make neighbors into enemies, it becomes harder to live out the ethic of Jesus. The Good Samaritan parable was quite offensive to those who first heard it. It remains disruptive and challenging today. Our neighbor is the one outside of our comfort zone, the one we least expect, the one we didn't invite to dinner. A recent study conducted by the Public Religion Research Institute showed that 91 percent of the average white American's closest friends and family members are white, and just 1 percent are Black. One of the most glaring statistics showed that, when asked to name their closest friends and family members, 75 percent of white Americans didn't name even one person who was not white.[10] That statistic continues to stun my students and explains a lot about why we are where we are.

CHOOSING OUR PATHWAYS

When it comes to the neighbor question, I often quote the Latin American theologian Gustavo Gutiérrez. The Peruvian faith leader says: "Who is my neighbor? The neighbor . . . *is not he whom I find in my path, but rather he in whose path I place myself* [emphasis added], he whom I approach and actively seek."[11]

Our pathways are often determined by others. They were created for you, so that you will never meet those people that Jesus calls your neighbors. In America, as I described in my own personal family history, our pathways are deliberately determined by race, economics, and culture. Our geographies are planned, by public policy, to segregate us from one another, to separate us from those who are different from us, the ones Jesus calls us to love.

Your path includes those with whom you share meals, talk about your kids, health, education, jobs, and your future. Your family paths include your children's classmates and their parents, your kids' teammates and the parents you watch so many games with. Are most the same as you—in terms of race, economics, and culture? Or are some different from you?

As I often share about my own pathway, I was a Little League baseball coach for eleven years and twenty-two seasons with both of our boys. I knew not only the many kids I coached, but most of their parents too. And our house was always the "club house" for the teams and their families. It was the place where we would have meetings and parties, where parents would leave their players before and after games if they couldn't make it to practices or a game on time. And it was the place where we celebrated our championships, passed out the trophies, and heard the stories from each player about what the team meant to them and how it became like "family."

When I would tell my white players how their Black teammates all had to have "the talk" with their own parents about how to behave in the presence of police officers, they were first stunned and then angry. It was a talk that they as white players had never heard, and something their own white parents often knew nothing about either. But just talking about "the talk" created a kind of solidarity between the boys and a concern for what their "neighbors" were experiencing. As they have gotten older, I am still in touch with many of them and we keep talking about the systemic racism they first heard about as twelve-year-olds.

Proximity is what creates the concern, understanding, solidarity, and even action to change. But to have proximity with neighbors outside your normal path, you have to place yourself in other pathways, as Gutiérrez teaches us. Those movements on all our parts are what will make all the difference. To seek out other pathways is hard; but it is also a discipline for democracy and an act of faith.

COMING NEAR

Some of the biblical translations of the Good Samaritan story speak of the Samaritan "coming near" to the wounded man by the side of the road. Coming near to the victim allowed him to see the man and his condition, and have "pity on him." *Proximity* is what most often creates understanding, empathy, and compassion. Some of you know those connections in your own life.

I will never forget when the emerging Sojourners intentional community initially arrived in Washington, DC, in 1975. Coming from Chicago, we were in two packed trucks that pulled up in front of the two houses, side by side, that we had rented but never seen. On the street to welcome us were a bunch of neighborhood kids who promised to help us move in if we gave them all the old mattresses they assumed would be in those old and abandoned houses. Of course, we said yes! They took many mattresses away and helped us carry all our stuff into our new homes. A couple of days later, after we were settled in, the kids came back and invited us to see what they had done with the mattresses. In the alley down the block from our new homes, all our mattresses, and many others, were spread end to end and the kids proceeded to demonstrate their amazing acrobatic skills. "We are the Afro-bats," they proudly told us, and over time, we saw them win many acrobatic tournaments in Washington, DC.

We began to tutor many of those children in our new houses and got to know them and their families over the next several years. Ultimately, the biggest family's rent was raised and rats had literally invaded their household. We invited them to move in with us in a third house we had set up. All nine children and their mom stayed with us for a year until they could find another home. I have vivid memories of tutoring one of the boys in reading by taking him down to the Lincoln Memorial—where he had never been before—and listening as he read the words of Lincoln's second inaugural address. I was deeply moved watching him successfully falter through the words of Lincoln's plan to heal a divided nation: "With malice toward none, with charity for all, with firmness in the right as God gives us to see the right, let us strive on to finish the work we are in to bind up the nation's wounds, to care for him who shall have borne the battle and for his widow and orphan—to do all which may achieve and cherish a just and lasting peace among ourselves and with all nations."

We spent a lot of time with these young people as they grew up; there were lots of laughing and crying, lots of conversations about family, hopes, fears, and dreams. And when people spoke of African American youth in the nation's capital, we immediately thought of Earl, Ronnie, Wesley, Theresa, Peaches, Isaac, and all the other kids with whom we had such close proximity. Proximity changes perceptions. We learned how to love our neighbors.

WHEN FAITH TRUMPS POLITICS

We need better stories. After Donald Trump came into office, he continued his anti-immigrant fear and loathing. He talked about "caravans" of immigrants coming from the south, from Mexico; about lepers.

When was the last time an American president talked about leprosy? Leprosy is a trigger; it sparks fear. In particular, he was trying to relate to evangelical white Christians who know what leprosy is from biblical stories.

So, when these asylum seekers came to America, needing survival and freedom from tyranny and threats to their lives, the Trump administration put them in cages. Literally in cages. And then that same administration tore those immigrants' children from their parents' sides and put the children and their parents in *separate cages*.

Imagine that you're seeking asylum, and you're frightened. You're in a dangerous situation in your own country; dangerous enough to gather your children and the few possessions you can carry and to walk thousands of miles to a new place, anxiously hoping for a safer and better life in a place where you have been told they will welcome you. But as soon as you arrive, they take your children away from you. Some of those families still have never been reunited. *Us and them* did that.

The Trump administration expected that most Americans would be indifferent to these arriving immigrants and even their children. After all, Pope Francis had shared his concern about the "globalization of indifference" to human suffering. But this time the Trump people were wrong and there was both moral outrage and pushback.

I was struck by how many of the countless protests that erupted all over the country drew young couples, often bringing and even carrying their own children. Their message was clear. These immigrant children are our children too; and we care about them too. Even conservative women from evangelical churches showed up with signs that read, "We care about children at the border, as well as children in the womb."

A number of Republicans were appalled by Trump's policy, as were some Christians who had been supportive of him up to that point. It was just too much. He had, indeed, crossed a line. I believe we have to reconnect with that outrage and empathy if we are going to save the soul of democracy.

THE MEETING THAT NEVER HAPPENED

When immigrant children were being separated from parents and placed in separate cages, I was invited to a meeting up on Capitol Hill. It was to be a private conversation with senators on both sides of the political aisle who were upset about this monstrous act. They were deeply troubled, but they didn't know how to intervene. The Republican senators, in particular, were unsure of how to proceed. Torn between their consciences and their politics, they knew they had to proceed carefully in light of the potential ramifications of criticizing a Republican president. They wanted a private moral conversation.

I arrived at the office of a Democratic senator and found a large group of senators gathered in his small private back-room office. It was crowded, so much so that a few of the attendees had seated themselves on the floor. It was important that this meeting remain confidential. All the senators who attended, both Democrat and Republican, were Christians and struggling to determine the wisest path forward. How could they honor their faith and take effective action? They felt deeply bothered by the matter and knew in their gut that this policy was wrong, in direct opposition to their faith.

What followed was a conversation about how they could fulfill their political duties without sacrificing their personal faith. We began to talk about the moral dimensions of this situation, and it wasn't long before the conversation turned to the central question of this chapter: *What does it mean to love your neighbor as yourself?*

I raised the Samaritan parable and what it said about loving people outside of our neighborhoods and our country. I offered my thoughts, but mostly I listened to the senators' earnest concerns about what it might mean to follow their hearts and the heart of their faith, and to confront the president. We had the kind of deep moral conversation that doesn't always happen in the halls of power. When I left the room, I did not know how they would proceed, but I knew that faith had been lifted up in the midst of politics.

Eventually, they came to a decision. And out of that conversation, and a number of follow-up discussions between some of those leaders individually, emerged a letter addressed to Donald Trump; one signed by Democrats, as expected, but also nine Republicans, which was quite unexpected. Here is the letter that was sent to Donald Trump at the White House:

Dear Mr. President:

We write to urge your administration to prioritize the reunification of families and to ensure that, from this point forward, the default position of the United States of America is to keep families together.

While we represent constituents from all faiths and political backgrounds, we have all heard one consistent message—the United States government should not separate children from their families except in extreme circumstances. As we work to find a permanent solution, we urge the administration to use all available resources currently at its disposal to reunite families as soon as possible.

Throughout our history, faith-based organizations have partnered with the federal government to help achieve its humanitarian goals. Faith-based organizations, including groups like Sojourners, Catholic Charities USA, World Vision, the National Association of Evangelicals, the Christian Community Development Association, Church World Service, and World Relief are willing and able to support reunification efforts and provide critical services for children and families in need. We encourage you to partner with the faith community to assist with family reunification and keeping families together in the future.

We remain committed to working together to fix our broken immigration system. Enforcement of our immigration laws should be a high priority, but we must also adhere to our core moral values as Americans.

Thank you for your attention to this important matter.

The message was clear and united: this policy is unacceptable to us. Don't do this again.

The letter didn't get a lot of press, but it certainly made its way to the White House. And because faith was invoked in politics and across party lines, it worked. Donald Trump never did that again.

At a moment of collective moral outrage, senators from both parties united their voices for what was right. These are the precedents that we can experience and witness to what is possible when we follow the example of the Good Samaritan and truly love our neighbors. We cannot achieve the common good or become "one body" and a perfect union if we just submit to the lines of race, religion, or political party.

A GOOD EXAMPLE FROM OUTSIDE MY TRIBE

In late 2000, I received a call from Austin, Texas. When I asked my team at *Sojourners* who was calling, they said, "Them!" After thirty-six days of recounts to determine the winner of a historically close presidential election, Republican George W. Bush had just been declared president by the Supreme Court over Al Gore, leaving many Democrats deeply distressed.[12]

The new president's team was calling with an invitation to talk about poverty and faith. I did not know what to expect when I arrived for this gathering in a basement of a Baptist church in Texas. I saw about twenty-five people, some of whom I assumed had voted for Bush, and others I knew had not—like me.

The newly named president arrived and said he mostly wanted to listen to help him understand how to relate to poverty, especially as a Christian. After the formal discussion, Bush lingered to talk further in smaller groups—some one-to-one. He came over to introduce himself and told me, "Jim, I don't understand poverty. I have never really known poor people or been around much poverty. I am just a white Republican guy who doesn't get it. Help me understand."

I suggested that he spend time listening to poor people themselves and with people who live and work with poor people in their neighborhoods and communities. After a bit, he looked around and yelled, "Gerson!" This was the first time I met Michael Gerson, President Bush's chief speech writer, whom I quoted earlier. Bush directed him to take notes on our conversation, and some of the language from our talk about poverty ultimately appeared in the new president's first inaugural address.

Later, I would make trips to the White House to further discuss the poverty issues and the formation of the president's new faith-based initiative to deal with it. Some of the people on the left flank in my tribe were critical of me for doing so. But faith and poverty, and what it might mean to love our neighbors, were being raised up. My brief time at the White House ended when Bush invaded Iraq. I was one of the first faith leaders to oppose the war on principles of faith. I wasn't invited back to the White House. But while I was clearly opposed to the war, I continue to commend George W. Bush for another policy that serves as a shining example of loving our neighbors, including those different from ourselves.

That was the story of the President's Emergency Plan for AIDS Relief (PEPFAR), the initiative Bush began to combat the HIV/AIDS epidemic in Africa twenty years ago, which saved twenty-five million lives.[13] In my view, this was the most important accomplishment of Bush's presidency and one that he still gets little credit for. A 2023 opinion piece by Nicholas Kristof and others at *The New York Times* echoes this sentiment: "With the anniversary of the Iraq invasion, there's lots of commentary about his miscalculations and failures, and there should be. But we liberals also have to acknowledge that the most important humanitarian program of modern times wasn't started by a progressive we admire but by a conservative evangelical whose policies we deplored."[14]

Mike Gerson led the way on PEPFAR in the White House, and Bono praised it from the stages of U2 concerts around the world. To take bold action to support the many millions of victims of HIV/AIDS, with all the surrounding rhetoric condemning homosexuality and immorality, was hardly an initiative one might expect from an evangelical president. Also forgotten by most people is that combating HIV/AIDS was the first stated cause for a young congresswoman and devout Catholic named Nancy Pelosi. Loving our neighbors, especially across the lines of our tribes and the factions of us versus them, will be a vital pathway forward if democracy is to be saved and secured for all of us.

On March 7, 2015, more than a decade after my opposition to the Iraq War suspended my invitations to the Bush White House, I was invited to the fiftieth-anniversary commemoration of "Bloody Sunday" at the Edmund Pettus Bridge in Selma, Alabama. Congressman John Lewis, who as a young civil rights activist was beaten almost to death that day by the horse-mounted troops of racist sheriff Jim Clark, had the blessing of introducing the new president Barack Obama. I was blessed to walk up the Pettus Bridge with Lewis and all the still living "foot soldiers" from that historic and courageous day, some now pushing walkers or in wheelchairs—along with President Obama, Michelle Obama, and their daughters Malia and Sasha.

All of a sudden, I looked up and there was former president George W. Bush and first lady Laura! They had not been a part of the event or press conference and, apparently, just wanted to be there on this historic day. George Bush walked over to say hello: "Jim, I have really missed our conversations!"

I had too.

THE ELEPHANT IN THE ROOM

Again, in nearly every political conversation and every debate in Washington, hardly anyone acknowledges the one thing we all know will inevitably come to pass. As I said earlier in this book, by 2040, America will no longer be a majority white nation. We are approaching the day when America might become the world's first true multiracial democracy; and certainly, there are those who perceive this as a great threat. But the reality is that this will be the challenge and the opportunity to truly realize the constitutional vision of "a more perfect union." And all of this directly relates to the Good Samaritan parable. To acknowledge and respect the shift in our demography, we need a shift of our idea of who our neighbors are.

For all the flaws of the documents conceived by our founding fathers, at their heart was a promise and a vision, likely beyond any of their imaginations. Granted, these were white men and property owners who wanted to take governance of their nation away from the king of England; but what they envisioned was ultimately more universal.

This vision eventually also applied even to white men who didn't own property. It much later applied to their wives and female partners and friends. And despite their enslavement and all other evidence to the contrary, it finally applied to Black people, who would not be clearly granted the right to vote until 1965, almost two hundred years later. And yet, those rights are still being threatened through voter suppression by people who continue to resist the perfect union promised for this nation. The battle is not over.

Faith communities can and should offer a moral compass that transforms American life, culture, and politics and goes deeper than politics, deeper than power, deeper than self-interest. It is through following the example of the Good Samaritan that we will finally realize this more perfect union.

NO EXCEPTIONS

Together, our faith communities are very diverse. And yet, despite the fact that we share in the love of God, most of us are not living, working, or building together for the sake of the gospel, or, as the gospel text says, for the kingdom of God. We fail to see that our Bible *and* our founding fathers shared a common vision: one body and a more perfect union.

We could and we should pull ourselves together for the sake of the nation. We could and should pull ourselves together for the sake of that kingdom witness, that gospel witness, that multi-faith commitment, at this very divisive and polarized time.

To Jesus' directive "Love your neighbor as yourself," we could add a postscript: "No exceptions." Love your neighbor as yourself—no exceptions. We could post this on churches, other congregations and gathering places. More important, though, we could live it. Because as faith communities, and as a nation, we are making exceptions when those social barriers still persist in white congregations in particular. That is what must change by nothing less than a direct and deliberate pastoral strategy in all of our denominations.

If we are to be of service to the world, we have to live by our faith with integrity, reaching out like good Samaritans to different races, different civic and religious communities, and, yes, to different political affiliations. That doesn't mean all our churches need to be individually fully integrated. Black churches can still remain the glue that holds together Black communities, for example. What it does mean, however, is that the body of Christ has different expressions that can and should be reaching out to each other and working together around critical issues in their communities.

Paul said, "There are different kinds of gifts, but the same Spirit. There are different kinds of service, but the same Lord. There are different kinds of working, but the same God works all of them in all men. Now to each one the manifestation of the Spirit is given for the common good" (1 Corinthians 12:4–7). This doesn't mean complete assimilation of differences. It means we must show the nation what it means for all of us to love our neighbor as ourselves, and that we must share our gifts for the good of *all*.

FOR A HEALTHY NATION

When we were in the middle of the pandemic, there was a tremendous need to increase access to vaccinations and overcome the reluctance and skepticism that many had about their effectiveness. Lack of access and lack of trust were keeping too many people away from their personal and public health protection—especially racial minorities whose experience with health systems, historically and personally, led to that mistrust. Many of us in the religious community viewed this as a matter of faith, a potential means toward pursuing the common good. Realizing that this concern crossed lines of color and faith, some of us came together to form a new coalition we called "Faith-4Vaccines."

Through countless phone calls and meetings, hours of planning and strategizing, and much prayer, we were able to come together and serve literally millions of people by offering vaccinations in our many congregations. With multi-faith medical teams in diverse religious congregations, from churches to synagogues to mosques, we became bound together to vaccinate those who had less access or genuine misgivings. Our wonderful coordinator was Dr. Mohamed Elsanousi with, as he would insist, lots of help from me and others.

The initiative was an unequivocal success, so much so that the White House eventually reached out to us. They had planned to form their own COVID faith caucus, but when they saw the good work we were doing they decided to just join with us.

We held a White House interfaith summit that was seen by hundreds of thousands of Americans—leaders across our faith communities. Those who tuned in witnessed the coming together of faith leaders, scientists, and those working in the White House to address the COVID crisis and ensure that *all* had access to the best care.

Of course, it was the *others* who were most in need. They had the most obstacles and the most apprehensions to overcome. One story illustrates this particularly well. Fully devoted to the cause, physician

Cameron Webb spent long days at the White House coordinating vaccination outreach to those with less access, while maintaining his regular hours as a doctor at night. One day, he shared with some of us his great frustration that despite all his expertise, knowledge, and skill, he still couldn't get his uncle Moe to get a vaccination! No matter what he said, Uncle Moe was not convinced.

But one day when Uncle Moe was getting his car washed, he looked across the street and saw a church offering vaccinations. He knew and trusted that church, and so he crossed the street, and he got vaccinated. He then called his nephew and shared the news, "I got vaccinated in one of those churches you're working with."

At a moment of crisis, Faith4Vaccines showed the way forward, how we could continue to be ourselves and stay true to our own faith and our own communities while coming together as one body, in perfect union, for something as vital as the public health of the nation. This we can do again and again across a whole range of issues that will determine the "health of the nation."

A POLITICS OF LOVE

As I have said, we have a present-day political situation that has us on a trajectory of fear, leading to hate, which results in violence. Just as I write in the spring of 2023, three horrible stories emerged about gun violence within just one week. A woman who had driven into the wrong driveway by mistake in Upstate New York was shot and killed; two young Texas cheerleaders who tried, also mistakenly, to get into the wrong car after practice were both shot with one in critical condition; and a sixteen-year-old Black teenager was shot when he rang the wrong doorbell in Kansas City, Missouri, looking for his younger brothers, and was then ignored by nearby households when he begged for help.

"Paranoia" is the word the best describes our contemporary situation, a very dangerous combination of guns and a complete lack of trust in one another—which is in such radical and horrible contrast to the Good Samaritan parable. In response to that growing danger, we need to rediscover what it means to love our neighbors.

What would a politics of love look like? How would we talk? How might we listen? How would we find empathy with one another? These are not hypotheticals, just as they weren't in Jesus' day. How do we see our neighbor in need? How do we respond as the Good Samaritan did, with mercy and compassion? We have to answer these questions if we want our faith professions to have any integrity.

What does the politics of neighbor love look like? We have to do something regarded as unnatural and somewhat surprising, as the parable demonstrates.

Back to Howard Thurman. In his classic book *Jesus and the Disinherited,* Thurman has four simple chapters on fear, deception, hate, and love. In his final chapter on love, Thurman concludes,

> Once the neighbor is defined, then one's moral obligation is clear. In the memorable story Jesus defined the neighbor by telling of the Good Samaritan. With artistry and great power, he depicted what happens when a man responds directly to human need across barriers of class, race, and condition. Every man is potentially every other man's neighbor. Neighborliness is nonspatial; it is qualitative. A man must love his neighbor directly, clearly, permitting no barriers between.[15]

That is what he calls love. "Love of the enemy means that a fundamental attack must be made on the enemy status. How can this be done? Does it mean merely ignoring the fact that he belongs to an enemy class? Hardly. For lack of a better term, an 'unscrambling' process is required."

I love Thurman's use of the word "unscrambling." That will now be required of all of us—unscrambling the false enemy status of those on the other side of all our divisions. That is what we need to talk about in our sermons, in the public statements of political leaders, in our local town meetings and neighborhood cafés, on our front porches, and at our dinner tables.

Howard Thurman goes directly to the church, as he should, and speaks as the minister of one of the first multiracial congregations in his time:

> It is necessary, therefore, for the privileged and the underprivileged to work on the common environment for the purpose of providing normal experiences of fellowship. This is one very important reason for the insistence that segregation is a complete ethical and moral evil. Whatever it may do for those who dwell on either side of the wall, one thing is certain: it poisons all normal contacts of those persons involved.

Thurman says, "The first step toward love is a common sharing of a sense of mutual worth and value. This cannot be discovered in a vacuum or in a series of artificial or hypothetical relationships. It has to be in a real situation." And that is what faith congregations are able and supposed to provide for people from all ways of life. "The common worship of God," Thurman says, "is such a moment. It is in this connection that *American Christianity has betrayed the religion of Jesus* [emphasis added]."

Those words were written in 1949 (hence the common references to "man"). But they are just as relevant today. The racial autocracies that rose up in Europe in the 1930s could not have existed without the support of the churches—like the German Protestant and Catholic churches that almost all Germans belonged to. In America, we are now in a similar situation. Only in our relationship to God and therefore also to one another can we overcome the divisive and violent barriers of race, wealth, and power. Our congregations are the places that will either provide a subservient accommodation to, or the overcoming of, these dangerous social barriers. If we fail at that, says Thurman, "The enormity of the sin cannot be easily grasped." But the "concept of reverence for personality, then, is applicable between persons from whom, in the initial instance, the heavy weight of statis has been sloughed off." What a wonderful piece of writing and what a hope for our con-gregations—to *slough off* the divisions that are crippling us. Let us find in the love of God and for one another the spirit and the power to just slough them off!

What Jesus is saying to us right now in the midst of our theologi-cal and political crisis is: love God. Love your neighbor. That's it. That's everything. Now go do it. And perhaps the Good Samaritan can show us the way.

3

MADE IN GOD'S IMAGE— OR NOT?

Then God said, Let us make humankind in our own image, according to our likeness.

—GENESIS 1:26

DO WE BELIEVE THAT ALL OF US—OF DIFFERENT RACES AND CULTURES, citizens or immigrants, Americans or from any nation, of every faith and no faith—are equally created in the image of God—or not? That's what Genesis 1:26 asks of us.

And what does the first chapter of the first book in the Bible have to do with voting rights?

Everything.

This early Genesis text is the moral foundation for voting rights—and all the human rights that any of us have. Will we dehumanize the "other," those who are not like us, or will we embrace the image of God (*imago dei* in Latin) in the equal humanity of all people, of all humankind? This is not just a theological question but a very practical one. Therefore, any strategy to make it harder for Black and brown, low-income people, and young people to vote is nothing less than *an assault on the* imago dei. That is why our spirituality is at stake here, far more than just politics.

KAIROS TIME

I believe that, in both a secular and spiritual sense, America has arrived at a "kairos moment." How do we finally make the moral transition from the beginning of slavery to the redemptive reality of a genuine multiracial democracy in the United States of America? The time has come. *Kairos* time.

The Bible counts two kinds of time. The first, "kronos," refers to our usual, tick-tock sense of life's passing. The second is God's time, "kairos," a critical moment when the world can change dramatically—even in a place as hostile to change as Washington, DC.

Kronos time often moves so slowly. But kairos, a time that can change the times, can create huge shifts in a moment, shifts that will reverberate for a long time—even for all time.

The word "kairos" is used eighty-six times in the New Testament. In Romans 5, Paul notes the kairos—"the perfect time"—when humanity was saved by Jesus' sacrifice. The theologian Paul Tillich called kairos the moment "when eternity erupts, transforming the world into a new state of being."

What will be our new state of being in America, if our fight for genuine multiracial democracy is won, or lost? The threats to democracy are more than just a question of equal citizenship, or even politics. If we believe that we are all of us made in the image of God—*imago dei*—then denying someone the right to vote is virtually silencing their God-given voice.

This is *why* Congressman John Lewis called the "precious" right to vote "almost sacred" when he addressed the 2012 Democratic National Convention. To suppress a vote on the basis of skin color is indeed *a throwing away of the image of God*. Any strategy that would negate people's votes because of their racial identity is a theological, biblical, and spiritual offense to God. A sacrilege.

Therefore, voter suppression and nullification are tests of both democracy and faith. As my dear friend and mentor Vincent Harding, noted Black historian and part of the inner circle of Dr. King's Southern movement, pointedly asked in many retreats he led, "Is America possible?" I believe that question has not yet been answered. This kairos time will answer that question one way or another.

BE QUIET, AND LISTEN TO WHAT GOD SAYS

The word "humankind" translated from the Hebrew does indeed mean all human beings that God created. Not some, but all. It is the starting place for all matters of human rights embedded in the many issues that now divide us. "Then God said, Let us make humankind in our own image, according to our likeness." We are made both in God's image and likeness—which conveys both our worth and our nature.

How has the moral imperative of this Genesis text been addressed by different people before? From the time in early America when Indigenous people and enslaved Africans were not regarded as fully human, to this moment when people of color still do not yet fully share power in a multiracial democracy—but now could. This is a crucial juncture to review and reflect afresh on this text from Genesis—central to both Jewish and Christian faiths, with parallel texts in other faiths.

Of course, the Genesis text is also philosophically—and, I would say, spiritually—tied to similar texts in the Declaration of Independence: "We hold these truths to be self-evident, that all men are created equal, that they are endowed by their Creator with certain unalienable Rights, that among these are Life, Liberty, and the pursuit of Happiness."

You don't have to be religious to see and understand equal human value, dignity of life, freedom, and happiness, or the flourishing of each individual to be central to the making of a good society. Even our political documents use sacred words like "created equal" and "unalienable rights," and "truths to be self-evident." Many consider these words in our founding political document to be grounded morally in Genesis 1:26. Our being created equally in the image of God undergirds every movement toward justice and respect for the dignity of every human life. Always has and always will.

"Then God said," begins the Genesis text, and, I like to imagine, *shuts up* all the other political noise that surrounds us. Be quiet! Listen to what God says! All of us are created equal and that spiritual reality must be named, *respected,* and reflected in our society and, yes, in our laws. The Genesis text is the biblical basis for a *theology of democracy* that we are developing throughout this book.

Those who want to prevent the coming of a multiracial democracy can't do so without the complicity, silence, or active support of churches. And to stand up for democracy, churches have to stand up to and speak out against its most dangerous and current threats.

As noted earlier, the rise of Nazism in Germany in the 1930s could not have succeeded without the support of the German churches that Hitler seduced and coerced into submission; and perhaps it was only the German churches or military that could have blocked and prevented the Third Reich; but both were easily co-opted. And here we stand again, now, in a different but parallel situation.

Those who want to dismiss the new restrictive voting laws as merely partisan—just trying to limit those who will likely vote for the other party—but not racial, must ask themselves these questions: Why does one party think that the majority of Black and brown voters will not be voting for them? Why do the poorest and most oppressed people in the country think that you are against them? It's time to be honest here.

DEMOCRACY COULD DIE AT THE BALLOT BOX

The process of sabotaging democracy has now become mainstream—with a whole political party committed to undermining free and fair elections. Harvard University political science professor Steven Levitsky, coauthor of *How Democracies Die,* says democracy can die at the ballot box. He makes the case that one of our two major political parties, the Republican Party, is no longer committed to accepting the results of elections, or even the peaceful transition of power.

In August 2022, Levitsky told me: "There is a powerful authoritarian reaction to the emergence of . . . a multiracial democracy, and that reaction is likely to lead us to a pretty serious constitutional crisis in years to come. . . . There is real risk of a stolen election in 2024."[1]

And, *voting is a problem for white Christian nationalism.* In their book *The Flag and the Cross,* Philip Gorski and Samuel Perry explain that the more closely someone identifies with Christian nationalism, the more likely they are to agree with the statement "We make it too easy to vote."[2]

The authors add, "Even after accounting for partisanship and political ideology, the more strongly white Americans affirm Christian nationalism, the more likely they were to respond to Trump's election loss with a view that voting access should be restricted even more." The research shows this same group believed "It's too easy to vote" after the 2020 election.

And, of course, white Christian nationalism wants to make it harder to vote in ways that most directly affect the most marginalized. The Lawyers Committee on Civil Rights (LCCR), an organization that tracks these issues over time, tells us, "Voting eligibility laws disproportionately burden communities of color, naturalized voters, and low-income individuals. Many states require additional documentation to prove voting eligibility, such as a passport, birth certificate, or naturalization papers."[3] Efforts to make voter registration easier and voting more accessible are routinely blocked by Republicans in Congress and state legislatures.

Perry warns:

> The threat of Christian nationalist violence like what we saw on January 6 is real. Yet because such threats are so obvious and shocking, and the role of Christian nationalism in them is so blatant, it makes confronting them more challenging. The threat of white Christian

nationalism as an ideological covering for voter suppression is perhaps more destructive because its influence is more subtle and its effects (electoral outcomes) are more consequential. Demagogues like Trump will no longer need to mobilize Christian nationalist violence after an electoral loss once they've ensured they'll never lose in the first place.[4]

As we read on in our Genesis text, we see that all human beings are called to have "dominion" together over God's creation. The better translation of the word is "stewardship," which has a very different meaning. But the white Christian nationalists want to bring the word "dominion" back—in the worst sense of the word as control and dominance. What they mean is that *some* people—white Christian people—are called to have dominion over other peoples, which is a deep distortion and an absolute heresy of the Genesis text. A precursor to white Christian nationalism was actually called "dominionist theology." Its abusive misinterpretation of the biblical word in Genesis is still alive and well in conservative white evangelical circles.

Old Testament scholar Walter Brueggemann suggests the biblical meaning of the word "dominion" here is like the relationship of a shepherd to sheep—to feed, care for, and protect them. Rather than the dominance of control, exploitation, and abuse, dominion has to do with a shepherd leader "securing the well-being of every other creature and bringing the promise of each to full fruition."[5] Caring for the creation and all of its creatures is what some biblical scholars call the first "great commission," or the "creation mandate," or the "cultural mandate," but one that serves all the creations and cultures that God has made. Jesus affirms that vision of "servant leadership" in calling his disciples to move beyond their own self-interests and personal agendas, then shows them what he means by washing his disciple's feet in John 13.

In his book *Genesis,* Brueggemann goes on to say,

Being made in God's image meant that humans were created to rule over creation in the way that God ruled over creation. Creatively using power to invite, evoke, and permit was what made Homo sapiens special and a reflection of God, because this is the way that God exercised God's power. God ruled as a servant-king, but not as a dictator-tyrant; so should the species made in God's image.[6]

Bad white Christian nationalist theology gets very practical and dangerous when it comes to voting rights. When white Christian nationalists claim an election was stolen, they are reflecting their belief that some votes don't or shouldn't count. As Philip Gorski told CNN, "It's the idea that we are the people, and our vote should count, and you're not the people, and . . . you don't really deserve to have a voice." He continued, paraphrasing the mindset of Christian nationalists: "It doesn't matter what the voting machines say, because we know that all real Americans voted for Donald Trump."[7] So curtailing voting rights is core to the ideology of white Christian nationalism.

THE GENESIS TEST OF OUR TIME

The battle over voting rights going on right now in America will determine every other issue that we care about. Issues like poverty, racial justice, policing and criminal justice, health care, human dignity on many fronts, the economy, educational opportunity, access to housing, the meaning of life and family values, liberty and freedom, immigration reform, gun laws, neighborhood safety, national security, and the defining questions of climate change, among others—will all be impacted and even determined by the success or failure of democracy shaped by voting rights. With all of this at stake, voting rights is also a faith issue, even a test of faith.

In the election of 2020, America had the largest voter turnout in US history.[8] That included the largest turnout of Black and brown voters; and their impact was felt all over the country. Part of that high turnout was, of course, due to the extension of voting access because of the pandemic—with more days of early voting, more permission for absentee voting, more assistance with disability voting, more conveniently located polling places and drop boxes.

So, why wouldn't that record turnout be a good thing? Why wouldn't making the most fundamental and critical act of citizenry—voting—much easier be celebrated as a great accomplishment?

As we have seen, there was no evidence of any significant or meaningful voter fraud in 2020. This has been attested by way of endless legislative inquiries, repeated voter recounts, court examinations, and decisions by judges appointed by both Republicans and Democrats—including unanimously by judges appointed by Donald Trump.[9] Despite that, Trump has created and continued the "Big Lie" that the 2020 election was "stolen"—an election he lost decisively.

Republican candidates for office now, unbelievably, are being vetted for whether they still support Trump and prove their loyalty to him by subscribing to the Big Lie, which is now central to the party's doctrine and strategy. It is stunning that a *majority* of Republican candidates in the 2022 election were "election deniers" who would not acknowledge that Joe Biden legitimately won the 2020 presidential election.[10]

FAKE FRAUD, REAL RACISM

Ironically, but not at all surprisingly, in 2021, the year following the biggest voter turnout in history, lawmakers in nineteen states passed thirty-four laws to restrict voting access and make it harder to vote.[11] In just a few months, many of those attempts to curtail voting rights succeeded. These new laws shorten the windows and days during which one can vote, make it more difficult to remain on absentee voter lists, limit ballot drop boxes, impose strict signature requirements, expand voter purges, make the locations of polling places more difficult to travel to for low-income minority people, and even ban the act of providing water and snacks to those lining up to vote! And as I mentioned earlier, the longest lines to vote are in Black and brown neighborhoods.

Even court rulings have described such states' laws for what they really are. For instance, in November 2021 a North Carolina superior court struck down a 2018 voter ID law that had been added to the state's constitution via referendum a few weeks earlier. The majority opinion ruling stated that the law "was motivated at least in part by an unconstitutional intent to target African American voters."[12] Similarly, a 2012 North Carolina election law was struck down by a federal appeals court, which stated the laws had been written by Republican legislators with "almost surgical precision" to thwart Black voters. Stacey Abrams, who many believe lost the Georgia governor's race in 2020 due to voter purges, says, "Voter suppression is no longer billy clubs and hoses and dogs. It's administrative rules, bureaucratic barriers. It's precincts that seem to close in the dead of night."[13]

Most dangerous and alarming, though, is how some of these laws, passed now in fourteen states, could give state legislatures or judges the right to oversee all elections and even overturn the results of local elections—if they so choose.[14] And, of course, these are majority Republican state legislatures, skewed that way to promote rural and white voters over urban ones. This is a partisan power grab, which likens to the old days of Jim Crow.

A compelling *Politico* piece on June 1, 2022, before the midterm elections, described the strategy as fourfold: recruit, train, challenge, and overturn elections with legions of antidemocratic activists from the national to the state, to the local, and down to the precinct levels—to allege "fake fraud," aim for voter desertification, and swing elections by making it harder for the votes of people of color to be cast and counted.[15] This strategy is all out in the open now.

This most threatening provision in the new voting laws is "voter subversion," or more precisely, as Dr. King called it in his 1963 "I Have A Dream" speech, "voter nullification." That is, erasing Black and brown people from democracy—from America—by erasing their votes in pre-dominantly white state legislatures.

An emerging strategy now includes new voter suppression laws; racially and politically motivated gerrymandering in redrawing voting district lines; blocking comprehensive immigration reform to prevent more brown voters; rejecting the voting rights of returning citizens after they complete prison sentences—going along with the hugely disproportionate mass incarceration of people of color. All this is painfully consistent with American racial history. Our divisions now are no longer just North and South, but more rural and urban and including metro suburban areas, which are becoming more diverse. State legislatures are still often controlled by white rural voters, so the threats to genuine democracy are very real. Important Supreme Court decisions on those subjects are being decided as I write, with the battles over their implementations still to come.

THE *IMAGO DEI* MOVEMENT

But, again, this book is *a call to action, to peaceful arms.* There are encouraging and growing signs of clergy and others mobilizing to counter this threat to voting rights. I was a part of founding one new network, Faiths United to Save Democracy (FUSD), which is multifaith, multiracial, and multigenerational.

Based in ten key vulnerable states where voter restriction and suppression laws threaten free and fair voting, the campaign began with educating and enlisting interfaith leaders, then meeting with state election officials, including secretaries of state, to send the message "We are watching."

Our efforts then turn toward voter registration and mobilization, to assisting voter turnout, and finally to *voter protection* by training almost one thousand "poll chaplains," so far, to protect the vote and voters on election day and help de-escalate potential conflict in critical places. The moral task of voter protection has linked "lawyers and collars" together and this mission has connected people both inside and outside of the religious community.

We are now holding regular meetings with leaders in Michigan, Wisconsin, Ohio, Pennsylvania, North Carolina, Georgia, Florida, Alabama, Texas, and Arizona and are building a movement of hope with practical consequences for democracy and the common good. Bishops, pastors, and preachers across our denominational and religious boundaries are enjoying being together and not just at election time.

It is very good news that clergy from many faith traditions are coming together in response to these new strategies of voter suppression. In many conversations with Black clergy, I heard reminders of how we have fought this fight before and, in the words of the old spiritual, "Ain't nobody going to turn me around!" Younger white clergy are joining in too, exemplified on a recent call with a new Presbyterian pastor in Georgia who shared what she tells her congregation, "This is the gospel! If you don't want to see our church get involved with voting rights as a faith issue, you better go somewhere else!"

I join in Zoom conference calls—virtually every week now—discussing how to take action against voter suppression, something churches were deeply involved in before and during the Civil Rights Movement. Our conversations sometimes become personal and emotional. Rabbis express how important it is to them to work with Black clergy again for the first time since the Civil Rights Movement. And imams expressed their gratitude for finally being included in an interfaith clergy network. Even after discussing the hardest issues, the calls end with fervent and bonding prayer, and along with it a great sense of hope. I am often called upon to do the "moral vision" that begins our calls. And I always start with the Genesis text of this chapter. "We are the *imago dei* movement!" I exclaim—always to a chorus of "amens." I love the spirit of our calls; we remind one another that "God is bigger than voter suppression."

Dr. Barbara Williams-Skinner, of Skinner Leadership Institute, is my closest ally in this work. Dr. Skinner, who is also the co-convener of the National Network of African American Clergy, serves as the coordinator of Faiths United to Save Democracy (FUSD). When asked what keeps her going, she tells the story of the time she got to meet Fannie Lou Hamer while hosting her to speak at a major Congressional Black Caucus event.

This was in the later years of the famed civil rights leader's life. Deeply honored to be hosting her, Dr. Skinner took the opportunity to ask: "You've given so much for so long and worked so hard, you've been attacked so often, and even savagely beaten. How do you keep going?" To which Fannie Lou Hamer replied, "When God tells you to do something, you just do it, baby!" Barbara quotes that response all the time!

Practically, the moral and spiritual battle for voting rights—to save both democracy and the church—*will require us all*. It means registering to vote and helping others to do so. It might mean getting parishioners to sign up to be a poll worker or volunteer. We need many people to help get other people out to polling places on election days. It will take some of us being trained to become poll chaplains or poll watchers to make sure nothing is going wrong; and to use their training to intervene if something does. It will mean talking about voting rights as a faith issue among your friends and family, in your congregations, and getting your pastor to preach about it from the pulpit.

We are at a point in time when fervent public praying for free and fair elections will be deeply necessary. If you are clergy, "show up" for democracy, for faith, and for the image of God in all our fellow citizens. Don't keep voting rights out of church as a political issue, but bring it into church as a religious issue. It is no violation of the separation of church and state to preach voting rights as a sacred duty and an image of God matter, and to pastorally assist people in securing their voting rights. All of us must join the *imago dei* movement for a diverse American future, and for a church that looks like the kingdom of God.

In response to the clear and growing threats to the votes of citizens of color, our "poll chaplains" are present at the most vulnerable polling places to provide truthful information, trusted assurance, moral presence, and practical protection for voters as needed. Wearing their pastoral garb, they have helped to defuse potential conflicts. They have escorted armed white men out of Black polling places by surrounding them with their clerical collars, visible prayers, and spiritual presence. They have circled pickup trucks with flying Confederate and Trump flags and rifles in the air outside of Black elementary schools serving as polling places, and with their religious authority persuaded them to exit the scene. We respond to threats by so-called voter challengers and interrogators. And these are much more than good civic actions. They strike a moral nerve in the culture and clock a kairos moment.

I love our "lawyers and collars" campaign. For these clergy, this is not merely a partisan or even just a political issue, but a moral and theological one; creating an obligation of faith for us. Almost one thousand poll chaplains were enthusiastic about being present on the scene for the 2022 election with many more planned for the 2024 election. I implore you to join and help with this *imago dei* campaign. Check out the FUSD Faiths United to Save Democracy Toolkit and see how you can help (turnoutsunday.com).

"THE PEOPLE HAVE SPOKEN"

Raphael Warnock's ability to put his faith into politics throughout his campaign and in his victory speech after his runoff election in January 2023—was, you might say, a powerful sermon. When was the last time you heard a Democrat say, "To God be the glory, for the great things God has done"? The senator reiterated his oft-repeated belief that "a vote is a kind of prayer for the world we desire for ourselves and our children." He thanked Georgians for praying with "your lips and with your legs, with your hands and your feet, with your head and your heart." Raphael Warnock is clearly a son of the Civil Rights Movement that always spoke of praying with your feet.

When Warnock cited, the night of his run-off election in 2022, what he called "the four most powerful words in a democracy: *the people have spoken*," it sent chills down my spine.[16] Then he went to the theological foundations of democracy when he praised the people for rising and standing up against all odds from the "ugly side of our complicated American story . . . because you believe as I do, that democracy is the po-litical enactment of a spiritual idea. The notion each of us has within the spark of the divine, that we were created in the image of God, *imago dei*."

Warnock also showed the kind of religion that can inspire but not dominate. After stating that a victory for democracy goes back to the Genesis text for him, he was respectful and careful to include those for whom religious language isn't comfortable: "And if you are not into that kind of religious language, that's fine. Our tent is big. Let me put it this way: each of us has value. And if we have value, we ought to have a voice. And the way to have a voice is to have a vote to determine the direction of your country and your destiny within it."

Amen!

4

LIES THAT DEMAND
OUR LOYALTY

Then Jesus said to the Jews who had believed in him, "If you continue in my word, you are truly my disciples; and you will know the truth, and the truth will make you free."

—JOHN 8:32

THE TRUTH—HOW TO FIND IT, TRUST IT, AND LIVE BY IT—IS CORE TO BOTH faith and democracy. And the truth problem we now confront may be the single biggest threat to our democracy.

Disinformation. Fake news. Alternative facts. Telling lies in the public forum has become so commonplace that it has spurred its own lexicon. Of course, bending the facts and using rhetorical smoke and mirrors to highlight the positive and gloss over the negative is not a new phenomenon, especially among politicians and other powerful individuals, corporations, and institutions big and small. Still, the idea of "truth" has become murkier than ever.

Today, more than any time in my seventy-five years, separating the truth from lies has never been harder for people. Even worse, some people are concluding that there is no truth anymore, or that it doesn't matter anyway, so let's all just pick our favorite lies. And powerful interests and ideologies have developed sophisticated messaging, media skills, and the technology of algorithms, to go after people who are open to the falsehoods that serve their interests, perspectives, or power.

Lies have become a hallmark of both political discourse and the way the news is delivered and consumed. There are countless spins or even downright contradictory reports on the same pieces of news, each carefully crafted to take hold of the target audience's attention by serving up just what they want to hear and what will justify their existing beliefs, prejudices, and judgments. Cable news networks focus on the stories and the angles that will draw the best *ratings* based on viewer biases. And talk radio shows daily appeal to our worst extremes and impulses. "Fair" and "balanced" are now antiquated words long out of date to many of our media platforms. The 1949 Fairness Doctrine of the Federal Communication Commission (FCC) required those who held broadcast licenses to offer differing viewpoints on controversial matters and important issues; it was abolished during the Reagan administration. The demise of the FCC rule helped lead to the increase in media polarization.[1]

And that polarization is no accident. Both the practice and publicizing of politics today play on the well-established human tendency to favor the attractive lie over the difficult truth.

JESUS' WORDS

Given this state of affairs, Jesus' message in John 8 is more critical than ever. What did he mean by "the truth"? His words went beyond, and much deeper than just saying, "Don't lie." He wasn't merely moralizing about right or wrong when he proclaimed, "You will know the truth *and* the truth will make you free." He was urging his followers to recognize that truth and freedom are *indivisible,* that you can't have one without the other. At the same time, he was exhorting us to recognize that the opposite was equally true. Without truth, we are slaves to our own delusions. Jesus makes clear that *the opposite of truth is captivity—the loss of freedom.* No truth, no freedom.

Even when we believe or endorse lies unwittingly, we are ensnared in a web of dishonesty, one that gradually kills our souls. We are trapped, and this is the very reason Satan is known as "the Father of Lies" (John 8:44). In John 8, Jesus urges the people gathered around him, his disciples, to seek truth, no matter how inconvenient and painful it may seem.

The only way to break our captivity is to learn anew how to know, love, and speak the truth that Jesus promised would set us free.

How do we do that?

The freedom Jesus promises is not just life after death but freedom for our lives in this world—here and now. New Testament scholar Tom Wright remembers singing freedom songs as a young man in the 1960s, and so do I! Wright says this about John 8:32:

> Verse 32 rings like a bell through much of Christian language: free from sin, free from slavery, free from the law, free from death, free from injustice, free from debt, free from tyranny. . . . The way to freedom is through the truth, and what matters is to know the truth. Tyranny and slavery of every sort thrive on lies, half-truths, evasions, and cover-ups. Freedom and truth go hand in hand.[2]

Many commentaries on John focus on freedom from the *slavery of sin.* Wright says, "It is the slavery that grips not only individuals but also groups, nations, and families of nations. It is the slavery we know as sin." He and I both grew up in religious worlds with a "small minded" view of sin, often relegated to mostly sexual sins. He says, and I agree, that "sexual sins matter" and can destroy lives, marriages, families, and communities. "But there is more to sin than sex," Wright says, "and sin as a whole is more than the sum of its parts. When people rebel against God in whatever ways, new fields of force are called into being, a cumulative effect builds up, and individuals and societies alike become enslaved just as surely as if every single one of them wore chains and was hounded to work every day by a strong man with a whip."[3]

"Fields of force" is a powerful phrase that can illuminate the spiritual nature of America's sin of historic racism. This passage, and the many commentaries on John 8:32 and following, have got me thinking how sin is slavery *and* slavery is sin, and how the two are so deeply connected in America. The brutal physical chains that enslaved African Americans wore led to the destructive moral chains on the sinners who held them and denied their humanity. We have described how America's original sin of white supremacy still endures and evolves, and those chains in the nation still continue for both Black and white lives. Lies sustained those chains—and still do. And *only the truth can set us free.*

Therefore, we all ask: What is the truth, and how can it set all of us free? Throughout John's gospel, as many commentators also point out, it is Jesus himself who is the "truth, the way, and the life" (John 14:6) and he can set us free. And the way to do that, says Jesus, is to continue in "my words." Tom Wright says to be "infected with the disease of sin" puts us in "darkness" but, by hearing and receiving Jesus' words, we can be set free. The text goes on to show that even those who say they believe in Jesus can still be stuck in the darkness of sin unknowingly. "The same is true today," says Wright, "that even those who are members of churches are not automatically in God's favor. What if the people called to carry Jesus' light into the world are themselves infected with the darkness?"[4]

These are questions for us all as readers, leaders, and pastors. And it is critically important that a new generation learns how to find the truth.

THE NEWS, THEN AND NOW

Let's apply the gospel truth principles practically.

When I was growing up, we all got our news from a few anchors on the "big three" major broadcast networks—ABC, NBC, and CBS. News then was like a town meeting, where we all received the same information and considered the same arguments, trusting that the only agenda was to present the facts, what was happening in our country and world. Sure, they made mistakes, sometimes showed their biases—especially mostly white reporters with racial biases and the Black news that was seldom reported; but we basically trusted them to present the general news as it had occurred and without a deliberate attempt to mislead us.

My family gathered each night for a half hour after dinner to tune into the *CBS Evening News with Walter Cronkite*. Cronkite famously signed off each evening: "And that's the way it is." And America believed him. A poll taken in 1972, ten years after he assumed his role as a CBS news anchor, declared Cronkite "the most trusted man in America."[5] We didn't always agree with everything that he said and we weren't always happy with all the news he reported, but mostly we believed that what he said was, in fact, *the way it was.*

The trust in shared media that we once took for granted has gradually, and now completely, eroded over the years. In fact, television news is now the second-least-trusted institution in the country, according to a recent Gallup poll.[6] Alarmingly, Congress earned the top spot. In both cases, powerful interests have caused a distrust of truth. The news, once a means of getting the populace onto the same page, has been replaced by media outlets split along ideological and political lines. With some admirable exceptions, too many so-called news sources play to the darkest fears and most deep-seated prejudices of the consumer, each spewing venom in the direction of "the other." Many have grown tired and distrustful of "the media" and have begun seeking out other news sources. Unfortunately, this disavowal of mainstream media has turned many toward extremely partisan news sources with even less oversight and accountability.[7]

"The left" and "the right" seem to be living in parallel universes. There is a real difference between deliberate lies and regular bias. But we do see each claiming their own set of truths and facts irreconcilable with the other. Kellyanne Conway, former senior counselor to Donald

Trump, all but owned this phenomenon when she referred to "alternative facts." Each side's audience is rarely exposed to the perspective of the other and too often reject it outright when they are. Of course, there is only one alternative to truth, and that is a lie.

THE VOCATION OF TRUTH TELLING

The vocation of journalists is to tell the truth. This is a mission of the church as well. There are vocational parallels here. And there are still many courageous journalists who work hard to fulfill that mission of truth telling. In some countries that costs journalists their lives; and even in America they are increasingly becoming the targets of those powerful people who want to deny or cover up the truth. There have also always been great truth tellers who are pastors and preachers. But now, truth telling from pulpits is far too rare and, when some pastors do tell the truth about current events and offer a biblical response, even they can become targets of congregants who don't like their "politics." And in the pulpits of white Christian nationalism, congregants who don't agree with the political right's agenda being preached can be targeted or even asked to leave.

I've had conversations with pastors whose congregations are increasingly divided along political lines, using different media sources, resulting in battles erupting on church listservs and in newsletters. When I ask what one side does when hearing about big stories and events from the other side, they say, "They never even hear those stories; don't know those events and circumstances ever existed; and wouldn't believe it if they heard."

Other pastors tell me how they work mightily to correct rumors and fears on their church listservs. Feeling a need to *pastorally* intervene, they ask parishioners to please not spread unverified information.

Recovering the vocation of truth telling is one of the most important missions for pastors now. For that, we will need both Scripture and important research to help make our vocation of truth telling more possible.

ITCHING EARS AND CONFIRMATION BIAS

Despite our growing skepticism toward politics and media, there is reason to suspect that we are nevertheless more susceptible to media influence than ever before. Cable news networks and political elites capitalize on the appeal of dividing people into enemy camps, and the fact that the American populace is perhaps at its widest political polarization ever attests to their success in doing so.[8] A recent study by the Pew Research Center revealed that Republicans (77 percent) and Democrats (72 percent) agree that they can't agree on anything, even the most "basic facts."[9] It is not surprising, then, that both sides are incredulous that anyone in their right minds could endorse or support the leaders and policies of their opponents—ever.

It would be easy to take the lead of Trump and scapegoat the media. And yes, political leaders and the media are selling their unique versions of "truth" while at the same time mercilessly debasing the "lies" of "the other." But without a willing buyer, they would go out of business. So, what is going on here?

It turns out that as divided as they are on everything else, left and right sometimes have more in common than they'd like to believe. I don't believe there is a moral equivalency between the networks on either side of the debates, but while the overt lies of the right are increasingly frightening, the repetitive ideological biases of the left and their selection of "truths" become annoying and exhausting. Again, both recognize that there exists a seemingly impassable chasm between them. What's less obvious, though, is that both are subject to the same cognitive blind spots that fuel their perception of moral and logical superiority and prevent the building of any bridges. In other words, both are captive to their claim on "truth."

Psychologists refer to this tendency of cherry-picking the information that proves us right and discarding what challenges our presuppositions as "confirmation bias." Recent research out of Duke University indicates that this tendency is very much at play in relation to political issues.[10] In the study, participants chose a political position on a number of issues before being presented with only affirming evidence, only conflicting evidence, or evidence for both sides. Regardless of their initial stance, participants' opinions remained relatively unswayed by the evidence presented. Most telling, of course, was the fact that participants rated evidence upholding their original position much more favorably than that which contradicted it. This finding held regardless of prior knowledge on the issue or the novelty of the reasons presented.

This tendency to proclaim the superiority of self-justifying information, in combination with starkly partisan popular media and social media algorithms designed to feed the user the news and evidence they prefer, creates *a perfect storm of group polarization*. To make matters even worse, social media networks tend to connect like-minded individuals as "friends," further narrowing the views to which people are exposed. In her book *#Republic: Divided Democracy in the Age of Social Media,* Harvard Law professor Cass Sunstein puts it this way: "It seems plain that the Internet is serving, for many, as a breeding ground for extremism, precisely because like-minded people are connecting with greater ease and frequency with one another, and often without hearing contrary views."[11]

Around 65 AD the apostle Paul wrote a letter to his apprentice Timothy in which he cautioned, "For the time will come when people will not put up with sound doctrine. Instead, to suit their own desires, they will gather around them a great number of teachers to say what their itching ears want to hear. They will turn their ears away from the truth and turn aside to myths" (2 Timothy 4:3–4).

Discerning the truth in today's world is exponentially more challenging than ever before, certainly more than it was when Paul offered his warning to Timothy two thousand years ago. But that is precisely why his counsel is more critical now than ever before. The strategic manipulation of "itching ears" will draw our people into more falsehoods, and it is only the pursuit of truth that will set us free.

BIG LIES AT THE HEART OF FASCISM

"What happens when truth doesn't matter anymore?" That is the question Obama posed to all Americans and especially Republican leaders who continued to push the failed and debunked "Big Lie" Donald Trump promoted both leading up to and following his failed bid for reelection. Let's remember the facts, the truth, here. According to a *New York Times* investigation, more than 370 Republican candidates running for office during the midterm elections of 2022 questioned and, at times, outright denied the results of the 2020 election despite overwhelming evidence to the contrary, including the admission of the former president himself.[12]

In our public forum together at Georgetown, January 6 committee member Congressman Jamie Raskin named that infamous insurrection day as "the most heinous and dastardly political offense ever organized by a president and his followers and his entourage in the history of the United States."[13] In the enormously important and unexpectedly impactful public hearings, the January 6 investigative congressional committee repeatedly exposed how Donald Trump and his handlers denied election results and hatched a plan that combined legal maneuvers, unlawful offenses, pressuring local election officials to change vote counts, seeking to corrupt the electoral process with false "electors," and, ultimately, inciting outright violence in order to subvert the certification of the new president and reinstall an autocratic tyrant, with martial law if necessary. As I write, the founder of the Oath Keepers, Stewart Rhodes, was just sentenced to eighteen years in prison, convicted of "seditious conspiracy" by helping incite the violence that day.

His group, along with the Proud Boys, tried to obstruct the congressional certification of the 2020 election. Apparently, they were "standing
by" as Trump had asked them to do in a presidential debate. As some
historians have commented, here was the first American president who
was an *insurrectionist*, instead of a *constitutionalist*.

A scheme of this magnitude and kind had never before been seen
in American history.

In our Georgetown forum, Raskin said the committee's findings
would "blow the roof off the house." Perhaps Raskin's story of Vice President Mike Pence refusing to get into a Secret Service limousine—to help
him escape the violence-filled Capitol, because he didn't trust where
that Trump-controlled car would take him—made the most dramatic
point of where we were in this country. As the January 6 committee
went deeper into its investigations, I noticed that Raskin kept quoting
Thomas Paine, an American Founding Father: "For as in absolute governments the King is law, so in free countries the law ought to be King,
and there ought to be no other."[14]

A scheme like the one attempted by Trump, along with the incessant
pathological propagation of falsehoods during his presidency (30,573
lies over four years for anyone who's counting[15]) and suppression of truth
that preceded it, are part and parcel of the fascist playbook—a reality
that even many of those on the liberal political side against Trump still
do not seem to fully comprehend. This is not merely a narcissistic cult, but
textbook fascism. And white liberals continue to underestimate how
race is at the core of it. Promoting the idea of truth's nonexistence is
one of the primary means by which autocrats have historically sought
to establish their power. Strongmen and dictators encourage their followers to depend on them for truth and to reject anything that contradicts what they say to be true. Let's be clear: all presidents "spin," and
are selective with facts and truth. But Trump took spin to a different
level; he wanted to undermine the truth itself.

I often use the example of the famous debate that the Roman em-
peror's representative in Jerusalem, Pontius Pilate, had with Jesus on

the day of his death. They were discussing the meaning of truth and, when Pilate realized he was losing the debate, he said to Jesus, "What is truth?" We will never find it, this line of reasoning goes, so let's not bother to try. Autocratic tyrants always seek to deny or distract from the truth and its implications. Like Pilate, they want to "wash their hands," as the Roman leader did, and move on. And then he just killed Jesus.

Despite Pilate telling the crowd that he didn't "find a case against this man," Jesus was crucified. Because of a troubling dream, Pilate's wife warned her husband, "Don't have anything to do with this innocent man." Don't you often wonder what the wives of tyrants really think when they stand alongside their husbands smiling?

Let's go back to *How Democracies Die* by Steven Levitsky and Daniel Ziblatt.[16] These two democracy scholars point to four key indicators of authoritarian behavior: (1) the rejection, in words or action, of the democratic rules of the game; (2) the denial of the legitimacy of political opponents; (3) toleration or encouragement of violence; and (4) a willingness to curtail the civil liberties of opponents, including the media. It is both obvious and frightening how these historical conditions apply today.

LIES LEAD TO VIOLENCE

Leading up to January 6, Trump incited his followers to violence, even after privately and angrily acknowledging to White House chief of staff Mark Meadows that he had lost the election, saying, "I don't want people to know that we lost."[17] But he continued to message his followers to come together in Washington for a "wild time." He called on his vice president to decertify the election, unconstitutionally, which Pence finally decided not to do; but the president's subsequent text led his followers to scream, "Hang Mike Pence," and even erected gallows with a criminal noose right outside of Congress. Should this plot have succeeded, the defeated president's followers like General Michael Flynn were calling for the imposition of martial law with Trump staying in the White House.

The nation witnessed the worst attack on the US Capitol since the War of 1812, but this time from an internal enemy; with five people killed, 140 injuries, and untold trauma among Capitol police; congressional staff hiding under their desks and members and senators hiding up in the galleries or running to find places to hide in the building; all setting a dangerous precedent.[18] But in his first town hall meeting for the 2024 election with CNN, again candidate Donald Trump praised the January 6 events as a "beautiful day" of "patriots" with "love in their hearts" who are now being "persecuted." Trump promised his followers that he would pardon "most" of the people who had already been or will be criminally prosecuted and convicted, if he wins the White House back.

It is very important to remember that all of this hinged upon a lie— and still does—one Trump and his followers so desperately wanted to be true that they would resort to violence to avoid acknowledging the truth. And sadly, the events that have followed portend more violence to come.

We are now seeing so many ways that lies lead to violence, with untruths leading to the undoing of a society. Armed militia groups, like the Oath Keepers and the Proud Boys and other local groups, now threaten African American, Hispanic, and LGBTQ+ events with *The New York Times* reporting some of those being canceled out of security fears.[19] Armed protesters camped out in front of the home of Arizona House Speaker Rusty Bowers, a Republican and former supporter of Trump who refused to unconstitutionally change the state's electors from Joe Biden to Donald Trump.[20] Georgia election poll worker Wandrea ArShaye "Shaye" Moss, the target of a baseless conspiracy theory of voter fraud promoted by Trump's sons, also testified to the June 6 committee hearings about the vicious, hateful, sexualized, and racialized taunts and threats directed at her and her family.[21]

Paul Pelosi, husband of Nancy Pelosi, then the Democratic Speaker of the House of Representatives, was attacked with a hammer by an assailant, whose confession left no doubt as to whether this violence was "political." While he may be "deranged," as these perpetrators of such violence often are, he was motivated by the same hate and lies and conspiracy theories he heard on the internet.[22] In a Georgetown forum with then Speaker emerita Nancy Pelosi, I asked of her, "There may be students here who are considering a life of public service but may be put off by the extreme polarization and even violence that threatens the lives of our public servants. What would you say to them?" Her answer was based on two words: "calling" and "courage." Her engagement with students that day was something to behold, and all could see that these young women and men were listening.

But even in the case of a brutal assault on Paul Pelosi, Republicans remained largely silent. The question of why can only be answered by going back to the historically supported truth that Donald Trump is literally a fascist—and it is past time to recognize and name him as a racial autocrat. He has taken over the base of his party, and most Republicans are afraid of him and his loyal political constituency. And indeed, as many have pointed out, silence in the face of evil is indeed complicity.

Hannah Arendt, a political philosopher, author, and Holocaust survivor, wrote that strongmen "replace competency with loyalty."[23] Totalitarianism requires the destruction of the truth.

REPLACING THE GREAT REPLACEMENT THEORY

In his commentary on John 8:32–33, pastor and theologian Brad Braxton speaks of its meaning to the Black community. On the anniversary of Juneteenth, which he calls a "liturgical moment," Braxton writes:

> Freedom—the quest for it and the denial of it—lies at the heart of the African American experience. In the dark night of slavery, church mothers

moaned for it, and preachers intoned for it. For many enslaved African Americans, freedom was worth more than life itself. Thus, the spiritual declared, "Oh freedom, oh freedom over me/and before I'd be a slave, I'll be buried in my grave/And go home to my Lord and be free."[24]

Braxton explains exactly what we have to do. "Preachers can use John 8:31–36 to explore sensitively the 'chains' that shackle so many people," he says. "If we live by these truths, the ultimate 'Emancipation Proclamation' belongs to us." John 8:32, therefore, becomes the great gospel emancipation of truth setting us free. This deeply theological affirmation and spiritual motivation is the only force that is big enough and strong enough to set us all free. It is the spirit and power of Jesus' words in John 8 that will equip us to lovingly persuade the persuadable and defeat those who insist on enacting a racist, violent vision for America.

On May 14, 2022, Payton S. Gendron, a white eighteen-year-old, drove three and a half hours to a predominantly Black neighborhood in Buffalo, New York. He was armed with an AR-15 and dressed in body armor and a military helmet mounted with a camera to livestream what would follow. Less than a minute after he had exited his car, he commenced executing the plot he had begun to devise four months prior, one aimed at murdering as many African Americans as he could. By the time he surrendered to police, Gendron had wounded thirteen and killed ten human beings in what FBI director Christopher Wray called "a targeted attack, a hate crime, and an act of racially motivated violent extremism."[25]

Two days before the attack, Gendron posted a 180-page, ranting manifesto online, in which he directly appealed to the language of the "Great Replacement," a conspiratorial theory claiming a concerted effort among left-wing and Jewish elites to engineer demographic shifts to threaten white identity, power, and existence in America. *Here was the lie that led to his violence.*

Clearly, these ideas did not originate in the empty mind, heart, and soul of this ignorant young man. Unfortunately, such baseless fear and hate mongering has found its way even into mainstream media.

Less than a year before the attack, many Republican pundits publicly criticized what they perceived to be an inadequate response of President Joe Biden's to an influx of Haitian refugees at the border of Del Rio, Texas. But Tucker Carlson of Fox News took it a step further, running a segment on-air in which he suggested that Biden fully intended to allow free passage of immigrants into America as part of a concerted effort to "change the racial mix of the country."[26] He went on to explicitly declare this as part of "the Great Replacement, the replacement of legacy Americans with more obedient people from faraway countries." Carlson's report represented an unabashed example of white grievance politics and the ideology of white supremacy taken mainstream by a large faction of the Republican Party now under the control of former president Donald Trump.

Trump's claims and lies about the dangers of people of color in America were not new ones. In the 1978 novel *The Turner Diaries,* which the FBI calls "the bible of the racist right," neo-Nazi William Luther Pierce describes a violent revolution in America that ends in white victory over racial minorities.[27] The book's message was said to be the inspiration for the Oklahoma City bombing in 1995, which killed 168 people. At a 2017 rally in Charlottesville, Virginia, that would turn deadly, white supremacists gathered under the rallying call of "Unite the Right" and marched through the streets chanting, "Jews will not replace us!" A small group of faith leaders, some of them friends of mine, courageously took up the call to also go to Charlottesville and tell the truth and, at night, found themselves surrounded in a church by armed men carrying guns and shouting slogans and threats at them. Trump said there were "good people" on "both sides" of the conflict.

Those who have espoused replacement theory, whether indirectly or directly—and the fear, hate, and violence it inspires—have blood on their hands. And GOP leaders who won't name and condemn white supremacy are morally culpable.

The Dominion Voting Systems case against Fox News for fraud, for lying about their machines and accusing them of efforts to steal the 2020 elections, was the most truth-revealing media scandal for a long time.[28] The case showed how Fox owner Rupert Murdoch as well as top Fox anchors like Sean Hannity, Laura Ingraham, and Tucker Carlson were deliberately lying about the validity of the 2020 election in order to preserve their network's top ratings.

Wherever it is, in local congregations, school meetings, or community gatherings, those who know what is true need to find the courage to speak up against what is untrue. Lies are best interrupted by people who know the people who are being lied to.

My favorite story in response to the caravans of immigrant lies comes from a church in rural Georgia where the pastor's wife is also a member of the choir. Every Sunday morning the choir practices before the service. And every week, as their practice is ending, just before the service, the choir director leads a prayer with the gathered group in preparation for worship. One Sunday morning, the woman who led the choir prayer included a statement along the lines of, "Oh Lord, please protect us from those caravans of immigrants coming with the drugs, violence, and diseases they will bring to us! And God, please protect the soldiers who are protecting us from them!" In the middle of the prayer, the pastor's wife interrupted and said, "Stop. That is not true and we cannot tell lies in church!" I love that example! Anyone can be a truth teller. And they can tell the truth wherever they are.

It's time to confront and replace conspiratorial rhetoric with what we know to be true. The Bible says and we say we believe that all human beings were made in the image of God (Genesis 1:26); that the diverse body of Christ was meant to be united together by being reconciled to Christ (Galatians 3:28); and that only the truth can set us free (John 8: 32). If we believe these things, it is time to say so in the places where our influence and relationships count.

THE WHITEWASHING OF HISTORY

One of the greatest obstacles to the pursuit of truth in America today is the growing pressure for a deliberate suppression and denial of our country's history of slavery and racism. In the name of parents' rights in education, with school district and board meetings becoming public forums, state legislatures are opting to edit out the inconvenient truths ingrained in our nation's story.

The trend of "whitewashing" American history took its inspiration from a September 2020 letter published by Donald Trump ordering federal agencies to cease diversity training and the discussion of topics like critical race theory (which is seldom taught before college but makes a great rhetorical scapegoat) and, of course, any conversations about white privilege. In the letter, Trump asserted that agencies "should begin to identify all available avenues within the law to cancel any such contracts and/or to divert Federal dollars away from these *un-American* [emphasis added] propaganda training sessions."[29] It wasn't long before parents, school districts, and state legislators took note and followed suit, especially in the South, but elsewhere too.

According to PEN America, a nonprofit dedicated to protecting free expression in America, 137 bills across thirty-six states were passed in 2022 to suppress teaching on topics such as race, gender, American history, and LGBTQ+ identities.[30] This marked a 250 percent increase over the previous year, when fifty-four bills were passed across twenty-four states. Some states have gone so far as to pass laws that prohibit schools from teaching courses that make white people "uncomfortable." Yes, they explicitly use that word. In his Stop WOKE Act, for example, Florida governor Ron DeSantis threatened harsh consequences including termination to any teacher who taught lessons that caused people to feel "discomfort, guilt, or anguish" on account of their race.[31] Remember how lies promise to protect us?

Other state legislatures are also passing laws that would prevent such history being taught. Governor Glenn Youngkin successfully ran on such a platform in Virginia; he vowed to combat the teaching of "inherently divisive concepts."[32]

I watched the media debate in the Virginia governor's race about what constitutes culturally sensitive and legitimate educational content for the populace of the DC metro area where I live. White Loudoun County mothers said that they didn't want their children made to feel guilty—as though they were the ones responsible for slavery. They argued for a more positive depiction of America that highlighted our success and how far we have come. Racism is declining, they insisted, and is only a personal problem *some* people still have, and not a structural problem anymore. In particular, the use of the term "systemic racism" is seen as problematic. Every person has an equal chance to succeed now, they like to say.

While it is reasonable for parents to be concerned about, for example, how and when their third-graders are taught about sex, there is far more going on when it comes to race. Whether one chooses to acknowledge it or not, Black history *is* American history, and what happened before and at the founding of our nation is a real and necessary part of our story.

Histories of slavery and racial discrimination are being taken off our school shelves. Books by prominent African American authors like Maya Angelou, Nobel Prize winner Toni Morrison, and Isabel Wilkerson are being removed.[33] Some schools have even targeted the biographies of paragons of Black history like Rev. Dr. Martin Luther King, Jr., and Rosa Parks.[34]

There are presently at least fifty groups with local or regional chapters that collectively number at least three hundred members who are actively lobbying for book bans at the national, state, or local level.[35] Seventy-three percent of these groups have formed since 2020.[36] And they have been very successful. Between July 2021 and June 2022, there were 2,532 books banned across 32 states and 138 school districts. That is all truly alarming for the state of both the quality of our children's education and for our multicultural democracy.

Where in the Bible does it say that truths need to make us feel comfortable? Where does it say to seek truth, so long as it doesn't make us feel guilty? In fact, the Bible says the opposite. The truths that we most need are often the hardest to hear. But that's why they are necessary to challenge and change us, to make us open to the Word of God, which opens the way to forgiveness and redemption. Truth, Jesus said in John's gospel, paves the path to freedom; ignorance and lies block the way forward.

Do these mothers and fathers really understand what they are saying? Denying the real and painful history of this country ensures that their children will exist in a present that has no answers to the sins of the past.

I believe that to be afraid of telling our kids the truth is to underestimate them. White children don't all crumble under the weight of the bad and ugly presented alongside the good of American history. What discomfort they do feel often transmutes into compassion, righteous anger, and a determination to make things better. When our high school baseball players heard how one of their beloved Black coach's chances at playing Major League Baseball was hijacked as the result of an unjustified and racially motivated arrest in college, they were furious and committed themselves to finding ways to change the systems that led to this injustice. The story didn't make them feel guilty; it made them feel angry and motivated them to do something about these terrible wrongs.

When children hear the unadulterated truth about slavery and the continued reality of racism, many are inspired to become the "abolitionists" of their own time, activists who want to change their country and make it more just. Perhaps it is their parents who still don't want to deal with the racial inequality that has, in fact, sustained their privilege.

In a *New York Times* review of a book entitled *American Inheritance,*

Jon Meacham offers a critique of Florida governor Ron DeSantis's Stop WOKE legislation. Meacham writes:

> The messy, difficult, unavoidable truth of the American story is that it is fundamentally a human one. Imperfect, selfish, greedy, cruel—and sometimes noble. One might wish the nation's story were simple. But that wish is in vain. Influential white Americans knew—and understood— that slavery was wrong and liberty was precious, but chose not to act according to that knowledge and that understanding. . . . And it was a choice: one made for convenience. Slavery and racism were not externally imposed forces that lay beyond human control. They were, rather, economic, political, and cultural constructs that served the purposes of the powerful—in this case white people—and because of this, they stood for centuries.[37]

We must face what can legitimately be called "hard truths." But growth emerges from that struggle.

As citizens, parents, and members of local communities, we cannot wait and hope for these issues to be resolved on a national level; rather, we must go local and make our convictions known to neighbors, congregants, and community members.

REDEEMING HISTORY

Many years ago, I traveled to Montgomery, Alabama, to visit my friend Bryan Stevenson, the founder and executive director of the Equal Justice Initiative. Bryan invited a group of faith leaders to Montgomery for an annual retreat we have, in order to have conversations about how we might indeed build a more just future together. As a Christian himself, he made clear that we first had to acknowledge the past and name it for what it was before we can move to a different and better future.

Bryan contends that the lynching of Black people represented the ultimate undermining of faith in God who created us all in God's image. Lynching is a refutation of the gospel itself. Then he took us to some of the sites where Black people had been lynched by white people in Montgomery, Alabama.

Of course, such sites extended far beyond Alabama, even into the North. But these places of infamy are often unresearched, undocumented, and unmarked. At the lynching sites, Bryan invited each of us to take dirt from the earth beneath the trees where the victims were hanged and put it into glass vases. We brought those vases back to the Equal Justice Initiative center, where they were stored until they were eventually put on display at the National Memorial for Peace and Justice, which opened to the public on April 26, 2018, to commemorate the thousands of lynching victims in the United States.

On that inaugural day, Bryan Stevenson was enacting his vision to place a marker in every spot where a lynching had occurred in the United States. He wants every site to be a reminder of where we've come from, the atrocity that was committed, and the cost that was paid, so that we may recommit to the different country we need. Bryan hopes for a deep reckoning that might repent and reestablish unity in the life of the church and in the life of our nation.

Tragically and to the shame of the church, many of the lynchers were professing Christians, and after executing a Black man under cover of dark on Saturday night, or with a large cheering crowd including women and children, would attend church on Sunday. And they saw no contradiction between their abhorrent actions and their profession of faith in Christ.

"I am not interested in talking about this history because I want to punish people," says Bryan. "I'm interested in talking about this history because I want us to be liberated. I want us to get on the other side of repentance and experience redemption, and restoration and reparation and recovery. But those are words that can't happen until we give voice to the pain and the anguish and the sin and the burdens that we have created by our silence."[38]

A LIGHT IN THE DARKNESS

One way to address our own biases head-on is to seek out multiple opinions, conservative and liberal alike. Listening to diverse voices is absolutely critical. By actively paying attention to the perspectives of those outside our tribes, we preempt our natural tendency to jump to customary, convenient, and comfortable conclusions. And of course, we must then commit to really listening, even when what we hear evokes discomfort.

Bad religion provides easy and self-serving certainty; good religion leads us to deeper reflection. And that is where our true freedom lies.

Our faith communities cannot simply exist in the same parallel universes that control our society at large—with the messages preached in one church standing in stark contrast to what you might hear in another. All too often, and increasingly, those sermons have more to do with political and racial identity than truth and theology. Some pastors go as far as saying, "If you don't agree with the politics that we preach from this pulpit, I don't want you here." Some megachurch pastors are actually calling Democrats "demons."[39]

In John 3:19, Jesus declares, "Light has come into the world, but people loved darkness rather than light because their deeds were evil." Clearly, there is much "darkness" in our midst today. But remember the opening chapter of John's gospel where the coming of Christ is described: "The light shines in darkness, and the darkness has not overcome it" (John 1:5).

Light often appears when and where we least expect it. And our faith instructs us to believe that darkness will not have the last word.

I find it very hopeful that *John talks about both "truth" and "light" more than any other gospel.* And he connects the two. Lies lead to living in the darkness, but truth allows us to live in the light. It is a wonderful thing to come out of the darkness and into the light—to leave the lies behind and embrace the truth. Then, and only then, will we be free. The Rev. Dr. Martin Luther King, Jr., said it best: "Darkness cannot drive out darkness; only light can do that. Hate cannot drive out hate; only love can do that."

5

JESUS' FINAL TEST OF DISCIPLESHIP

When the Son of Man comes in his glory and all the angels with him, then he will sit on the throne of his glory. All the nations will be gathered before him, and he will separate people one from another as a shepherd separates the sheep from the goats, and he will put the sheep at his right hand and the goats at the left.

Then the king will say to those at his right hand, "Come, you who are blessed by my Father, inherit the kingdom prepared for you from the foundation of the world, for I was hungry and you gave me food, I was thirsty and you gave me something to drink, I was a stranger and you welcomed me, I was naked and you gave me clothing, I was sick and you took care of me, I was in prison and you visited me."

Then the righteous will answer him, "Lord, when was it that we saw you hungry and gave you food or thirsty and gave you something to drink? And when was it that we saw you a stranger and welcomed you or naked and gave you clothing? And when was it that we saw you sick or in prison and visited you?"

And the king will answer them, "Truly I tell you, just as you did it to one of the least of these, who are members of my family, you did it to me."

Then he will say to those at his left hand, "You who are accursed,

depart from me into the eternal fire prepared for the devil and his angels, for I was hungry and you gave me no food, I was thirsty and you
gave me nothing to drink, I was a stranger and you did not welcome
me, naked and you did not give me clothing, sick and in prison and
you did not visit me."

Then they also will answer, "Lord, when was it that we saw you
hungry or thirsty or a stranger or naked or sick or in prison and did
not take care of you?"

Then he will answer them, "Truly I tell you, just as you did not do
it to one of the least of these, you did not do it to me." And these will
go away into eternal punishment but the righteous into eternal life.

—MATTHEW 25:31–46

This is my own conversion text; it brought me back to faith. Often referred to by biblical scholars as "the parable of the sheep and the goats,"
it is the final of three parables about divine judgments. This one is about
what will happen when the son of man, Jesus, returns in all of his glory.

These parables are divine judgments about human life choices. And
in this final and most comprehensive parable, some standing before
Jesus will be rewarded for their choice to serve those who are the most
vulnerable. They will "inherit the kingdom prepared for you from the
foundation of the world." And some will be punished. The text uses the
Greek words for "accursed," for "damnation." They will be sent away
from Jesus—that separation perhaps being the worst outcome—for
ignoring, neglecting, and perhaps even exploiting those whom Jesus
calls "the least of these."

It is still striking for me how *surprised* the people who heard the
words Jesus spoke—both to the sheep and the goats—were about the
basis for this final judgment. "When did we see you hungry, thirsty, naked, a stranger, sick, or in prison?" they all asked. "Are you really saying
that *you were there* among the poorest and most vulnerable people—
the ones in great need?" "Yes, that was also me," Jesus says.

The text is not just about individuals, but also uses the word "nations." Peoples of many tribes and places—alleged believers and non-believers alike—will be judged by Jesus' words here. It is a very broad judgment and one of the most serious and ultimate in all of Jesus' parables. Jesus is usually not perceived as "judgmental" in the way many religious people are; but he renders real judgment here. And the ultimate judgment in this last teaching—before he left for Jerusalem to be crucified and then resurrected—is about serving those most in need.

I believe that white Christian nationalism has failed Jesus' final test of discipleship. White Christian nationalist leaders and their churches almost never speak of the poor, of God's priority of a "preferential option" for the poor as Catholic social teaching calls it, or offer any "good news" to the poor as the evangelical revivalists of the nineteenth century did, or the Black churches have always done. While the least of these are central to Jesus' final test of discipleship, calls to serve the poor and the most vulnerable are almost completely absent in white Christian nationalist circles. Occasionally, some voluntary charity is offered, but never a call to justice for the "least of these."

A BIBLE FULL OF HOLES

After my years as an activist at Michigan State University, I attended Trinity Evangelical Divinity School in Deerfield, Illinois, just north of Chicago. There, alongside my fellow seminarians, I wrestled with the biblical views of the poor and how at odds they were with the priorities of many churches. At one point, we did an experiment to try and grasp just how central these biblical issues are to the Christian faith.

We took an old Bible and set out to find every single Scripture about the poor and the oppressed, about wealth and poverty, about injustice and justice. Then we took a pair of scissors and cut every verse that we found out of the Bible: every single verse about the poor was removed.

When we were done, all of those verses had fallen to the floor—about *two thousand* verses in total! We were left with a Bible full of holes.

When all God's calls for justice were taken out, the Hebrew prophets almost disappeared from the Bible. We found Amos preaching, "I hate, I despise your festivals, and I take no delight in your solemn assemblies. . . . Take away from me the noise of your songs, I will not listen to the melody of your harps. But let justice roll down like waters, and righteousness like an ever-flowing stream!" (Amos 6:21–24). That had to be cut out of our old Bible. We found Isaiah saying, "Is this not the fast that I choose, to loose the bonds of injustice, to undue the thongs of the yoke, to let the oppressed go free, and to break every yoke? Is it not to share your bread with the hungry, to bring the homeless poor into your house, when you see the naked, to cover them, and not to hide yourself from your own kin?" (Isaiah 58:6–7). Isaiah also had to go. We saw Micah asking a core question, "What does the Lord require of you but to do justice, and to love kindness, and to walk humbly with your God?"—so we were required to take that out too. Whole portions of other prophets like Jeremiah, so many Psalms where we see God uplifting the poor, and the wise words of Proverbs saying, "Whoever is kind to the poor lends to the Lord, and he will reward them for what they have done" (Proverbs 19:17) also all had to be removed. One of every sixteen verses of the synoptic gospels (the first three) had to be cut out, and one of every seven verses in Luke's gospel. Our old Bible was now holey, instead of holy.

For years, I used that Bible as an illustration when I spoke. I would hold it up and say to American churches, "Brothers and sisters, this is our American Bible. It is full of holes from all that we have paid no attention to. We might as well each take a pair of scissors to God's Word for all that we have chosen to ignore." White Christian nationalism has cut out of their Bibles all of the Scriptures that lead faith to justice.

When television personality Glenn Beck had his highly rated show on Fox News, he urged people to leave churches that preach "social justice." Said Beck: "I beg you, look for the words 'social justice' or 'economic justice' on your church website. If you find it, run as fast as you can. Social justice and economic justice, they are code words. Now, am I advising people to leave their church? Yes! They talk about economic justice, rights of the workers, redistribution of wealth and, surprisingly, I love this, democracy."[1]

Beck, who is a Mormon, said the message of social justice has infected all faiths. He called it a "perversion of the gospel." Beck advised people who attend churches where pastors preach a message of social justice to report it to their bishop or other church authority.

Then this very loud and noxious broadcaster decided to put some of those "social justice" perpetrators on his famous blackboard to remind his listeners day after day of who they should look out for. And after a blazing attack on me personally, Beck put me on his blackboard and began to regularly assail me on his show.

My wife Joy would tell me every day what Beck had just said about me, some of which was so crazy and bizarre that she found them almost comical. She had never heard of Beck or watched his show before, but some friends kept telling her that I had become one of Beck's prime targets. Then some ugly and threatening messages came at me and my family from some of Beck's listeners who were on America's extreme far right wing, including some who quickly went to hate and could even turn to violence against Beck's accused enemies.

We were encouraged to inform our young boy's elementary school to look out for them and become ever more attentive to their movements. Eventually, a friend of ours who was a mother at our school, a cancer survivor that our boy's classes had reached out to support, and who was also a Fox News commentator, confronted Beck directly to say we were "a great family" and that he should stop attacking me—which he finally did.

The point of this personal story is that all the biblical passages described here are a great threat to those who defend injustice and whose purposes are directly linked to the wealth and power of those who want ever more control of our society and systems. They are the ones who want to continue to take these two thousand scriptures out of the Bible, and attack those who lift them up. And that is why it is so important to continue to lift them up—despite potential blackboards you might find yourself on.

Putting those passages calling for compassion and justice back into the Bible is not a political or partisan act. Rather, it is to literally restore the Word of God to our lives, our churches, our communities, and our nation. Eventually, the Bible was put back together in "The Poverty and Justice Bible" published by the American Bible Society in 2008, where all the verses that had been ignored and literally been cut out by us as seminarians were put back into the Bible in orange, so they could clearly be seen.[2]

Some of the versions used by groups like World Vision and others referred to our story from Trinity Evangelical Divinity School. And I was invited to speak in Australia at the launch of the new Poverty Bible with Prime Minister Kevin Rudd, so this became a global phenomenon.

It was those Scriptures, and Matthew 25 in particular, that brought me back to faith.

REUNITING WITH THE *REAL* JESUS

In the introduction, I shared my conversion story that led me outside of the church and the faith that had raised me. In the spring of 1970, during my senior year of college, I was thinking deeply about what my future would look like. This was a time of great societal upheaval, over the war in Vietnam and fights over racism and poverty. We were on the heels of brutal US bombings of Cambodia and the shooting and killing of student protesters at Kent State University. I was on the front lines of protests that shut down the campus of Michigan State University and many other schools, with a national march we helped mobilize that drew hundreds of thousands of students to the US Capitol and the White House; Richard Nixon reportedly watched us from his White House window.

My involvement in these protests and social movements late in high school and through my college years convinced me that I wanted to be in the business of social change. But the more I considered a life of activism, the more I realized I didn't have an adequate foundation to stand and build on.

Like many student activists of that era, I was seeking answers, reading the works of revolutionaries like Karl Marx, Ho Chi Minh, and Che Guevara. But ultimately, their philosophies left me unsatisfied. I needed something deeper, not merely political analysis and critique but a moral framework that would guide my spirit and shape my path toward bringing about the changes I envisioned for my country and our world.

During those college years, I remained dissociated from the church. I saw no reason to reconcile the points of contention that had led to my decision to break ties and the church's desire to happily let me leave. If anything, I was further repulsed by the perspectives of many Christian groups at Michigan State who showed either obliviousness to the causes I cared about, or believed we should "bomb those commies to hell," as one Campus Crusader told me. Others said they were praying about the war before taking a stand, which they never did. Still, while I had left the church, I had not quite given up on Jesus, and his presence from my early life on still sometimes whispered its way past my religious disenchantment and into my moral consciousness.

Without any association with the Christian groups on campus, and certainly with no connection to my church back home in Detroit, I started reading the Gospel of Matthew, the first book of the New Testament. I soon came upon the Sermon on the Mount in Matthew chapters 5–7, beginning with the Beatitudes, where Jesus delivers his central message to his followers. He describes the new way of life he has come to bring as a new order called "the kingdom of God" to change both our lives and the world, through his disciples in the world. I later learned that the Sermon on the Mount, with the Beatitudes, was the basic catechism, the first teaching that was shared with the earliest believers in

Jesus—the *curriculum* that the early church universally used to instruct new converts as to how they were supposed to live in following Jesus.

I soon realized that in a "young" lifetime of faithfully attending my white evangelical church in Detroit, I had never once heard these Beatitudes of Jesus preached. This foundational sermon, the one which tells us how we are to live and what it means to be Jesus' disciples, had somehow been skipped over in my Christian upbringing. But the more I read, the more I understood that the Sermon on the Mount literally turns the world upside down. And tragically, to this day, it gets little attention in most white evangelical churches.

My church actually believed that this sermon from Jesus was for another time and a future "dispensation," meaning it was only meant to be lived after we got to heaven. Not much help for changing things here on earth! More recently, the Sermon on the Mount has been said by the religious right to be "too soft" for this kind of world. And some of the megachurch white Christian nationalist pastors have literally said they prefer a tough guy like Donald Trump to fight for their agenda.

THE UPSIDE-DOWN KINGDOM

In seminary, I read Donald Kraybill's *The Upside-Down Kingdom,* which is still, for me, one of the clearest descriptions of the new order that Jesus brought.[3] Kraybill points out how Jesus' kingdom of God turns the world's values of selfishness, consumerism, individualism, militarism, power, and domination upside down. Therefore, one of the saddest and most dangerous things about white Christian nationalism, and the churches that willingly or unwittingly support it, is how *white Christian nationalism literally turns Jesus' kingdom of God wrong side up.* White Christian nationalism has nothing good to say about the poor, and poverty is often described as a character flaw. In fact, Christians are responsible for some of the cruelest things being said in America about "those immigrants" or those "on welfare." And their individualistic, nationalistic, and racial interpretation of religion—leading to the prosperity gospel, the embracing of military power, the white ethnocentricity, and pride of nation—all directly conflict with Jesus' teachings about the kingdom of God.

In Matthew 25, Jesus speaks of *what we do, or don't do, for the poorest and most vulnerable; is what we do, or don't do—for Him.* This was divine poetry for me when I first encountered this text because it fundamentally changes our relationship to millions of people in the world. And Jesus put himself, his life, at the center of their lives. *He* was the "stranger," a Greek word that translates quite literally to "immigrant or refugee," at the center of our polarized political battles today. Jesus says that those who have welcomed the stranger, fed the hungry, given the thirsty something to drink, clothed the naked, visited prisoners in jail, or cared for the health of the sick were his true followers. He was *with* them, and if you wanted to be with Jesus, you had to be with them too. He told his would-be disciples: I will know how much you love me by how you treat them. And those who had offered the gift of their presence and care to the least of these would inherit the kingdom of God.

Jesus made very plain what he was saying to all those gathered around him; all of who apparently believed themselves to be his followers. I was always very struck by that reality in the text. The people he was addressing *all* thought they believed in him. They had followed the rules as they understood them, and thought they had done what was necessary to earn their salvation. And they obviously were confused: Lord, when did we see you hungry, thirsty, naked, a stranger, sick, and imprisoned? We didn't know that was you, Lord! Had we known it was you, we would have done something—like maybe formed a church social action committee.

But, in Matthew 25, Jesus shows white Christian nationalism adherents the fault in their ways. He explains, "Truly I tell you, just as you did it to one of the least, who are members of my family, you did it to me." It was when they cared for the poor, the disenfranchised and the marginalized, that they cared for him. "It *was* me," Jesus showed us. I often refer to Matthew 25 as the "It was me text." How you treated those who had nothing to offer in return, that was how you treated me, he says.

As a student, this was the most radical thing I'd ever read—more radical than the revolutionaries we young activists were all reading at the time to guide us. Jesus was calling for a complete reversal of the current world order. I began to see how the kingdom of God confronted the materialistic, militaristic, and racial values of American culture. In his transforming Sermon on the Mount, the ones whom Jesus calls "blessed" were both the poor and poor in spirit, those with the capacity to weep and mourn over human suffering, those who are meek and humble, those who hunger and thirst for righteousness (justice), those who are merciful (compassionate), those who are pure in heart (integrity), and those who are the peacemakers (who resolve conflicts rather than start them). Jesus' words cut to the heart of economics and politics. This was a different value system than the one I had grown up with in my white American church.

One day, many years later, when I was fortunate to climb that hillside overlooking the beautiful Sea of Galilee, it seemed so small. I sat there quietly for a long time, pondering how Jesus' sermon was intended to change the world, to turn our lives right side up. And Matthew 25 became Jesus' final test of discipleship: how we treat the poor is literally how we treat him.

In his commentary on Matthew 25, Tom Wright speaks of its overriding theme of justice. He says,

> Justice is one of the most profound longings of the human race. If there is no justice, then deep within ourselves we know that something is out of joint. Justice is hard to define and harder still to put into practice; but it has never stopped human beings and societies seeking it, praying for it, and working to find ways of doing it better. And "justice" doesn't simply mean "punishing wickedness," though that is regularly involved. It means bringing the world back into balance.[4]

The world "balance" is important. All the imbalances I saw as a young activist were deeply motivating me to change things. Wright goes on to say, "Part of the biblical image of the coming of the son of man is the announcement that justice will at last be done." This is how the rule of Christ in the kingdom of God would be exercised—through justice. Wright goes on:

> Should we not say, then, that this scene of judgment, though in this picture it is spoken of as a one-off future and final event, may actually refer to what is happening throughout human history from the time of Jesus' resurrection and ascension to the present. . . . Jesus is portrayed as launching his followers on their dangerous and vulnerable mission.[5]

This new order is both now and coming. When is the last time you heard a white Christian nationalist MAGA pastor talk about justice from the pulpit—justice for the poor, for the immigrants, for those being discriminated against? The only words that relate to "justice" are predictions of punishment for all those who oppose their political agenda. In the Bible, as many scholars have pointed out, the word for "justice" and "righteousness" is often the same. But white Christian nationalist preachers translate righteousness into only personal piety, and ignore the biblical language of justice altogether when it comes to the people who are other than them.

ICONS OF GOD

Making these connections across church history is important. In an article titled "The Least of These—Martin Luther King's Advocacy for the Poor," African American scholar Albert Raboteau says that King's arguments for the poor, based on Matthew 25, go right back to some of the church's earliest bishops:

Like the ancient "Fathers of the Church" King emphasized that "the least of these" are children and "icons" of God, whose treatment is the measure of our "salvation or damnation" as persons and as a nation. Like them he argued that excess wealth is "robbed from the poor." Like them he cautioned us against the ineluctable tendency of consumption to addict us to status and power. Like them he exhorted us to "move from being a thing-oriented, to a person-oriented" society.[6]

Raboteau quotes historian Peter Brown in lifting up fourth-century church bishops like St. Basil of Caesarea and St. Gregory of Nyssa, who were "lovers of the poor" and thought of themselves as "guardians of the poor." When I first discovered these unusual bishops in the history of the Catholic Church in my seminary days, I wondered why I had never heard of them before. St. Basil said:

Who, then, is greedy? The one who does not remain content with self-sufficiency. Who is the one who deprives others? The one who hoards what belongs to everyone. Are you not greedy? Are you not one who deprives others? You have received these things for stewardship, and have turned them into your own property! Is not the one who tears off what another is wearing called a clothes-robber? But the one who does not clothe the naked, when he was able to do so—what other name does he deserve? The bread that you hold on to belongs to the hungry; the cloak you keep locked in your storeroom belongs to the naked; the shoe that is moldering in your possession belongs to the person with no shoes; the silver that you have buried belongs to the person in need. You do an injury to as many people as you might have helped with all these things![7]

Around the year 369, St. Gregory of Nyssa preached on "almsgiving" in the spirit of the Matthew 25 text: "Do not look down on those who lie at your feet, as if you judged them worthless. Consider who they are, and you will discover their dignity: they have put on the countenance of our Savior; for the one who loves humanity has lent them his own face, so that through it they might shame those who lack compassion and hate the poor."[8]

Soup kitchens and shelters for the homeless after famines and disasters were implemented in keeping with the bishop's preaching; the aid even included job and skill training to help people get work!

Raboteau reminds us that Dr. King was killed while in Memphis in support of the sanitation workers' strike for better wages: he had just begun a poor people's campaign. And his words "echoed these ancient church teachings." King was "a twentieth-century exemplar of a very old tradition." Raboteau goes on to recount how, similarly, in 1962, King preached, "I see hungry boys and girls in this nation and other nations and think about the fact that we spend more than a million dollars a day storing surplus food. And I say to myself, 'I know where we can store that food free of charge—in the wrinkled stomachs of the millions of people in our nation and in this world who go to bed hungry at night.'"

Howard Thurman, King's spiritual mentor, who called for genuine faith to lead to social action, found a "touchstone" in Matthew 25. He calls the incoming of the kingdom of God into the world "a precipitous movement of God invading human history."[9] The announcement that this kingdom is at hand means "a sovereignty inclusive of the entire human race" and "the invasion to the will, to the love of God." He paraphrases the response to Jesus' words, imagining what was going through his listeners' minds, understanding how we often act in contrary ways to what is good and true:

But I didn't know that it was important. For some reason, I was so involved in the living of my life, in handling my own affairs, in doing my thing, that I did not refer my deeds to my center [a word Thurman often uses for where God wants to be in our lives]. I referred my deeds to some other aspect of my life. To my anxieties, it is out of these that I acted. It is out of my fears that I acted. It is out of my ambitions that I acted. It is out of my pride that I acted, always getting my clue as to what I should do from something less than my center. Something less than that which is at the core of me.[10]

And in stark contrast to the white Christian nationalists, St. Augustine, the fourth-century bishop of Hippo in northern Africa, said that governments without justice are robbers of the poor, and an unjust law is no law at all.[11]

WHERE DOES BURGER KING MOM GO TO CHURCH?

Some years ago, I walked into a Burger King to grab a bite on the run when I saw something that struck me as unusual. Three children sat in a corner booth, with their school books, papers, and pencils on the table, clearly doing their homework. As I watched, I saw a worker hurry from her register at each lull in the action to help these kids for as long as she could. Then she would rush back to the next customer who approached the counter or drive-thru window.

Here was a working mother trying to balance her job with helping her kids with their schoolwork. Given her low wages, she was likely struggling with more than just making the time to fill hamburger orders and help her children with their homework. She was undoubtedly also making impossible choices about what to prioritize and what to neglect. Pay the rent or go to the doctor to get a prescription for a sick child or relative? Put food on the table or keep all the bills up to date? Buy winter boots for her kids or school supplies?

And maybe, I thought, she's working multiple jobs to make up for her inadequate wages, forcing a whole other set of compromises in trying to balance her full work schedule with her children's school and life schedule. Who will read her children a story before they go to bed and tuck them in when her work hours run well past their bedtime? How will the kids get to school when she works the early shift, and how will the bills get paid if she misses a shift? Making sure kids get to the places they need to go is a challenge for all parents, but it is so much harder for low-income and often single moms.

Burger King mom, as I would come to refer to her in the sermons and talks she inspired, lived a life of continual predicaments, compromises, sacrifices, and crises. It was clear to see she was doing all that she could do—none could question her devotion to her children—but her circumstances dictated that her "best" was often not enough, and many poor single moms feel that way. The reality of modern-day politics is that the soccer mom takes far greater priority than the Burger King mom. In states like Georgia, Michigan, and Pennsylvania, suburban moms are courted by Democrats and Republicans alike as the potential "swing vote" to determine who will hold the power. These are overwhelmingly white, affluent women, and politicians are all competing for their votes.

Meanwhile, the desperate circumstances of the Burger King mom, the one who truly needs assistance, are much less talked about or just ignored. The low-income women working in our fast-food restaurants, cleaning industry, and hospitality business are most likely to be women of color, many also immigrants; and a part of the most underrepresented groups in US politics. They belong to the low-income demographic, the group with the lowest levels of both voter registration and turnout. As such, neither party holds much vested interest in the success and well-being of those mothers and their families.

With so much to worry about and the resources of time and money being in such short supply, it is no wonder low-income people have a hard time investing in the voting process. Logistical obstacles are only compounded by the sense that they are not the political priority. With Republicans looking after their wealthy donors and constituents and Democrats championing the middle class, the poor understandably find little reason to believe that the outcome of elections will make much difference in their lives.

But could the lack of attention to the poor among politicians actually reflect that their circumstances are improving? Is it that there are other issues that are truly more pressing? Hardly. The poverty rate, including that among children, has steadily climbed over the years.[12] Many people are still without health insurance.[13] The number of people who can't find affordable housing is on the rise.[14] And the national minimum wage has not changed since 2009 when the dollar was worth 28 percent more than it is today.[15] However, in response to COVID, a pandemic rescue bill added a major extension of the child tax credit that reduced child poverty by almost half! But after the pandemic was deemed "over," that critical CTC expansion was allowed to expire, and child poverty went back up—doubling!

How comfortable do you think Burger King mom would feel in a white Christian nationalist church?

JESUS AND MONEY

Jesus was no stranger to the topic of economics. His parables and sermons ran the gamut from giving (Luke 6:38), wealth management (Luke 16–17), and controversy over wages (Matthew 20), to a parable about a lost coin (Luke 15:8–10). Perhaps the Sermon on the Mount best sums up the economics of Jesus. Consider how often, each and every day, our lives are shaped by consumer values that bring us everything we watch, listen to, or read ("brought to you by . . ."). Then reflect upon the key portions of Mathew 6 in Jesus' sermon: "Do not store up for yourselves treasures on earth, where moth and rust consume and where thieves break in and steal, but store up for yourselves treasures in heaven, where neither moth nor rust consumes and where thieves do not break in and steal. For where your treasure is, there your heart will be also."

Whom do we finally serve? We can't have it both ways. "No one can serve two masters," says Matthew. "You cannot serve God and wealth" (Matthew 6:24).

The advertising that fills our lives has one purpose: to make us worry—about everything—how we look, how we feel, what we eat, what we drink, and everything else about our lives. The heart of Jesus' message in his Sermon on the Mount is to stop worrying:

> Therefore I tell you, do not worry about your life, what you will eat or what you will drink, or about your body, what you will wear. Is not life more than food and the body more than clothing? Look at the birds of the air: they neither sow nor reap nor gather into barns, and yet your Father feeds them. . . . Consider the lilies of the field, how they grow; they neither toil nor spin, yet I tell you, even Solomon in all his glory was not clothed like one of these. (Matthew 6:25–26, 28–29)

And perhaps what we most worry about is tomorrow instead of just living in today. Jesus gives us the values of his new order of the kingdom of God: "So do not worry about tomorrow, for tomorrow will bring worries of its own. Today's trouble is enough for today" (Matthew 6:34).

Do you ever hear the preachers of the prosperity gospel—who consider those with more wealth to be "blessed" and those with less to be without adequate faith—sound anything like the preaching of Jesus here in his last teaching in Matthew 25, before he went to Jerusalem where he would be crucified, buried, and resurrected? There is a profound tension between Jesus' message and the false gospel of white Christian nationalism. It is not surprising given the context that this was Jesus at his most urgent, and he spoke in an uncharacteristically judgmental manner. He chose exclusionary language, in part, so that his listeners would see clearly that they were not being inclusive. There are two groups of people, he said: goats and sheep. And he asked plainly, "Which one are you?" In doing so, he beseeched people to seek wholeness and healing through their connection and communion with the ones always left out and left behind.

IT WAS ME

Matthew 25 was Jesus' final exam—his last teaching before he was killed as an enemy of the state. And in his moment of crisis, his measure of his followers' faith was: "How did you treat me?"

Undoubtedly, the mother at Burger King was no stranger to living in need. She worked a job that could not possibly keep up with the cost of living for herself and her three children. And Jesus says, "That was me." Today that mom is hungry and needs nutritional support including through SNAP, the Supplemental Nutrition Assistance Program that we know as "food stamps," but many in politics keep trying to cut people out of receiving SNAP. Jesus says, "I was that mom whose kids were hungry."

While city and state governments ensure clean drinking water in the white suburbs of places like Flint, Michigan, and other cities, the Black neighborhoods in Flint found their family's tap water full of lead and asbestos, unsafe to drink. Mothers in my home state kept trying to make us care that their children didn't have clean or safe water to drink or bathe in as the pipes full of lead never seemed to get fixed over weeks, months, and years. I could hear Jesus saying, "It was me who was thirsty in Flint."

And let's talk about our nation's Southern border. Many politicians want us to close it off to the incoming "strangers." Consider the farmer in Guatemala who can no longer feed his family because climate change has rendered his land unable to produce food. Gangs threaten to kill his wife and rape his daughter if he keeps refusing to hand over his son to be a boy soldier. With violence all around, and unable to protect and feed his family, this father gathered his family and left home. They took only the possessions they could carry on their backs to make the thousand-mile walk to find a new home in America, which they were told took in asylum seekers who found their lives in peril. But when they made it to the United States, they were put into cages, then separated from their children who were put into separate cages. Stripped of possessions, work, and even their children—the farmer and his wife must have felt like naked strangers.

"I was that Guatemalan farmer, that stranger, and I was the one made naked," says Jesus. "They did not welcome me and instead used me as a political pawn and rallying cry to validate their constituencies' fears: 'Build a wall to keep out the immigrants—the people like *me.*' They created fear and incited hate and violence, even in my name, against the bodies of my family."

Jesus is also the man, the woman, and the child sick and without money to afford health care, go to the doctor, get preventive care, or get the prescriptions they need. Jesus is the person whose loved ones' health hangs forever on the brink of the next accident, illness, or disease. Jesus says, "That was me too." Then he says, "I was the one persecuted by the criminal justice system, a Black person five times more likely to be pulled over without cause than a white person[16] and imprisoned like one in every three Black men are in America.[17] I had inferior legal representation, longer sentences, higher bail, and more parole time after my sentence was over. It was all me."

WHITE CHRISTIAN NATIONALISM'S FAVORITE VERSE ABOUT THE POOR

There are always those who say that we can't do anything about poverty. In fact, ironically, there is a biblical text in the next chapter of Matthew that is abused to support that cynical view that nothing really can be done for poor people.

Matthew 26:6 begins the story of Jesus' anointing at Bethany. In a discussion with his disciples he says, "For you always have the poor with you." What does that mean? In a newsletter and blog post from *Food for the Hungry,* Wendy McMahan describes how this sentence is misinterpreted to justify our continual neglect of the poor: "You can't overcome poverty. It's a useless cause. Don't waste your money on it. Even Jesus said so." Sadly, I have sometimes asked audiences what the most famous text in the Bible about the poor is—and this one comes up again and again; more even than the Matthew 25 text we have been reflecting on.[18]

Let's briefly take this sentence on. First, the disciples are all sitting at the table in the house of Simon the leper. Think about that. Jesus and his followers were always hanging out with the poor and marginalized— even the lepers—and not enjoying the hospitality of the local chairman of the Bethany Chamber of Commerce. A woman anoints Jesus' head with costly oil, and some disciples complain about it. But Jesus is grateful for her warm care and worship and says in effect: "Look, as my disciples you will always be with the poor, like tonight, as that is what we always do—you will always be with them and they will always be with you. Just don't begrudge this woman her act of worship and thanksgiving." Jesus knew that he would be killed the next day.

And the words he uses in the text are actually drawn from Deuteronomy 15:11: "There will always be poor people in your land. Therefore, I command you to be openhanded toward your fellow Israelites who are poor and needy." Openhandedness is the biblical response to poverty. But when Jesus' followers are *not proximate* to the poor and oppressed, they completely misunderstand this text and actually use it to further ignore them.

The good news is that many religious leaders and communities across the theological and political spectrum are now responding to the vacuum of political leadership on poverty and income inequality. While divided on other issues, more in the faith community are increasingly united in their focus on poverty as a defining moral and biblical issue.

Evangelicals, Pentecostals, Catholics, mainline Protestants; Black, Hispanic, and Asian American churches are all coming together, and working with other faith traditions too to make poverty a religious issue again, even at the ballot box. Maybe Burger King mom will finally have someone speaking for her and her kids.

We must continue to ask: "How are the poorest and most vulnerable being treated?" This is finally the moral test of any economy. And that is clearly how the biblical prophets of God judge those who claim to be governing political leaders, and that's what will distinguish the true disciples of Jesus. And it makes both moral and common sense that the well-being and flourishing of all of us is the best thing for both democracy and the common good.

SCAPEGOATING THE LEAST OF THESE

French anthropologist, philosopher, and literary critic René Girard argues that, like many forms of human behavior, our desire is mimetic.[19] In other words, we often imitate others. He suggests that rivalry, envy, and comparison are largely the result of this tendency and that the possibility of violence arises with those conflicts. Violence, in turn, threatens the stability of a community and the common good.

Girard argues that humans sometimes seek a solution, one he called the "scapegoat mechanism." In an unconscious effort to restore harmony, those in conflict unite in opposition to a symbolic—and innocent—victim. By projecting their hostility and frustration upon another individual or group, they preserve the solidarity of their own group.

We are still reeling as a country from the blatant scapegoating tactics leveraged by Donald Trump to draw the support of his followers. Statistics reported by the FBI reveal that hate crimes, which had been falling in the years leading up to his presidency, surged by 20 percent while Trump held office.[20] The increase in hate-motivated murders was even more pronounced, reaching their highest numbers in three decades.[21] Most of these crimes were committed by white offenders against victims who were most often targeted based on their race or religion. The greatest threats to our safety and security now come from white terrorist individuals and groups in the United States, according to law enforcement officials.

This is no coincidence. Trump gave voice to the greatest fears and worst instincts of his followers from the outset of his campaign. He claimed that "Islam hates us," and at the time of his proposed ban on Muslims entering America he declared that they represented "an extraordinary influx of hatred and danger coming into our country."[22]

In the five days that followed, anti-Muslim violence rose by 90 percent. He responded to the outrage against the killing of George Floyd by Minneapolis police with a tweet that harkened back to a statement made in the 1980s by a Miami police chief known for racialized policing: "When the looting starts, the shooting starts."[23] There was never any presidential remorse over the death of Floyd.

It is no surprise, then, that African Americans were among the groups with the greatest increase in victimization while Trump was in office. And of course, he blamed Latino immigrants for any number of ills of American society, championing a wall he groundlessly claimed would be paid for by the Mexican government. This open antagonism resulted in a marked increase in hate crimes against Latinos, including the El Paso massacre that left eleven dead.[24]

Just after the 2016 election, I began getting many calls from faith groups working with immigrants and refugees, and from Black church pastors and others working with young Black men being racially profiled by police. They all worried about those they served being *scapegoated*. They could see that this new administration was politically targeting these groups and that this intolerance would embolden those all too ready to act upon their existing prejudices.

I began to hear stories of many church workers who were being threatened with prosecution for ministering to immigrants. I spoke to the head of a church medical clinic who confided in me that she was caring for a number of undocumented people. When they showed up sick and in need of help, her priority was to serve these individuals' medical needs, regardless of their immigration status. As such, she didn't check their documentation.

For this, she was threatened by Immigration and Customs Enforcement

(ICE) agents who wanted to know who she was treating, and whether she had checked their documentation. They then insisted on interrogating her patients and demanding their documentation. In her case and in others like it, churches were told that their members would be legally liable and would be arrested and prosecuted for helping undocumented people in need. These threats have even been made to national faith-based charity groups, with attacks against them by Republican members of Congress. In fact, I have spoken to individuals who have been threatened with prosecution for simply taking an immigrant to church, a clear abuse of a federal law intended to prevent individuals from "harboring and transporting" illegal immigrants. But despite the threats, these Christians kept treating the sick and taking people to church if they wanted to go!

Sadly, scapegoating became a more common inclination not just in politics, but also in churches. As Senator Cory Booker points out, "Often people wield religion as a way of distinguishing themselves, to indulge in that which Jesus warned us about in judgment of others, not humble servants or unconditional love, but to use religion as a weapon against others."[25]

And most tragically, white Christian nationalism and the churches that support that heresy and ideology—explicitly or implicitly—have adopted the scapegoating mechanism against the poor. Indeed, white Christian nationalist churches regularly abide by this us-versus-them theology that's almost indistinguishable from the toxic culture of modern politics and flies in the face of the new reality that Jesus sought to inaugurate in Matthew 5 through 25. They see the stranger and they do not welcome him. They see the hungry, thirsty, naked, sick, and imprisoned, and they do not help them, but *blame them* for their problems. During recent debates on the debt ceiling and spending, an extreme Republican caucus accused poor people of manipulating and gaming the system—with little evidence for that—while, at the same time ignoring the tax behaviors of the wealthy who actually do manipulate and game the systems they control—with much evidence for that. From the Matthew text, we see Jesus in desperate need and, just as the world did before, people make him the scapegoat.

But Jesus was the final scapegoat so that no other would be needed. He willingly volunteered his life as a means of sacrifice; the lamb slain. In essence, Jesus said, "I will be the final scapegoat so you no longer have to scapegoat your brother." And there are, gratefully, many in the church who want to live by the spirit of his teachings. Only the coming back to Jesus can save the churches from white Christian nationalism.

A MATTHEW 25 MOVEMENT

I encountered more and more faith leaders in the churches, and out-side of them, who told me, "Jim, this is the text that God is giving us to address the issues at hand." Matthew 25 was becoming a unifying text and commitment, even a movement, for diverse people. Black and His-panic pastors, Jews and Muslims, and, of course, nonreligious people all wanted to protect the least of these from the increased jeopardy they were now facing with the scapegoating tactics of Trump and his minions. In conversation after conversation with pastors and activists about the problems they were facing in trying to serve the most vulner-able, the Scripture of Matthew 25 kept coming up. And gradually, in our discussions, the idea of a new *Matthew 25 movement* began to emerge. We gathered to talk and pray about its application, even organizing re-treats to contemplate its implications. Over time, the movement began to organize around three groups of marginalized and targeted groups: immigrants threatened with potential deportation and the dissolu-tion of their families, Muslims questioning whether they had a place in Trump's America, and young people of color being racially policed in Black and brown neighborhoods—including from youth groups in Black and brown churches.

Just as the movement began to take form, we got word of a Pente-costal pastor in Southern California named Reverend Noe Carias who had been arrested and threatened with deportation. Carias had been in America for decades, having arrived illegally with his parents at age thirteen. Since then, he had married; his wife was a US citizen, and they had two children who, by birth, were US citizens. Carias established an Evangelical Assemblies of God church in Los Angeles; he had been its pastor and a leader in the community until the time of his arrest. He had been granted temporary conditional residency under President Obama's DREAM Act, but his status had been revoked when Donald Trump rescinded the act in 2017.

Rev. Carias faithfully checked in with ICE every year, but this time, he was put in an orange jumpsuit and told he was being deported back to Guatemala. His wife and children were waiting for him in the ICE office with plans for dinner, but he never came out. Rev. Noe was held in detainment, but during that time, the Matthew 25 community, referred to in Los Angeles as "Mateo 25," rallied around him with vigils and marches, diverse readers' letters to influential people, visits with political leaders, press conferences, and endless prayer.

In late September 2017, Rev. Carias was released from detention after two months (fifty-nine days). Many other prisoners said they had come to Christ through his presence in jail. But, of course, he was an exception. Many targeted immigrants didn't have enough support to avoid deportation. They were sent to countries they might not have seen since they were small children; and their families were left behind.

Many Muslim leaders were also worried about their fate in this new political climate where they were suddenly being threatened with removal. Muslim students and many international students were prevented from returning to America even after holiday visits to their home countries.

But law students at Georgetown, some of them in my classes—with other law school students from around the country—headed to local airports to support their Muslim classmates who were now under attack. I was also moved to see both Jewish and Christian faith leaders deciding to stand by their Muslim brothers and sisters. They pledged that if these Muslims were required to nationally register, as was being threatened, then they would be first in line to say, "I, too, am a Muslim."

These inspiring enactments of the Matthew 25 movement produced a great sense of relief, not only among those under threat, but for those who came together in solidarity in support of the least of these. They experienced a sense of community that transcended the fellowship of their typical ingroup. And they experienced empowerment in realizing the strength they had when they came together in the spirit of Matthew 25 to care for those who were in jeopardy.

The focus on Black youth, with the increased dangers they were experiencing, continued to grow. I was on a speaking tour with a new generation of young Black activist leaders in South Africa when Michael Brown, an unarmed Black teenager, was shot and killed by police in Ferguson, Missouri. News of the incident spread rapidly around South Africa, hitting the country and young Black people there very hard. When I came home, I went to Ferguson to meet with the young leaders organizing and leading the protests. At their invitation, I went to a very publicized event at the now infamous Ferguson police station, where Cornel West and I helped lead a march of clergy and young people. We took our vigil right up to, face to face with, the heavily armed police, and we were arrested. The view of those young leaders that defined the movement was that until Black lives mattered, all lives would not matter.

Their perspective again mirrors that of Jesus, made clear in Matthew 25: how we treat the marginalized separates Jesus' true disciples from those who just pay him lip service. From Jesus' point of view, the world isn't top-down, but bottom-up. This is also the message at the core of the Black Lives Matter (BLM) movement that so many miss, refuse to acknowledge, or reject outright.

Ironically, many of these young activists were almost entirely unchurched, unlike their predecessors in the Civil Rights Movement. In fact, I was told by a number of church leaders that not only did these new activists not come up through the churches, but they didn't feel welcome there. And yet, these were the very individuals now living in the spirit of what Jesus says in Matthew 25.

A few months after the shooting of Michael Brown, some of the young Ferguson leaders joined with a group of national pastors and heads of faith-based organizations and denominations who comprise our Faith Table for our annual retreat, which we chose to hold that year in Ferguson. With great authenticity and passion about their cause and their mission, the young leaders bared their souls and their lives to us in very vulnerable ways. And the church leaders who *heard* these un-churched Black activists were deeply moved by them. In particular, I remember the response of Reverend Otis Moss III, pastor of Chicago's Trinity United Church and son of Otis Moss, Jr., a close colleague of Martin Luther King, Jr. Otis 3, as he is now called, spoke movingly to the young people on the night that we shared together.

"You know," Otis said, "I preach prophetically, which I learned from my father, from Dr. King, from my history, and from my tradition. . . . But I've been preaching from a place of comfort inside the walls of my church, and I want to change my relationship to the young people on the streets around my church and in my city of Chicago." Rev. Moss told these young street leaders, "Tonight has been transforming for me." Otis Moss III returned to Chicago with a fresh outlook on his own ministry and to deeply engage with the Black Youth Project, the equivalent of Black Lives Matter in Chicago.

Out of this, a bond of trust was formed, as Rev. Moss and Trinity took their faith into the lives of street youths, and some of the leaders of the Black Youth Project began showing up at church. Church and street communities that have too often been disconnected could form a bridge that would help heal the divides in the community, and connect those who served but also those who wanted to be of service in the streets. In Chicago, pastors like Otis 3 and his colleague on the south side, and Reverend Julian DeShazier, pastor of the University Church, are leading the way. Julian, a young leader and friend who gives me great hope, is also known as J.Kwest, an award-winning musician and rapper with a growing audience. One day when my two boys met Julian in our home after a Sojourners board meeting, they asked, "Dad, what is J.Kwest doing in our house?!" DeShazier, with the help of other pastors like Otis Moss III, helped support the street leaders around them to establish the first hospital trauma center in one of Chicago's toughest and most violent neighborhoods to save lives critically at risk.

BUDGETS AS MORAL DOCUMENTS

With the prevalence of poverty still in America, we must ensure that the priority of the poor is given a clear and strong moral voice—not just in private service but also in public policy. If you really read the Scriptures and if you are one of the 90 percent of members of Congress who claim to be Christian, you will see that the God of the Bible is not simply a God of charity, but a God of justice.

To address this need, a number of us as faith leaders assembled over a decade ago to form a nonpartisan coalition called the Circle of Protection. We are comprised of diverse leaders from a variety of theological, political, and ethnic backgrounds. The COP brings together the National Council of Churches and its mainline Protestant denominations, and the National Association of Evangelicals with their many evangelical denominations—two groups who rarely come together for anything. We are also joined by the United States Conference of Catholic Bishops (USCB), Catholic Charities and Catholic Relief Services with their direct and effective work among the poor, along with many active faith-based social justice organizations like Sojourners, Bread for the World, and the Friends Committee on National Legislation (FCNL). In the COP, we regularly apply the meaning of Matthew 25 to concrete issues of federal spending for the least of these. We are a broad circle of churches and faith organizations whose church bodies together represent almost one hundred million members. Our mission is to call upon our elected political leaders to make *a circle of protection* around the least of these and all those most vulnerable lifted up in the two thousand biblical texts. We often call ourselves the Matthew 25 coalition (circleofprotection.us).

What unites the coalition is a focus on how decisions are made on Capitol Hill in regard to the budget and its spending for poor and low-income families and children. For many years now, we have come together to raise up the notion of budgets as "moral documents." That term and perspective originated in a meeting, years ago, with Senate Democrats who were at a stalemate with Republicans in trying to address the polarities that defined their party positions—even back then. In the continual battles for or against taxes and spending, the two sides had reached a deadlock. The Democrats asked, "How do we get beyond just being considered tax-and-spend liberals?"

After the long meeting, I suggested we reframe the whole conversation around the idea of a *budget as a moral document.* This phrase has stayed in the air throughout the years and, in fact, has even been used on Capitol Hill by people who don't realize that it came from a conversation with the faith community. It simply means that whether it is for a family, a school, or a church; or for a local, state, or federal government; a budget tells us who and what is important. A budget represents who and what we care most about, and don't care much about. A budget reveals our true priorities and applies moral accountability to them.

During the Trump years, the Circle of Protection helped fight a sustained Republican push for roughly $2 trillion in cuts to poverty-focused programs.[26] Despite repeated budget brinkmanship with government shutdowns and fiscal cliffs, that partisan path achieved no significant cuts in effective poverty programs, which we were grateful to have played a faith role in.

And we have found that we need to speak to both sides of the political aisle about the prioritizing of the poor. I recall a dramatic Circle of Protection meeting in the Roosevelt Room of the White House with then president Barak Obama and his whole economic team. They were trying to determine what federal spending should be cut or saved in a process called the "sequester." After Dr. Barbara Williams-Skinner's opening prayer, the official representative of the US Catholic Bishops Conference, Bishop Ricardo Ramírez of Las Cruces, New Mexico, said, "Mr. President, we are around this table today because of a gospel text that does not say, 'As you have done to the middle class, you have done to me.' What it does say is 'As you have done to the least of these, you have done to me.'" Barack Obama said, "I know that text." I replied, "I know you do." And that's why, we explained to the president, we were asking for a sequester exemption for spending cuts in any programs that were effectively reducing poverty in America. His whole economics team exclaimed, "No, that is impossible," and we vigorously argued over specifics for the next hour. We lost the argument that day, and walked out of the White House feeling defeated.

Three hours later, I got a call from the counselor to the president. He told me the president had changed his mind, reversed the course, and informed his staff that he had decided to exempt all those effective programs for the least of these. He said the president told him to tell me it was the breadth of the faith leaders group we brought in for the meeting and, most of all, it was that text from Matthew 25. That decision affected hundreds of millions of dollars for millions of people who needed help. The president's chief counselor invited me to come in to talk about the agreement and strongly encouraged me to keep "knocking on the door of this White House—we critically need the continuing faith voice."

On the subject of Matthew 25, what has recently captured the attention of our COP was the child tax credit CTC (as was earlier mentioned) as part of the bipartisan American Rescue Plan that provided an expanded tax credit for each child a family had. Enacted in 2021, this allowed families to receive increased monthly payments for every child age six to seventeen in response to the COVID crisis. The result was a *massive reduction* in child poverty, down 46 percent[27] and lifting almost three million children out of poverty.[28] Even during a global pandemic and economic recession, the expanded child tax credit helped drive the child poverty rate to a record low of 5.2 percent, according to the Center on Budget and Policy Priorities.

Not only that, but the data overwhelmingly supported that families used the money from the child tax credit to pay for necessities like groceries, school supplies, doctor's bills, and rent. The bill demonstrated a simple truth that many have learned over the years, particularly those living on minimum wage: that the best way to reduce poverty is through *cash*. Simply put, people need money, and the child tax credit provided it in a regular way.

But despite its resounding success, as a result of the votes of all Republican senators and two Democrats, Senators Manchin and Sinema, the child tax credit was cut by Congress in several bills subsequent to its 2021 approval. Predictably, this reversed much of the progress made by the increased child tax credit, and child poverty then increased by 40 percent. For a family of four with two children, this cut meant $2,600 less in income per month. Following the expiration of the child tax credit, 3.7 million children, including 2.5 million Black and Latino kids, fell back into poverty.[29] Had Congress made the current $2,000 child tax credit fully refundable and available to all low-income families, the number of children experiencing poverty would have dropped by another 20 percent.

Sadly, such choices are typical of policymakers. And I would say that legislators who vote against such programs, arguing that the money will not be spent on necessities but wasted on drugs and other things, have one thing in common. *Such policymakers simply do not know any poor people and are not in proximity to their families and children, even in their own districts and states; or are just not listening*—be they Republicans or Democrats. Tax cuts to the wealthy and to large corporations remain the preferred norm; and cuts are rarely made to military spending, even though it's the most wasteful federal spending in the whole government; but a child tax credit that produces profound and measurable relief for low-income families is discarded. These are choices, moral choices, and, I would say, choices with religious meaning. The legislators should all reread Matthew 25.

A Republican governor, and a Catholic, once told me, "I have read

Matthew 25, and now realize that if I don't do policies that care for the poor, I am going to hell!" He wanted to talk about those policies in his state. The Scriptures clearly say that the princes and kings and governing leaders of this world will be judged not for their gross national product, or military firepower, nor for the impact of their nations' popular culture in the world, but, rather, for their treatment of the poor, oppressed, and most vulnerable.

POVERTY *BY* AMERICA

Historically, a widening gap between the rich and the poor represents a dire threat to democracy. And at the same time, the accumulation of extreme wealth goes hand in hand with autocracy. In fact, wealth is part of the payment made for loyalty to the autocratic rule. This is the case for both Putin and Trump, who reward those who sing their praises and punish those who disagree with them. Authoritarian movements *depend* on rising inequality and the resentments it provokes to support dictators who proclaim themselves as the sole means of relief.

It's time to reimagine what a human rights economy would look like. It's time we measure our economic well-being based on the well-being of the people from the bottom up. Our political success is dependent on our economic success, not the kind valued by our policymakers, but the kind of success valued by Jesus.

In the spring of 2023, I spoke with Matthew Desmond, a sociologist at Princeton University whose research focuses on poverty in America. In his new book, *Poverty, by America,* he explores why the United States, the richest country on earth, has more poverty than any other advanced democracy.[30] He says we need to go beyond talking about the *conditions* of poverty, and dig deeper into the *causes* of poverty. Desmond makes it clear that the deepest problems of poverty are not just a lack of adequate assistance to the poor—which, of course, is very real—but the actual exploitation of the poor—which is beneficial to others, including our affluent selves, Not just poverty *in* America but poverty *by* America.

Desmond writes that we are "conditioned to assume the worst about one another when it comes to receiving help from the government." He calls this "capitalist propaganda."

The truth is that all of us, up and down the economic strata and structures, particularly in relationship to health and well-being, experience real feelings of vulnerability, especially for ourselves and our loved ones. Most all of us will know vulnerability at some time in our lives when we feel out of control, helpless, and even hopeless. How can we connect our vulnerability with the vulnerability of the poorest and most vulnerable among us? Only with proximity. It's time to put the two words together—"vulnerability" and "proximity." Matthew 25 is about *proximity* with the "least of these." And for Christians, this is also a discipleship issue, and even a judgmental issue from the one we call Savior and Lord.

Almost one in nine Americans live in poverty.[31] More than thirty-eight million Americans cannot afford basic necessities and more than *one million schoolchildren* are homeless, living in motels, cars, and abandoned buildings.[32, 33]

Desmond writes, "Today, the wealth gap between Black and white families is as large as it was in the 1960s. Our legacy of systematically denying Black people access to the nation's land and riches has been passed from generation to generation." And he offers this alarming statistic: in 2019, the median white household had a net worth of around $188,000, compared with $24,000 for the median Black household. Desmond told me, "It's impossible to write a book on poverty in America without also writing a book about racism in America. They go in lockstep."[34] He calls for a new moral movement of "poverty abolitionists" that could build momentum for new policies that actually would not just sustain people in poverty, but would begin to overcome it.

FROM A CHRISTIAN COLLEGE TO A
HOMELESS CHURCH

I was invited as I often am to speak at a midwestern evangelical Christian college. I knew it was a very conservative place, and was glad for the opportunity to offer the students a different perspective than they would usually hear. They were very responsive in chapel that day, as were many of the faculty. But apparently, the response from the school's leadership, board, and donors was quite different. They were very angry that the typical conservative political agenda of the school wasn't held up, and alternative visions of the gospel of Jesus were lifted up with such positive feedback from the students. And, to my great surprise and sadness, I learned that the chaplain to the school, who had invited me to speak, was fired! I had gotten to know him a little when I was at the college, really liked him and enjoyed our conversations. Still a young man, he had been at the school for several years, had a deep sense of mission to the students, and wanted them to hear the message of Jesus, being aware how that might counter the conservative politics of the school's leadership. He was also a family man, with several young children. And now he was literally put out of a job with no place to go.

I really felt terrible and called immediately to speak to him and ask what might be next for him and his family. He wasn't sure where he would go; we discussed several options, and I promised to stay in touch. On a later call, I was astonished by what I heard from this young and committed pastor. First, he told me to stop apologizing for getting him fired! Then he described how he had found a new church to pastor.

He said there was a bridge on a local highway that he, like many others, would regularly pass beneath. Under it, there were always many homeless people sheltering. But he, like most others, didn't give the scene much thought, and just drove by. After he was let go by his Christian college, he had more time and was doing much more reflection. He began to take more notice of the homeless under the bridge when he passed by and, one day, stopped to meet the people there who couldn't find housing in their town. He found himself going to visit that bridge more and more and just spending time among the homeless, some of whom now became faces and names to him as he listened to their stories. Some had been to church, and some not, but now they had no church to go to. Eventually, over time and many conversations, with much prayer and discernment, this young pastor and the homeless people he had come to know decided to start a new church—right under the bridge!

He told me all about it with great excitement and a deep sense of new mission which he had found in meeting with, ministering to, and being ministered to himself by these people with nowhere to go. "It's just like you preached in chapel about Matthew 25," he told me. "I have never felt closer to Jesus at any time during my career as a pastor." This young follower of Jesus then thanked me for helping to get him fired from his old college!

LORD, WE KNOW THAT YOU'LL BE COMING THROUGH THIS LINE TODAY

Matthew 25 has continued to convert me as I return to it again and again. Being my conversion text, I have read every commentator on it that I can find. But I have a favorite commentator and prophet on this gospel text who taught me practically what it means: a woman named Mary Glover, whom I met soon after we moved to Columbia Heights, which at the time, was one of the poorest and most dangerous neighborhoods in Washington, DC.

Mary was a Black woman of modest means and few possessions. She had little education and worked as a cook at a local daycare center. But she was one of those people who are the glue that holds neighborhoods together. She was a spiritual rock, an elder—and became one for me. In a community riddled with poverty, violence, and chaos of all kinds, Mary was a beacon of light who was never afraid of the dark.

It took some time for us to settle into our new home and meet our neighbors. But talking together, we began to realize that there were many in our community—just twenty blocks from the White House—who didn't have enough food to get through the week. So, after gathering with a few of our neighbors, including Mary, we decided to start something new in the neighborhood—a regular weekly food line. Those in need could line up on Saturday morning for a bag of groceries, which we gathered as best as we could throughout the week from around the city.

As we became established, it was not unusual for us to open the doors at our new neighborhood center to two hundred people waiting in line for a single bag of groceries. But before we started sharing the food, we always took a few moments to join our hands and pray. It was Mary Glover who led us in prayer every Saturday morning, because she was our best prayer. As a Pentecostal believer she prayed in a way that left no doubt that she knew to whom she was talking from countless past conversations.

Mary Glover always prayed, "Thank you, Lord, for waking me up this morning. Thank you that the walls of my room were not the walls of my grave. And my bed was not my cooling board! Thank you. Thank you, Lord." Then she would conclude: *"Lord, we know that you'll be coming through this line today. So, Lord, help us to treat you well."*

Mary Glover's prayer was the best commentary on Matthew 25 that I had ever heard. She looked at the world the way Jesus did. That was her instinct. I often ask myself, Do I and we see Jesus in the lines coming through our lives and society the way that Mary Glover always did?

Everywhere Mary looked in our neighborhood, and in the world, she saw Jesus and an opportunity to extend her love and care. Jesus was saying, "I will know how much you love me by how you treat them." I continue to recite her prayer to keep me on track.

As the legacy left by Mary spread, her prayer words eventually came to be included in the World Council of Churches' book of prayers. And before Mary passed, my dear friend Ken Medema, a wonderful songwriter and singer, wrote and sang a song dedicated to her, which we played for her at a celebration of our Saturday morning food program attended by all the volunteers at our neighborhood center. "There's a cold Black Jesus with a hole in his shoe, on a DC street with no more to lose. He walks through the line and there he stands, when sweet mother Mary puts some food in his hands."

The economics that Jesus taught means *seeing* the people we look past, try to get around, or tend to ignore or disregard when they serve us food, clean our hotel rooms, or help us take care of our business. Seeing them, as Jesus suggests that we do, will not only change their lives, but can change our lives too. And that deeper kind of conversion to human solidarity will ultimately be the very best thing for democracy and the common good—of us all.

6

PEACEMAKERS, NOT
CONFLICT MAKERS

Blessed are the peacemakers, for they will be called children of God.
—MATTHEW 5:9

ON JANUARY 6, 2023, THE SECOND ANNIVERSARY OF THE VIOLENT INSUR-
rection on the Capitol, a number of faith leaders gathered just across
the street from the Capitol for a sunrise service and prayer vigil for
democracy. We gathered on that day not just to remember that terrible event in American history, but also to reclaim an important day in
the Christian calendar, the Day of Epiphany. On this day, every year,
the church celebrates the coming of the three wise men, ancient el-
ders who followed a star in search of new hope and new life, seeking a
manifestation of Christ the Messiah, who they believed was coming.
There they found, and presented their famous gifts, to a child wrapped
in bands of cloth and lying in a manger, a stable. I remember singing
as a child, "The star in the sky looked down where he lay, the little Lord
Jesus asleep on the hay."

We gathered at the Capitol intent on restoring the corrupted spirit
of January 6 with the revelation of the true Christ who stands in stark
contrast to the false representation and the heresy on display two years

prior, the idol made in the dark spirit of white Christian nationalism. The insurrectionists came to take, not give; to divide, not unite; to hurt, not heal. They came not to make peace in the name of truth, but to commit violence in defense of a lie. They carried not just Confederate flags, revealing the racism at the roots of their indignation, but Christian symbols—flags, crosses, and pictures of Jesus. And when they took over the floor of the Senate, they paused and offered prayers literally shouting Jesus' name.

The word "epiphany" means to see and realize something very important. In part, we as faith leaders gathered that day in realization of what we nearly lost two years before—our nation and our democracy. The use of Christian symbols and prayers at the US Capitol was a desecration of true faith for the false religion of white Christian nationalism. Again, historically, the misrepresentation of religion is always key to the purposes of extremist political power, especially in the rise of movements that are autocratic and fascistic. We decided that the use of religion to justify insurrection required an authentic *liturgy* to publicly restore the meaning of faith. I was surprised at how much attention our sunrise vigil got in the religious press.

Democracy requires us to treat fellow citizens, even political opponents and adversaries, as neighbors, whom Jesus told us to love. Unfortunately, we live in an age when so many can't look at one another and see themselves, and or look at one another and see God.

PEACEMAKING IS A VERB

Words matter. "Peace" is a word that is, at best, overused and misused and, at worst, abused. So how do we make sense of what Jesus is *saying* in Matthew 5:9? Jesus never said, "Blessed are the peace*lovers*." Why would he have bothered? Don't we all fall under that umbrella? But a preference for peace doesn't just produce it. We all think and say that we love peace, but what is just in our heads, and even in our hearts, is not enough.

Jesus also never said, "Blessed are the peace*keepers.*" Sometimes, peace is kept so that the status quo may *not* be disturbed. But there is no nobility in maintaining peace in the midst of injustice and oppression. In that case, peacekeeping amounts to nothing more than silent complicity.

Rather, Jesus told his disciples that God's blessings are reserved for the peace*makers,* those who work to overcome conflict. Jesus was not advocating passivity—he was calling his followers to an active pursuit of peace. Those who face conflict head-on and bring healing in its stead, said Jesus, are the children of God—a very special designation.

Of course, conflict is a natural and an inevitable product of human nature. We all struggle with selfishness and ego. We judge and compare. We desire superiority over solidarity. And when unchecked, these desires and propensities lead to conflicts of all manner: lying, cheating, stealing, and violence. So, whether it be between individuals, families, neighborhoods, cities, or nations, conflict happens—and it always will. That doesn't mean that we should just resign ourselves to conflict when it arises. In fact, it implies the opposite: solving and reducing conflict is forever necessary. But most human conflicts don't result in people getting killed. So how do we decrease the number of conflicts that result in injury or death? *Peacemaking* may be more crucial today because so much is now at stake.

The FBI reported a 30 percent increase in murders between 2019 and 2020, the largest increase in the nation's history, and rates have not dropped since.[1] Domestic terrorism (meaning threats and violence that originate in America) virtually doubled between 2020 and 2022, and has been growing for a long time.[2] Norms of civility in Congress, on Capitol Hill, and on both the national and state levels of governance have all but disappeared. After the 2023 State of the Union address, for example, the shouting of "liar" and other epithets at the president occurred with no apologies afterward; just fundraising letters to cheering constituents.

It is no coincidence that political violence and violent crime across society as a whole are on the rise. As public officials become more openly confrontational, their constituents are following suit.

THE BIBLICAL MEANING OF "PEACE"

What exactly did Jesus mean when he referred to peace?

In the New Testament, the word for peace is the Greek *eirene*. The word appears on ninety-four separate occasions and refers, in one sense, to a state of calm and tranquility. Specifically, *eirene* is defined as "exemption from the rage and the havoc of war." Beyond that, peace is always relational. *Eirene* exists when there is harmony in relationships, peaceful concord between people, and a resultant sense of collective safety, security, and prosperity for the community. The word also suggests a state of happiness, the natural outgrowth of peace and harmony. Where peace is human well-being and what we would call human *flourishing* abounds.

When the authors of the New Testament spoke of peace, clearly, they were referring to something deeper than the word as we typically use it—merely a lack of overt conflict. In a sense, the apostolic writers were speaking of a state of the soul and community that follows from communion with Christ, but this state was not just evident through their state of mind, but also through action. The true state of *eirene* manifests through the practices, disciplines, and behaviors of peacemaking.

In the Hebrew Scriptures, what many Christians call the Old Testament, the word "shalom" is virtually the same as *eirene*. It denotes wholeness, the making of right relationships, as well as the absence of war and strife in the social, political, and individual worlds. Shalom is perhaps most commonly understood as a greeting, used interchangeably with "hello" and "goodbye." The true spirit of the word, however, suggests something closer to a blessing. The person who bids "shalom" wishes "peace be with you," the same words spoken by Jesus when he first reunited with the disciples following his resurrection.

Biblically, peace is not just a wish of well-being to each individual, but a vision for the whole of new humanity, "that they may be one," as Jesus prayed in John 17. Jesus' life was devoted to the uniting of humanity, where service to one another *and* the collective—the common good—was indistinguishable from service to God. Our deep American individualism cuts directly against that, as does our previously mentioned American church heresy of always making faith only private. Peace is not something Jesus meant only for our heads and hearts, but also for resolving conflicts in our societies.

The one existing in a state of shalom intentionally promotes peace, the well-being of others, and the whole of humankind. In both the Old and New Testaments, a state of harmony and equity in relationships was the rightful aspiration of those who would be called the children of God.

Harmony and prosperity are also, of course, the antithesis of war. When strife, conflict, tension, and competition result in violence and war, there can be no *eirene,* there can be no shalom. These are the paths and the ways of life put forward throughout the Bible, as implied by the instruction of Psalm 34, "Seek peace and pursue it." Peace, as this and many other biblical passages contend, is the way of life devoted to freedom and justice for all.

Author and theologian Cornelius Plantinga beautifully describes the biblical concept of shalom:

> The webbing together of God, humans, and all creation in justice, fulfillment, and delight is what the Hebrew prophets call Shalom. We call it peace, but it means far more than mere peace of mind or a ceasefire between enemies. In the Bible, Shalom means universal flourishing, wholeness, and delight, a rich state of affairs in which natural needs are satisfied, and natural gifts fruitfully employed. A state of affairs that inspires joyful wonder, as its creator and savior opens doors and

welcomes the creatures in whom he delights. Shalom, in other words, is the way things ought to be.[3]

Certainly, shalom represents a peaceful state of affairs and being, but it is also an aspiration and a pursuit to restore the balance and harmony possible when we live one for the other. Martin Luther King, Jr., famously said, "True peace is not merely the absence of tension: it is the presence of justice." Justice, derived from the Latin *justitia,* means "righteousness and equity." And the connection between "peace" and "justice" is foundationally biblical. A little sign on my desk says it well, quoting Pope Paul VI in 1972, "If you want peace, work for justice."

There are many who love and seek to preserve peace but who ignore the justice necessary for *eirene* and shalom. They seek peace through creature comforts and sensual pleasures. They believe that by growing their savings, or securing their retirements, they will find happiness and fulfillment. Still others proclaim peace and self-satisfaction through personal piety. But shalom cannot simply exist only in the individual when there is injustice in the society and among the collective. *Eirene* cannot prosper when conflict and violence are considered someone else's problems. Because silence is, indeed, complicity. At root, peace, in the biblical sense, means the establishing, or reestablishing, of right relationships.

WAR IS NOT THE ANSWER

One of the bumper stickers we've released over the years at *Sojourners* read, "War is not the answer." They kept running out! But surprisingly, this seemingly obvious and innocuous message received significant backlash. Some considered this message naïve and foolish. In fairness, I never particularly liked the term "pacifism," and it's probably for a similar reason that some bristled at this seemingly simple antiwar slogan. All too often, pacifism and passivism—i.e., just being passive—in response to violence and war can look as much alike as they sound. Nonviolence cannot just mean what we are against, but also must show what we are for.

Peacemaking is never passive. It's an active pursuit that requires courage, conviction, and sacrifice. Facing conflict is the charge, the calling, and the distinguishing feature of the peacemaker.

Dorothy Day, the founder of the Catholic Worker movement and a beloved mentor of mine, believed that war was irreconcilable with the words of Matthew 25. As we saw in chapter 5, Jesus calls his followers to feed the hungry, give drink to the thirsty, clothe the naked, welcome the homeless, care for the sick, and visit the prisoner. "War does just the opposite," Dorothy said. "It makes my neighbor hungry, thirsty, homeless, a prisoner, and sick. . . . You just need to look at what the gospel asks, and what war does."[4] And what we call "victory" in conflict often comes to the faction that imposes the greatest afflictions on the other—and imposes the greatest cost to the health and livelihood of the opposition. Dorothy said, "The gospel asks us to take up our cross. War asks us to lay the cross of suffering on others."

This argument for peace against war has as much to do with *pragmatics* as notions of right or wrong. Ultimately, Dorothy was arguing that war escalates the issues of conflict that it purports to solve. We have to ask ourselves, What works best? It may be that conflict is inevitable, but war is not; therefore, isn't diplomacy and negotiations with more honest conversations always the better place to start? Shouldn't we first exhaust nonviolent means of conflict resolution?

Time and time again, that is not how the plot of war plays out. Societies rush to war, instead of considering nonviolent alternatives to resolving conflicts. Why? Because the latter requires patience—patience to clarify the problem, patience to listen to many sides of the conflict, patience to understand people's needs and feelings.

Yes, sometimes conflict needs to be resolved by the use of focused force. I supported this approach in places like Darfur in the South Sudan where vicious gangs had to be stopped. Policing with force, both nationally and internationally, is required where aggressors need to see people standing up to them; but war quickly becomes total with casualties and consequences on all sides. I recall long conversations with a British general who became a friend, who commanded the broadest peacekeeping and special forces unit in the British Army, and believed they could have halted the killings by the Janjaweed in Darfur. "Why didn't you?" I asked.

"Because when your nation has gone into too many wars in Arab countries, you can't go in again."

War often tries to be the solution to problems that are not fully understood. Peacemaking, put simply, tries to solve the problems that war promises to solve but fails to—and can even make the problems worse.

PEACEMAKING FROM THE BOTTOM UP

I've participated in countless debates in seminaries and universities about issues of war and peace, debates where each side puts forth the theoretical, theological, rhetorical advantages of "pacifism" or "just war." During one such debate at Fuller Seminary, I stood in one of two big debate pulpits, elevated high above the audience. And as we spoke, it suddenly hit me: What are we doing way up here? We belong on the ground and in the streets, where the conflicts are happening.

The true nature of a problem is often found where people neglect to look—through the eyes of the people, whose lived experiences situate them to understand what might actually work to resolve the most pressing conflicts.

A growing number of students are taking a renewed interest in the study and vocation of conflict resolution. Over time, scholars and practitioners have become more sophisticated in their understanding of the art and science of effective peacemaking, and these students are eager to bring those practices to bear on real problems and conflicts between families, neighborhoods, communities, and even nations.

A remarkable new grassroots campaign called the Catholic Nonviolence Initiative is gaining the attention of Pope Francis at the Vatican. It is a movement, especially from the global South—in Africa, South America, and southern Asia—and is mostly led by women who are engaging local conflicts in the midst of national conflicts. They are moving beyond the narrow language of "pacifism" and "just war" to actually working hard to find answers to violence.

And we have also seen the power of these nonviolent means of conflict resolution even in the United States. One was called the Gang Peace Summit. I traveled to Los Angeles after the 1992 rioting that followed the beating of Rodney King, as part of a World Council of Churches delegation of international leaders, to hold hearings to better understand the causes of the violent uprising. Through some friends, I found my way down to Watts to meet with members of the Crips and the Bloods who were seeking a ceasefire and a truce. After my time in Los Angeles, and meeting with gang leaders in other cities, a strong desire for a "gang peace summit" emerged and I was asked to help with this extraordinary event.

When these gang leaders from across the nation were searching for a place to have their summit, I suggested they call Reverend Mac Charles Jones, the pastor of St. Stephen's Baptist Church in Kansas City, Missouri. Their request became an answer to Mac's prayers of wanting to serve the street youth. In 1994, 125 Black and brown gang-involved leaders from twenty-five cities arrived in Kansas City! But, of course, there was immediate backlash. The local newspaper, *The Kansas City Star,* denounced the hosting of this out-of-town conference, bringing gang leaders and "drug dealers" into their city.

Despite the local opposition, the national Gang Peace Summit happened, hosted by the Black church of St. Stephen's with help from other churches, including St. Mark Union Church, led by a white pastor, Reverend Sam Mann. The intention was to provide these gang leaders with a safe space where they could engage in dialogue and seek mutual understanding on the issues that divided them and were literally killing them. Here were perpetrators of violence and sworn enemies beginning to recognize that they were perpetuating the very cycle that was destroying their lives and families through their constant wars. Their shared grievances and deep grief were enough to lead many who were present to take a step back and consider how they might disrupt that cycle through nonviolent means. "I'm so tired of going to so many of my friends' funerals," many told me. St. Stephen's Baptist Church provided that safe space. Other churches around the country could do the same where such protected space is needed for conflict resolution and peacemaking.

I will never forget when then Kansas City mayor Emanuel Cleaver, also a clergyman and now a congressman, invited the gang leaders to a prayer breakfast at City Hall, and stood with these angry young men for hours until he gained their trust. Or when Reverend Mac Charles Jones preached on the Sunday of their visit, from the parable of the prodigal son in Luke 15:11–32, where a father waited for his wayward son to come home. With tears in his eyes, Reverend Jones, a large father figure himself, made an altar call from his pulpit for these gang leaders to "come home." I'm not sure how many verses of "Just as I Am," (a traditional "altar call" song) we had to sing before one Crip and one Blood—who had been fighting each other in Kansas City—came down separate aisles to drop their "gang colors," something you can be killed for, right there in the pulpit with Mac's big arms wrapped around them. Out of this remarkable weekend, a multitude of youth organizations led by former gang leaders were born, allowing sworn enemies to finally begin to view the "other" as a brother or sister in the fight against common enemies. These gang leaders were not churchgoers but came to trust church as a place where they would be welcomed and encouraged to make peace.

Another great example is Barrios Unidos, an organization led by Daniel "Nane" Alejandrez, a former San Quentin inmate and gang leader who I met at the Gang Peace Summit. *Barrios Unidos,* Spanish for "neighborhoods united," recognized that exposure to education, arts, and technology had the power to transform the lives of young people whose circumstances deprived them of the opportunities many others take for granted. Barrios Unidos also offered former and current gang members the tools of conflict resolution that many came to embrace—practical behaviors and ways of proceeding they could bring to the street level.

Barrios always incorporates spirituality into this process, as "disciplines" of peacemaking and transformed living. Young men and women from indigenous communities began to connect with the traditions of their Native American ancestors, using rituals like sweat lodges to go deeper into the reflection and explore changes needed to address the current state of their lives and communities. Similarly, gang members from Christian backgrounds receive Eucharist at their gatherings. At Barrios festivals and training sessions it is powerful to see sweat lodges and eucharists occurring side by side, and even at complementary times, so some young people could attend both!

The most common theme that emerged from the gang summits and many dialogues around the country was a need for a deeper collective investment in solving the problems that always lead to poverty and violence. Many insisted that crime prevention had to include significant public investments in education for young people of all ages. Most had experienced firsthand the consequences of racialized policing and mass incarceration and identified the need for transformational reform of a criminal justice system that too often works to create, extend, and exacerbate the problems of poverty and violence. These young leaders also called for investments in the infrastructure of their communities and in local economies that would lead to real jobs, affordable housing, and access to health care as viable alternatives to the street hustles many took on as a last resort to support their families.

This wasn't about a utopia. This was about the desire for what most would consider a basic standard of living for access to opportunity. And it was about investments that could save not just lives but also money in the growing costs of rising mass incarceration. The issues experienced by these individuals are deeply ingrained and systemic; and addressing them through the lens of peacemaking requires imagination and commitment that matches the depth of the problems.

The Jesuit priest and antiwar activist Daniel Berrigan put it this way: "We cry peace and cry peace, and there is no peace. There is no peace because there are no peacemakers. There are no makers of peace because the making of peace is at least as costly as the making of war—at least as exigent, at least as disruptive, at least as liable to bring disgrace and prison and death in its wake."[5] Until we learn that *the moral equivalent to waging war is the waging of peace,* we will not see an end to conflict.

It is risky to throw yourself in, to speak up and speak out, even to make your commitment to peacemaking known at your family's Thanksgiving dinners where our own families sometimes exemplify the nation's ongoing divisions and conflicts. In my classes at Georgetown, how to do that always comes up as students prepare to go home for Thanksgiving. We discuss how the lessons of peacemaking that we are learning in class can be applied at home with our families and wherever else we have relationships in conflict. Our dinner tables should become venues for peacemaking in a divided country.

What if our peacemaking were to be extended to the churches that have been caught up in white Christian nationalism, whether they know the term or not? Instead of just critiquing or attacking, could we find some ways to reach out to them? Jesus calls us to peacemaking. White Christian nationalism calls us to conflict making. And that is the choice that we must offer to those who want to follow Jesus.

ANOTHER NAME

Tyre Nichols. That's the name that came up in my class the day after he was killed by the police. Here's another: George Floyd. And others: Michael Brown, Eric Garner, Breonna Taylor, Sandra Bland, Ahmaud Arbery, Trayvon Martin, Tamir Rice. The list goes on and on. There's always another name, and it's time we recognized the truth about all these names. White Christian nationalism doesn't hear the names of young Black people who are shot and killed by the police as victims.

If those churches were committed to truth telling, they would acknowledge that if Tyre Nichols had been a twenty-nine-year-old white man, he would not have been beaten to death by four police officers in Memphis, Tennessee, in January 2023.

Let's tell the truth—especially in our churches.

When Trayvon Martin, a teenager, was shot and killed by a volunteer security guard in Sanford, Florida, in 2012, I thought of my son Luke, who was then about the same age as Trayvon. If America were to be honest, almost everyone would understand that had that been Luke walking back to his father's house returning from a trip to a 7-Eleven carrying a bag of Skittles—even if he had been wearing the same hoodie that made Trayvon look "suspicious"—my white son would *not* have been profiled, stalked, and finally shot to death. Who can deny that Luke Wallis would not have been killed the way Trayvon Martin was? Instead, he would have come back to me, his dad, to watch a game together on TV.

We were in England visiting family when twelve-year-old Tamir Rice was shot and killed in Cleveland in 2014. A white police officer drove up to him and, nine seconds after opening his passenger door, opened fire and killed Tamir. Joy's family and friends all commented that our son Jack was "growing so big and strong. You look so great!" Nobody said that Jack, who was the same age as Tamir Rice, looked dangerous because he was so tall and athletic. But Tamir, who was playing with a toy gun in a Cleveland community park, looked "dangerous" to a white cop.[6]

Jack and I sat on a British couch and together read the story in *The Guardian* about the shooting of another Black boy. Again, I will say with absolute certainty that my white son would *not* have been shot and killed so quickly by a police officer even if Jack had been in that same park playing with that same toy gun. I know that the white cop would have talked to him to find out what was going on before shooting.

In a powerful op-ed in *The New York Times* shortly following the killing of Tyre Nichols, "Where American Democracy Isn't Very Democratic,"[7] Jamelle Bouie argues that the police are typically the public officials with whom low-income communities of color most interact, and therefore the ones who most directly impact the experience of their citizenship. The police are the "government" in poor minority communities. Bouie says, "The middle-class residents of a moderately affluent suburb are likely to experience government in ways that affirm their sense of agency and political belonging, whether at a polling place, their child's school, or a local government office." He cites a 2017 article by political scientists Joe Soss and Vesla Weaver in which they observe that residents of low-income communities are not treated like "citizens facing social barriers or as victims needing protection from slum landlord predation, violence, and misaligned service provision, but as 'criminal targets' in need of surveillance."

The statistics play this out. Black people are five times as likely as whites to be pulled over without cause[8] and twice as likely to be searched.[9] Blacks are about half as likely as whites to have a positive view of police treatment of racial and ethnic groups or officers' use of force. In fact, 30 percent of Black men report that they have been the victim of police brutality.[10] It should come as no surprise, then, that the majority of the 1,096 people killed by police in the US in 2020—the highest number since 2015—were young Black men.[11]

We need to make churches safe places to discuss the problems and failures of policing in our communities.

MAKING POLICING PERSONAL

It's time to get personal with peacemaking because violence is so personal to those who experience it. In my classes at Georgetown, we make all this personal on our "policing day," after we read and discuss the national patterns in the systems and culture of policing. Every student is asked to tell their own personal and family stories of policing. The unplanned and unscripted results are the same every year and tell the human story of American policing all across the country.

A white student from an elite private school in Washington, DC, said that before coming to Georgetown, she had no personal policing stories to tell; but she did have one that involved one of her best friends, another white girl who we will call Susan, who was dating a Black boy, let's call him Sean. Walking together one day, in downtown DC among the monuments, Susan and Sean were approached by a white male police officer who asked the white girl in a very reassuring tone, "Are you okay, ma'am?"

Puzzled, Susan said, "Yes." Then, realizing what was going on, she replied, "What do you mean, am I okay?"

The officer then turned to the young Black man and in a very different tone of voice, demanded, "Are you on substances!"

"No," Sean said.

"Are you carrying them?!"

"No," the Black teenager replied.

But the white cop ordered, "Down on the ground," which Sean, very frightened, did immediately.

Also scared, Susan called her boyfriend's mother, a top Black lawyer in DC who quickly told Susan to yell to Sean what to do and not do—to say and not say—terrified now herself that her son was in great danger. Sean was clean, and was allowed to stand up. There was no apology, but rather a "You're lucky this time!" The white policeman never asked to search Susan's purse. If he had, he would have found an obvious bag of marijuana; but then he might have just called Susan's mother.

A Black student reported that she had been dating a white high school classmate and when they were pulled over by a police car, with him driving, they were quickly let go. By contrast, when her brother, dating a white high school girl, was pulled over, he was pulled out of the car, then verbally abused and pushed around. Students in mixed-race families with "white-passing" siblings told their stories of being left alone by the police, while their darker-skinned brothers were continually harassed. A white-passing student described his parents having "the talk" about police with his darker brother, while he just listened. Or a busload of high school students who were pulled over on their way to watch a school game and all the white kids were quickly allowed to get back on the bus while all the students of color were questioned and searched. One middle-aged student who took my class remotely during COVID spoke of being stopped and pulled over "more times than I can count" in Brooklyn, but one day was so frustrated he showed his NYPD police sergeant's badge and called in his supervisor to report the cop who had stopped him—for no reason. These personal and family stories of policing always reflect and reinforce all the national data the students had just studied.

There is, without a doubt, a police culture and system that targets young Black and brown men and women—treating them as suspicious, dangerous, and likely criminals. Such policing practices completely disqualify the biblical notions of shalom, destroy the meaning of *eirene* in the New Testament, and prevent the possibility of living with a sense of safety, dignity, and peace for those young people and their families. That should be simply unacceptable and irreconcilable for those who claim to be followers of Jesus. So why isn't this topic being addressed in every white congregation in America? Police brutality should not just be an issue for churches to take sides on, but rather we need to reach out to the persons affected, their families, and to the police who need help in learning how to better resolve historic prejudices—including theirs.

It could be argued that those who pledge to serve the public should be held to higher standards than those in the general population, but too often, the opposite is true. Peace cannot be realized when police departments train their officers to act as *warriors* first and *guardians* second, if at all. Warriors are a militarized, occupying force intent on control and punishment. They are an invading army. Guardians, on the other hand, ensure the peace of the communities they serve—and preferably also live in. They cultivate relationships with those whose lives and livelihoods they commit to keeping safe. They are present not just during moments of crisis but days of ordinary life-building relationships with the people they are called to serve and protect. And, of course, police are protecting guardians in some white and affluent neighborhoods, but become invading warriors in Black neighborhoods. Faith communities could help teach police officers how to be the guardians we all need, and not the warriors we all fear. I know several pastors who serve as police department chaplains with this exact goal in mind.

A friend and former staffer at *Sojourners,* Chris LaTondresse, is now a county commissioner with Hennepin County in Minnesota. The large county has installed social workers in every police department, to do the work in situations that they are better trained for, resulting in rave reviews from all those towns and cities—including the police departments. Change can happen.

If we care about peace and if we take Jesus seriously, then transformational public safety and police reform is one of the primary fronts on which peace must be won. And faith communities can be vitally involved. Perhaps, Ella Baker, the famed Civil Rights Movement leader, said it best in 1964: "Until the killing of Black men, Black mothers' sons, becomes as important to the rest of the country as the killing of a white mother's son—we who believe in freedom cannot rest."[12]

THE CRIMINAL (IN)JUSTICE SYSTEM

George Chochos, a former inmate at Sing Sing prison, is now working on a PhD in theology at Georgetown University. In addressing my ethics class, he replaced the term "criminal justice system" with "criminal legal system" because, as he put it, "there is no justice there." On average, Black men receive 20 percent longer sentences than white men for the same crimes.[13] This is the case regardless of the criminal histories of the two groups. Black people are nineteen times more likely to be wrongfully convicted of drug crimes than white people, and 87 percent of those framed for drug crimes by corrupt police officers were

Black.[14] They are also seven times more likely to be wrongfully convicted of murder[15] and account for 58 percent of exonerations for crimes of which they were wrongfully convicted—despite comprising only 13.6 percent of the population.

Studies consistently show that race is the single most important factor in determining which defendants are sentenced to the death penalty, especially when defendants are Black and victims are white, instead of the other way around.[16] And perhaps the most stunning statistic is that one in every three Black men will spend time in the criminal justice/legal system. Black people face injustice at the hands of the criminal legal system by every conceivable measure.

Given the devastating toll of incarceration on the individual—and their families and communities—these inequities represent irrefutable acts of violence against people of color and against any concept of peacemaking that establishes right relationships. Those who are imprisoned are twice as likely to suffer serious mental illness.[17] They often struggle to find employment upon their release and, in many states, returning citizens lose the right to vote.[18] Those who have been incarcerated are more vulnerable to disease and see a two-year decline in life expectancy for every year served in prison.[19] And there is no "peace" by any biblical definition in prisons—just confinement. Most fundamentally for faith communities and their pastors, these crucial matters must not be reduced to partisan politics but become our deep pastoral concerns and prophetic obligations.

One of the most articulate spokespeople for biblical peace in relation to the criminal justice system is Bryan Stevenson, who I wrote about earlier in the book. Bryan shared one particular story that pulls the veil off bias in the criminal justice system:

> I was in a court in the Midwest just a few years ago, and I had my suit and tie on. I sat down at the defense counsel's table to do a hearing, my first time in this courtroom. I was there early, the judge walked in, and when he saw me sitting there, he said, "Hey, hey, hey, you get

back out there in the hallway. I don't want any defendant sitting in my courtroom without their lawyer." And I stood up and I said, "I'm sorry, Your Honor. I didn't introduce myself. My name is Bryan Stevenson. I am the lawyer." And the judge started laughing. And the prosecutor started laughing. And I made myself laugh because I didn't want to disadvantage the young white kid I was representing.[20]

Whether this was the result of a cognitive bias or outright racism, it clearly demonstrates the prejudgment of the likely criminality of an individual on the basis of race. So, what's at issue is equal justice under the law—that is all and that is everything. Equal treatment, safety, and security for *all* of our sons and daughters. The mother and stepfather of Tyre Nichols were President Biden's guests at the 2023 State of the Union, one month after their son was beaten to death by the police. They spent an hour and a half with the president prior to the proceedings, and Biden shared something Tyre's mother said to him during that time. "My son was a beautiful soul," she said, "and something good must come from this."

Whether this comes to pass depends on *whether we truly believe in peace*. Our commitment must go beyond only outrage to a convicted belief in the rightful place of peace, wholeness, well-being, happiness, prosperity, and flourishing—*shalom*—for Tyre Nichols and every other human being.

THE PARENTS ARE CALLING

Guns. Gun violence. America is getting tragically used to—numb to— endless mass shootings and individual gun killings. This may be the most urgent issue of peace in America and it is past time for faith communities to offer more than their thoughts and prayers. I turned on the late evening news one night to current videos from my own Michigan State University where students had just been attacked by a gunman;

three were killed. I saw hordes of police going through a building where I once attended many classes and the student union building where I often hung out and we organized student protests against the war in Vietnam.

Fifty thousand students attend Michigan State University, and *all their parents were calling*. That happens all the time across the country now where shootings occur in schools, in congregations, at concerts, social gatherings, in grocery stores, and on street corners; parents and family are always calling to see if their most beloved ones are okay, or injured, or dead.

More places and more names. Sandy Hook Elementary School, in Connecticut where, on December 14, 2012, twenty-six young children and their teachers were killed. Marjory Stoneman Douglas High School in Parkland, Florida, where seventeen students and staff were murdered and seventeen more injured. Covenant School, a private Christian school in Nashville, Tennessee, where, while I was writing this book, three staff members and three nine-year-old students were gunned down with assault weapons.

We now see some politicians appearing in campaign ads holding guns in their family pictures and, even more bizarrely, we now see photos of smiling white megachurch pastors on the steps to their pulpits with AR-15s in their hands. Even days after the Nashville school shooting, the Facebook page of Andy Ogles, the Republican congressman representing the district where the shooting took place, still displayed a Christmas card photo of him and his wife and two of his three children holding automatic rifles in front of the Christmas tree.[21] As I write, a cadre of House of Representatives members have introduced a bill wanting to make the AR-15 our "national gun."[22] I vividly recall being in a meeting at the White House about the killings in Buffalo when all our phones went off with the news of a mass shooting in Uvalde, Texas. Nineteen children and two adults were killed by another mass shooter.

My Georgetown students were all talking and worried about the MSU shootings the day after, as was my own son who attends another college. Students all over the country were trying to come to terms with the reality that these shootings could easily happen at their own schools. I asked them if they too have had shooting drills and practiced "lockdowns," and most had since kindergarten. I also asked if they wanted that to be accepted and normal now for their children and grandchildren, and if they wanted to be the parents who were calling. They were unanimous in their "nos," but didn't know what to do.

There were 647 mass shootings—almost two per day—reported in 2022 by the Gun Violence Archive, a nonprofit research group that tracks gun violence.[23] Many families have lost loved ones to military weapons of war in the hands of civilians, weapons so destructive that parents in Uvalde, Texas, had to supply DNA to identify their children, mutilated beyond recognition.[24] And yet, Governor Greg Abbott and the Texas Legislature loosened gun laws following the shooting, including a 2021 bill passed to allow permitless carry.[25] Meanwhile, parents in the state are now being asked to provide DNA from their children up front to preempt the problem of identifying the dead.

Despite all this, views on gun reform are split along ideological lines in the nation's capital, a split that only grows wider with each mass shooting.[26] The impasse is largely driven by Republicans politically beholden to, and in bed with, the National Rifle Association and gun manufacturers whose money continually blocks the public will from being implemented. Americans overwhelmingly support, by over 88 percent, universal background checks for purchasing guns, as well as stronger "red flag" laws to identify individuals with histories and mental health issues who shouldn't have access to guns. And a strong majority, 67 percent, favor outright bans of military-style weapons among ordinary citizens[27]—a ban which, when implemented in 1994, resulted in dramatic reductions in mass killings, and when lifted ten years later, led to a sharp increase in shootings and death.[28]

In 2021, a year that saw eleven mass shootings per week on average,[29] gun companies brought in record profits.[30] Meanwhile, politicians bow to the NRA and win elections with the financial backing of the gun manufacturers who offer massive political donations. Here lies the biggest problem: our public acceptance of such indefensible weapons in civil society. Clearly, politicians will continue down the path of enabling gun manufacturers until they are held accountable. On June 25, 2022, Congress took a step in the right direction in passing the Safer Communities Act, the first federal gun-safety law in thirty years.[31] Attending the White House celebration of the still so inadequate legislation left me feeling ambivalent—of course, this was something beyond nothing; but it left so much work to be done toward protecting our children and loved ones.

The new federal legislation will not even require full background checks let alone commonsense gun regulations. And of course, it does not address assault weapons, a fact that did not go unmentioned by Dr. Ray Guerrero, Uvalde's sole pediatrician and the one responsible for treating eight children on the day of the shooting, some who he had known since they were infants and five of whom succumbed to their injuries. Some children, Dr. Guerrero told us on the White House lawn that day, could only be identified through their parents' DNA, after military-grade weapons ripped through their fourth-grade bodies. Hearing that from their doctor hit harder than all the statistics did. He opened the White House event by saying, "Let this only be the start to the banning of assault weapons. Start the change—where weapons of war are never allowed in our communities."[32]

Even conservative Supreme Court justice Antonin Scalia said in *District of Columbia v. Heller,* "The right secured by the Second Amendment is not unlimited. [It is] not a right to keep and carry any weapon whatsoever in any manner whatsoever and for whatever purpose."[33] This is not about responsible gun ownership and purchasing guns for hunting. It's about commonsense policies like universal background checks on all gun purchases, with required waiting periods and gun safety training as necessary; and extreme risk protection order laws to enable law enforcement, educators, and social and mental health workers to protect families, children, and communities. It's about banning assault weapons like the two AR-15s that the Uvalde gunman bought to celebrate his eighteenth birthday, a week before he entered Robb Elementary School and opened fire.[34] We cannot look the other way, knowing that six of the nine deadliest mass shootings in the United States since 2018 were by people under twenty-one whose brains and capacity for regulating emotions and impulses have not yet fully developed.[35]

In 2020, the most recent year for which the Pew Research Center offered complete data, there were 45,222 gun-related deaths, more than any other year in American history.[36] Guns are now the number-one killer of children and teenagers; and those gun deaths of our young people now outnumber the totals for both police and soldiers killed in the line of duty.[37]

This bears repeating: guns are now the leading cause of death for children and teenagers. Let's call it a moral fact and draw a moral conclusion: *we are not protecting our children.* If the cause of the number-one killer of our kids were food poisoning or inadequate seat belts, we all know that we would quickly deal with those dangers. After the mass shooting of children more than a decade ago at Sandy Hook, author Garry Wills wrote:

Few crimes are more harshly forbidden in the Old Testament than sacrifice to the god Moloch (for which see Leviticus 18:21, 20:1–5). The sacrifice referred to was of living children consumed in the fires of offering to Moloch. Ever since then, worship of Moloch has been the sign of a deeply degraded culture. Ancient Romans justified the destruction of Carthage by noting that children were sacrificed to Moloch there. Milton represented Moloch as the first pagan god who joined Satan's war on humankind:

First Moloch, horrid king, besmear'd with blood
Of human sacrifice, and parents' tears,

Though for the noise of Drums and Timbrels loud
Their children's cries unheard, that pass'd through fire
To his grim idol.

PARADISE LOST 1.392–96

Read again those lines, with recent images seared into our brains—
"besmear'd with blood" and "parents' tears." They give the real meaning of what happened at Sandy Hook Elementary School. That horror
cannot be blamed just on one unhinged person. It was the sacrifice
we as a culture made, and continually make, to our demonic god. We
guarantee that crazed man after crazed man will have a flood of killing power readily supplied to him. We have to make that offering, out
of devotion to our Moloch, our god. The gun is our Moloch. We sacrifice children to him daily.[38]

Until we make gun violence a matter of faith, a violation of everything
the Bible says about peace, the shootings will continue. This, indeed, is
most *deeply a spiritual issue* and not just a political one. It is outrageous
that the white Christian nationalists among us are some of the biggest
supporters of guns—more and more of them. In the face of America's
deadly epidemic of gun violence, what do Jesus' words "Blessed are the
peacemakers" mean to those who claim to be his followers?

Practice must follow church preaching. I suggest we instigate boy-
cotts of the National Rifle Association and any company involved in
gun manufacturing—in all our denominational and educational institutions. No investments in guns. What if we also helped to support legal efforts to sue gun manufacturers for the deaths they have caused?
And we need to create new networks of pastors and churches willing
to preach and teach about the morality of guns. Hopefully there are
new efforts underway, like the one in Pennsylvania, where up to 250
faith communities have become involved in memorializing the many
victims of gun violence and addressing the crises in their state.[39]

Both the pastoral comfort and the prophetic power of faith voices need to be heard alongside the parents who have lost their children.

We are required to make gun safety a single moral issue on which to vote and ensure that we impact the thing that politicians care most about—their reelection. Peacemaking requires that we look for new ideas and strategies. After mass shootings in the United Kingdom and Australia, even conservative governments passed strict gun safety laws—and the mass shootings stopped.

I spoke to the annual meeting of the Democratic Lieutenant Governors Association and suggested they could help move the gun debate and decision-making away from Washington, where it is stuck, to the states where a new national debate could be had. Popular legislative agendas and public referendums could mobilize public opinion, faith communities, and new constituencies like the MSU alumni and other groups of parents and citizens, state by state. We have seen local and legislative fights over guns go in different ways, but we have yet to see many congregations of faith enter into those political battles with a message of faith. That needs to change—now.

A WITNESS FOR PEACE

Starting in 1983, Sojourners was deeply involved in trying to stop the Contra War in Nicaragua. The Reagan administration formed and funded a mercenary army from the former dictator Anastasio Somoza's defeated military to fight the new Sandinista government. They mostly attacked civilians. But US religious volunteers in Nicaraguan villages found that their very presence stopped the violent attacks of the US-funded Contra War using the *Somocistas,* supporters of Somoza.

Therefore, with many other local and national groups in America, and even internationally, we launched Witness for Peace, ultimately sending nearly five thousand North American peacemaking, nonviolent army troops into the war zones of Nicaragua and successfully stopping some of the worst violence against civilians. I was chair of the WFP advisory group and convened the first official trip to a town called Jalapa, on the country's northern frontier. I vividly remember our first bus trip through the back roads with mortars exploding over our heads—a very dramatic and emotional journey. But once we arrived, the violence stopped as it did over and over again wherever Witness for Peace teams were sent—because the US-funded contras knew they would get into trouble if they hurt or killed faith-based Americans there to help the Nicaraguan people at the invitation of their local religious leaders.

During the 1980s, many faith organizations committed to peacemaking met annually at Kirkridge Retreat Center in the hills of Pennsylvania. At one of our Kirkridge peacemakers' retreats during the Nicaraguan conflict, I had a call from Dr. Gustavo Parajón, a deeply respected Nicaraguan physician and Baptist clergyman. His health and community care organization, CEPAD, was the primary partner with our Witness for Peace teams. I will never forget that call.

Gustavo said that religious leaders in Nicaragua had solid intelligence that the Reagan administration, worried that they might lose their White House–led Contra War, was considering an invasion of Nicaragua. And, as people of faith, they were very worried about the potential loss of lives. I was stunned, but even more stunned by what came next. I was ready to support our Nicaraguan friends in any way I could. But Rev. Dr. Parajón then informed me that the Nicaraguan faith leaders had all been praying, and God had told them—that we, as faith leaders in America, should stop the invasion! "How do we do that?" I asked incredulously.

"God didn't tell us that, but just to ask you to stop it," said my dear friend Gustavo.

I took that message back to our peacemakers' group in retreat, and they were as stunned as I was. We decided to pray. After much prayer and wrestling with a seemingly impossible task that we had now been called to, we decided to focus on what each of us would do if there was a US invasion. We each made a *pledge* to go to our local congressional office and refuse to leave until the Reagan administration either stopped the invasion or, at least, took it to Congress for a public debate. We understood that such an action would lead to arrest.

We left the Kirkridge retreat with that commitment, and an agreement to share our decision with everyone in our organizations and to ask others to join us if they also felt called to this; because, obviously, just a handful of religious leaders being arrested would make little difference.

Our Pledge of Resistance quickly ended up with 86,000 signers—people ready to do nonviolent civil disobedience in response to a US invasion of Nicaragua! In this time before the age of the internet, we created a phone tree to activate those who had pledged and a phone test showed that we could mobilize the nearly one hundred thousand people in about twenty-four hours. We were all overwhelmed by this massive response to peacemaking, but we learned that just a few people making a commitment could result in many more people also signing up.

At a subsequent meeting with the under secretary of state for Latin American affairs, I informed the US government of our Pledge of Resistance, our promise, and our capacity to put 86,000 American persons of faith in jail—which could become a serious "domestic cost" for a foreign invasion. When asked by a *TIME* reporter waiting outside the meeting what his response was, I quietly said, "He was sobered."

Fortunately, there never was a US invasion of Nicaragua, beyond the White House–armed intervention in the Contra War. Later, a person who was in the room for the internal administration discussions about an invasion informed us that our pledge with the commitment *and* capacity to mobilize tens of thousands of clergy was a big part of the conversations. Catholic sisters, clergy, and lay church leaders—all wearing their religious garb, collars, and crosses as they were led away to jail—proved to be "a serious deterrent" to the invasion. And when Reagan's funding for the Contra War was finally voted down in Congress, his state department blamed "the churches" the next day, and we were quite happy to share the blame for ending the brutal, and what I would call terrorist, violence of the Contra War. And our church friends in Nicaragua were eternally grateful for our fellowship in peacemaking.

THE CHILDREN OF GOD

Clearly, not all acts of peacemaking will result in a direct and quick change of US foreign policy. But most will help preserve or improve some human lives. Big changes or small ones, they all begin with a personal decision to act and bear the cost of acting. I have learned that the number of people who respond is not predictable; but our own choices open up possibilities for others' new choices. All those acts of peacemaking are "blessed" and will include us in the circle of the "children of God."

This is the time for the peacemakers to be who Jesus calls them to be. Activist and Black Lives Matter leader Brittany Packnett says, "My question is, are you willing to take a risk with me knowing that your risk might look different from my risk? Your risk might look like getting teargassed with me. It also might look like having a conversation with your white friends and family and knowing that they're not all going to like it."[40] In other words, we have to be willing to sacrifice on behalf of the collective shalom. Not just despite the decisive conflicts we now face—but because of them—we need those who are willing to take the risks of *waging peace.*

Peace is not a violent battle to be won, but a sacrificial work to be done. And the path and promise of a multiracial democracy will not take place without a committed band of peacemakers.

7

OUR COMMUNITY
IS NOT A TRIBE

*There is no longer Jew or Greek; there is no longer slave or free; there is
no longer male and female, for all of you are one in Christ Jesus.*
—GALATIANS 3:28

IN 1807, BRITISH MISSIONARIES FACED A DILEMMA. ON ONE HAND, THEY knew from the books of Matthew and Mark that they were to be "fishers of men," delivering the unsaved to salvation through Jesus Christ. On the other hand, the same gospels and epistles that proclaimed the good news also contained far too many passages that might inspire the enslaved to question their subservience. They feared that exposure to the Bible might incite an uprising among the enslaved whose labor was depended on to sustain British and American profits. So, what did they do? They edited, leaving only half the New Testament and just 10 percent of the Hebrew Bible Scriptures that they called the Old Testament.[1]

They retained verses like Paul's appeal to the enslaved to "obey your earthly masters with fear and trembling, in singleness of heart, as you obey Christ" (Ephesians 6:5). But they omitted statements Paul made elsewhere that were harder to reconcile with the institution of slavery. And very significantly, they discarded the entirety of Exodus—they didn't want to give the enslaved the hopes that God might deliver them from bondage as he had done for the enslaved Israelites who fled Egypt. And of course, Galatians 3:28 had to go. The text for this chapter is in *none* of the revised slaveholders' Bibles. "There is no longer slave or free," Paul said in a direct challenge to the social hierarchy, "for all of you are one in Christ Jesus." Ultimately, the missionaries wanted to satisfy their Christian duty to save the souls of the enslaved, but they wanted to do so on their own terms, not God's.

That is why this verse, which New Testament scholar Darius Jankiewicz refers to as "the Magna Carta of the abolitionist movement," was fundamental to the argument of Christians who advocated for the abolition of slavery. And it is why those who wanted to uphold slavery were so insistent on the removal of this Galatians text from the Bibles that slaves might read.[2] Both groups clearly recognized the implications of this verse—that subjugating another human being is irreconcilable with the idea that all peoples are equal in the eyes of God. The slaveholders wanted to keep the enslaved from believing that they were fully human, and therefore eligible for reconciliation in Christ.

And yet, pro-slavery advocates tried to rationalize their hypocrisy by adopting the view that Paul intended for the enslaved to take heart in their spiritual equality while accepting the social order of which slavery was a part. But "abolitionists viewed this passage not only as a proclamation of spiritual equality but also the seeds of social and racial equality," Jankiewicz writes. Galatians 3:28 calls Christians to seek unity and equity here and now.

Unsurprisingly, Black Christians agreed, and often heralded this Galatians text. "Racial segregation is a blatant denial of the unity which we have in Christ," said Martin Luther King, Jr., in 1957. "There is not a single passage in the Bible—properly interpreted—that can be used as an argument for segregation."[3] King understood that unequal treatment of Black people represented a direct affront to the equality Jesus came to bring. And sadly, you don't hear much about Galatians 3:28 from the white Christian nationalists.

ALL OF YOU ARE ONE

"When King was arguing for the things that he was arguing for, it wasn't reducible to Black people," said Eddie Glaude, James S. McDonnell Distinguished University Professor at Princeton University.[4] "It opened doors for poor people, women, LGBTQ—a range of folks." Indeed, the spirit of King's message and Paul's letter to the Galatians proclaim oneness that encompasses all human-made distinctions. He called for an end of division by race when he said, "There is no longer Jew or Greek." He disqualified the validity of class and race distinctions when he declared, "There is no longer slave or free." And he abolished inequality on the basis of gender by saying, "There is no longer male and female." Race, class, and gender shape oppression all over the world, and the apostle Paul upends and transforms them for the new social relationships and community that Christ came to bring.

On gender divisions, one such claim that is prominent in the church today is complementarianism, the idea that women ought to have roles that complement men rather than holding the positions of authority supposedly intended for men. Proponents of complementarianism believe that only men should be ordained in the Christian church. Such views are particularly common among those ascribing to the ideology of white Christian nationalism. Results of a 2023 recent poll administered by the Public Religion Research Institute (PRRI) indicated that seven of ten people drawn to white Christian nationalism also believe that wives should submit to the authority of their husbands.[5] Structures of patriarchy, both inside and outside the church, are central to the message of white Christian nationalism.

And yet, by declaring that "there is no longer male or female," the apostle Paul insists in no uncertain terms that men are not superior to women in the eyes of God. In doing so, he unseats the claim of men to hold sway over women in the church, in society, and in relationships—if male and female are of equal worth in the eyes of God, then so, too, should they be in the eyes of men and women.

Paul's words here in Galatians are therefore a challenge to the complementarianism that has created a void in Christian leadership and a hindrance to family life by preventing women from exercising their equal rights to authority and to using their fullest gifts. "This verse shows that the church has, in past generations, maintained unbiblical support of a paternalistic church and family order," writes Christian theologian Paul King Jewett. "This has kept Christian women from rising to their God-ordained place of equality of position and authority alongside men in the leadership of the church and in the family."[6] While some of Paul's writings in other epistles conform to particular situations and even controversies in those settings, the Galatians text is more *theological* than pastoral and clarifies the vision of transformation of gender relationships brought about in Christ. And, significantly, that was very evident in the ways Jesus himself treated and related to women, and even how the apostle Paul shared leadership in the earliest Christian communities with several women.

A CREED AND BAPTISMAL RITE

Most scholars believe that Galatians was one of Paul's earliest letters, written around 48 AD, and many think this passage came to serve as the *baptismal invocation* of the early churches.[7] Jesus' earliest and most immediate followers considered Galatians 3:28 a foundational text for the establishment of the church. Some ask whether this text refers only to relationships among Christians or whether it applies to relationships in general, in society. Biblical scholar Jakobus M. Vorster ascribes to the latter perspective, believing Galatians provides what he calls "a Christian foundation for the promotion of human rights and equality in contrast to patriarchy, racism, and exploitation caused by human sinfulness."[8] What is true for Christians, theologically, can be applied more broadly to social issues of human equality. And many Christian leaders agree with Rev. Dr. Martin Luther King, Jr., who believed the church should be a model for society.

The apostle Paul was declaring a new order of community and social relationships. In Christ, all these barriers—the most basic divisions that characterize all human societies—are overcome. At the same time, he was proclaiming a manifesto on the *vocation* of this new community and the very foundation of its common identity as those reconciled together in Christ. Such a community would not accept the old order marred by the divisions of race, class, and gender instituted by humans. Instead, they would proclaim and demonstrate the kingdom of God with unity that spans their diversity.

The significance of this text being chosen as the baptismal formula and a public proclamation of faith in the early church cannot be overstated. Some scholars even believe this text was *one of the first creeds* of the early church.[9] A creed is a foundational belief or doctrine of the church, so to see unity in Christ, over all our worldly divisions, as one of those earliest foundations is extraordinary. Imagine these early communities following an itinerant, brown-skinned Palestinian rabbi named Jesus and pledging publicly, at every baptism, to break down and overcome all the barriers that defined the social order.

Essentially, these earliest Christians were drawing a line in the sand and saying, "If you don't want to be a part of the kind of community that breaks down these divisions, we're not the right place for you." Essentially, the early church's central basis of exclusivity was its commitment to radical inclusivity. But is that how Christians are perceived by society as a whole today, especially in America? Do we say publicly, as the leaders of the early church did, that we are a community that breaks down and overcomes all society's divisions, and if you don't want to be part of that radical new unified community you should go somewhere else? Sadly, it would be stunning to hear that clear word of inclusivity from American churches today; but imagine how powerful and transformative it would be. It would completely change the perception of Christianity in America—a transformation that we urgently need.

Today, some of the most visible and loudest representatives of the church are the cruelest, those who espouse the views of white Christian nationalism, cherry-picking the so-called Christian ideals that maintain their power and threatening to defend those ideologies by violent means if necessary. In a clear alternative to the meaning of the Galatians passage, white Christian nationalism says, in effect, that their religious community and social order is intended only for us—white Christian Americans. Many in the wider society, especially a younger generation, are taking notice of where the churches are coming down on these critical choices of division or inclusion. My students are watching.

WHY PEOPLE ARE LEAVING THE CHURCH

A 2020 Gallup poll revealed that the number of Americans who were members of a house of worship dropped below 50 percent for the first time in eight decades.[10] David Campbell, professor and chair of the University of Notre Dame's political science department, calls this decline "an allergic reaction to the religious right."[11] Campbell's research suggests that many have turned away from religion—*because of* the right-wing political forces of white Christian nationalism, and have tragically equated white Christian nationalism with the whole of Christianity. It is a very sad day when some of the meanest and most hateful messages in our society are coming from people and groups who call themselves Christians. And therefore, it is vitally important to demonstrate that there is a true Christian faith in deep opposition to the partisan agendas of a false white, wealthy, prideful nationalism, and patriarchal religion. We must offer an inviting and hopeful alternative vision to that mean-spirited white Christian nationalism to restore the meaning of Galatians 3:28.

Young people, many of whom grew up in the church, especially re-sent imposing oppressive versions of religion on political issues like LGBTQ+ rights, women's rights, and forcing narrow ethnocentric faith into public classrooms. Ultimately and ironically, the growing public regard for inclusivity underlies the painful rejection of the church by many. The secular world is saying, "If you don't want to be the kind of community that breaks down these divisions, then you're not the right place for us."

But many young people are drawn to an alternative to bad religion. Many of my students check the "none of the above" box in religious affiliation questionnaires. But on the last day of class, they often share how they are more open and even drawn to faith than they were before. We have discussed the role of religion—both bad and good—in relation to our society and social movements in particular. We had not hesitated to be very critical about the negative consequences of religion in so many areas of people's personal lives and our public life. But we also discussed how bad religion is not true faith and that the latter can be reclaimed. And we had dug deep into the positive role of faith communities in the most important movements for social reform and change in American history in particular. I teach that the answer to bad religion is not no religion; but better religion. Some students say they are attracted to different and better religion, and that they had never heard about the Black church before, or about Catholic social teaching (even at a Jesuit university!); but really responded well to both. "I thought this is what Christianity was supposed to be," some say, echoing my earliest experiences with Black churches as a teenager.

Ruth Braunstein, a professor of sociology and director of the Meanings of Democracy Lab at the University of Connecticut, also believes that the mass exodus from the church also reflects a distaste for the blatant hypocrisy on display among the far religious right.[12] "Christian nationalism does appear to be pushing people out of religion," she says. "But at the same time, it's not just doing that. It also appears to be leading people down a variety of other paths that don't involve fully dissociating themselves from religion or religious belief and practice, but rather reworking those in ways that feel both politically and spiritually comfortable." So Braunstein sees a trend in which too many of those attending church practice a distorted version of the gospel, one intended to establish and protect their tribe and territory, and the general public has become further alienated as a result. "They've created a self-fulfilling prophecy where they say society is secularizing, but because of the extremely defensive posture they've taken, they've actually pushed people out of their own ranks and turned them into a nonreligious sort of people who they would now characterize as part of that secularizing society." What a dangerous irony.

By supplanting the gospel of unity with a false gospel of political power, white Christian nationalism has exacted a great cost to the reputation of the church. Its proponents judge political candidates not by their values and character, but by whether they will be powerbrokers for their ethnocentric self-interest and justifiers of their entitlement to governing the country they still believe to be promised as their own. Their brand of Christianity represents a blatant perversion of Paul's letter to the Galatians.

A DEFINING MISSION OF UNITY

The church was always meant to move beyond tribalism. The letter to the Galatians is a treatise on unity, establishing that this new community in Christ would not be just for the first Jews who decided to follow Christ; and that these new believers, these outsiders, would not be bound by Jewish law. In fact, this stood in direct opposition to the Judaizers, a group who wanted all the new believers to be subject to Jewish law as a condition of their unification and salvation. The Judaizers were saying, in effect, "Assimilate to our ways and accommodate our laws," to which Paul answered, "We Jews and Gentiles are now one, bound not by racial and ethnic ties, but by our oneness in Christ."

Perhaps an ancient form of Jewish nationalism echoes in our modern Christian nationalism today?

The society at the time of the Galatians letter was marked by rigid hierarchies and divides between the haves and the have-nots, and those who were free and those who were enslaved. And, at the same time, Jewish and ancient society generally was starkly patriarchal; by law, culture, and practice, inequality was assumed and women were subordinate to men. Yet not only were there women like Mary Magdalene, Joanna, and Susanna among Jesus' closest followers, and Paul ministered alongside a number of women in these early Christian communities. These women were exercising leadership in the new churches, acting in concert with men to preach the good news and to pull diverse communities together. At one point, Paul refers to Phoebe as *diakonos,* a Greek word that is grammatically masculine and one he uses to describe his own ministry. In this society where inequality among men and women was taken for granted, this was a new community indeed.

Paul's vision represented a radically countercultural movement, turning all of the accepted structures and practices of Jewish society upside down. And his conception of one unified body is not limited to the book of Galatians. In fact, scholar Bruce Hansen calls it "the most prominent refrain in the Pauline corpus."[13] It is also written in Colossians 3:11, "There is no longer Greek and Jew, circumcised and uncircumcised, barbarian, Scythian, enslaved and free, but Christ is all and in all!" It is proclaimed again in First Corinthians 12:13, "For in the one Spirit we were all baptized into one body—Jews or Greeks, slaves or free—and we were all made to drink of one Spirit." And its influence is also seen in Romans 3, Romans 10, First Corinthians 1 and 7, Ephesians 6 and 8—transforming personal and social relationships is a constant theme in the New Testament.

It also ties back to the Old Testament Hebrew Scriptures, beginning with Genesis 1:26, the passage we discussed in chapter 3 that says that all humankind was created in the image and likeness of God. Unity serves as the foundational principle of not just the origin story of the church, when the Spirit came down at Pentecost, resulting in diverse languages and infusing courage into the disciples of Jesus. This unity was the created purpose of humankind itself, from the very beginning. It underlies the story of the Good Samaritan, where the person who would have been viewed as a lower-class "other" saw an *other* in need and treated him with love and compassion—in the spirit of a common humanity. The reconciliation of all to equality and accord is the fulfillment of a promise that encompasses the entire arc of the Bible, from Genesis to Revelation where John the apostle envisions the end of time: "After this I looked, and there before me was a great multitude that no one could count, from every nation, tribe, people, and language, standing before the throne and before the Lamb . . . with palm branches in their hands" (Revelation 7:9). Here was all humanity, worshiping God together—but *in all their different languages and tribal diversities.*

Despite the revolutionary witness of Jesus' life and the many texts that echo the spirit of Paul's words in Galatians, most contemporary Christians don't know how central racial inclusion and integration were to the mission of the early church. The breaking down of cultural and racial barriers was not a casual suggestion but a *defining characteristic* of this new community and movement in following Jesus. Pulling humanity together, by reconciling them to God and to one another, was the purpose for which Jesus gave his life and the calling of all those who would follow in his footsteps.

Yet in America, the power of the few continue to be built upon the backs of the disempowered many, just as they were when Paul penned Galatians over two thousand years ago. And too often, our churches collude in exploiting the divides that serve their self-interests. Though the Bible has this unifying central theme, many Christians continue to ignore and disregard the parts that confront their hypocrisy and call into question their right to defend their place atop the social hierarchy. They function more like clubs, fraternities, or tribes than real communities and appear more interested in keeping people out than bringing them in. Christ came to dismantle those social hierarchies. And it could not be clearer or more compelling from the Galatians text and early church history that the community that God creates is not from one tribe—but from many tribes who have come together.

"MOM, THEY'RE GOING TO KILL YOU."

Jean Marvin's children had heard the threats from those seeking to force her resignation from the Rochester, Minnesota, school board, and they were afraid.[14] She, like many other local government officials, was now trying to reconcile her desire to serve her community with death threats and frightened children, exacerbating the normal challenges of long hours and late meetings at no pay. Her daughter told her, "They know where we live, Mom. They're going to kill you."

A recent national poll found that almost half of all local officials surveyed have experienced harassment and violent threats during their time in office.[15] As a result, many are choosing to leave their positions or refraining from running for public office or reelection. And because women and minorities are disproportionately targeted, that means the perpetrators are successfully disrupting the realization of a truly representative democracy.

In addition, threats of violence have also served as a deterrent to voters. Ahead of the 2022 midterm elections, two in five voters reported that they were worried about threats of violence or voter intimidation.[16] And though it's unclear how many of those voters stayed home, it's reasonable to assume that some were turned away by the sight of the armed militia who showed up at many polling places in defense of the Big Lie.[17]

Of course, none of this is an accident. In the 2022 midterm elections, voters in Republican strongholds elected many of the officials who pedaled the very lie that inspired the violent attempt to overturn the popular vote on January 6, 2021. Moreover, a leaked membership roster for the far-right antigovernment militia the Oath Keepers included forty-eight state and local officials, ten serving as state lawmakers.[18]

And, the same leaders who claimed the election was stolen continue to sell false narratives claiming their entire way of life is at risk. They allude to the great replacement theory, that their own white culture, prosperity, symbols, and lives are in great jeopardy. They call Democrats who support LGBTQ+ rights "groomers" and make outrageous and baseless claims about rampant pedophilia among the left. They frame books and classroom teachings about the history of race relations in America as a way to shame white people for their race.

At the same time, mainstream and social media promulgate the stories and analyses that get the most attention, which are often those that draw the most outrage. "Ideas that were once confined to marginal fringe groups now appear in mainstream media," says Rachel Kleinfeld, senior fellow in the Carnegie Endowment for International Peace's Democracy, Conflict, and Governance Program. "White-supremacist ideas, militia fashion, and conspiracy theories spread via gaming websites, YouTube channels, and blogs, while a slippery language of memes, slang, and jokes blurs the line between posturing and provoking violence, normalizing radical ideologies and activities."[19]

Extremist violence is going mainstream. Kleinfeld points out that since the 1960s, violent extremists—groups like the Weathermen of the 1970s, the United Freedom Front of the 1980s, and Army of God from the 1990s—tended to be made up of young, unmarried men with no children and no jobs. But now the pattern of violence is coming to resemble the 1920s, when political violence was normalized in many white, lower- to middle-class, often Christian families, contributing to the revival of the Ku Klux Klan.[20] "What we've seen more recently is a very different demographic, and it's older. It's people with kids who are married, who have jobs. And, alarmingly, some of the people who go to and belong to churches are actually more likely to believe in conspiracy theories like QAnon."

What is not new, though, are the factors underlying this resurgence of widespread extremism. Kleinfeld explained to me that two steps of propaganda historically underlie the incitement of political violence that extends beyond the fringes to the masses. The first is dehumanizing other people—calling immigrants "criminals" and "rapists," referring to Democrats as "libtards" and "snowflakes," demeaning Black people by referring to their African countries of origin as "shitholes." The second step is to paint these others—"the vermin," "groomers," "pedophiles," and the like—as threats to our society and way of life.

"Then you claim that you're defending your own community against that threat," said Kleinfeld, "because people are much more willing to commit violence to defend, to keep their women and children safe, to keep their community or their values safe." Claiming self-defense reframes the violence of resistance as a heroic act. Under these circumstances, otherwise moderate individuals come to consider violence as *necessary*. Indeed, there are many today who feel threatened, afraid, and ready to defend what they believe is at stake. A 2021 poll of 1,700 registered voters revealed that 47 percent of Republican respondents agreed with the statement, "A time will come when patriotic Americans have to take the law into their own hands."[21] Many of these individuals view political violence as an act of civic duty. "In America, we have a long culture going back to the revolution in which it's been heroic for white men, in particular, to wield arms to protect their communities," said Kleinfeld. "And so picking up on the language of '1776' and those kinds of rallying cries makes people feel that they're doing something important, like they're doing something for their country and their community that's patriotic."

VIOLENCE OR BELONGING

Americans have historically had multiple group identities, which sometimes helped balance one another. They could be church members, union members, members of hobby clubs, sports league parents, PTA

194 THE FALSE WHITE GOSPEL

meeting participants across racial or political lines, or community organization members just trying to make life better. But now politics is
coming down to a single white national identity for many who feel increasingly threatened by people of other identities. In her incisive and
very alarming column in *The Hill,* "American Democracy Is Dodging
Bullets," Kleinfeld describes how those "bullets" are no longer just met-
aphorical, but include a New Mexico Republican candidate for the state
legislature, allegedly spearheading the shootings of opposing lawmakers' houses, including the piercing of a ten-year-old girl's bedroom.[22]
These threats have risen tenfold in the last few years against members
of Congress, and have also dramatically escalated against mayors and
local office holders, now including election staff workers and voting
poll volunteers.

Such violence increases in elections that are perceived as having high
stakes, where identity issues are central, and where weak electoral safe-
guards make perpetrators believe they can get away with things. Kleinfeld proposes key ideas to help defuse political violence in the United
States: election credibility, electoral rules, prevention and redirection
of anger, and political speech. Leadership is absolutely key here. The
way political leaders talk is central to the accelerating or decelerating
of political violence. Trump's infusing the language of threats and violence into politics, from his campaign through his presidency, and
ultimately to January 6, has caused political violence to skyrocket in
America. But when leaders of both parties are willing to diffuse violent
rhetoric, political violence will go down.

In a conversation we convened with faith leaders, Kleinfeld told us
that there is also a spiritual core to these dangerous problems and the
faith community has an absolutely crucial role to play. Her research
shows that a foundational issue beneath the violence is the *sense of belonging* that many people don't feel anymore—belonging somewhere,
and to other people. Many people have lost both their sense of meaning *and* belonging, and are therefore very vulnerable to the political
tactics of using fear in order to bring people together. I spoke with a

former militiaman at the White House Summit on Hate in the fall of 2022. He said he was never motivated by political ideology. "I was just a kid smoking weed in an alley, all by myself. My parents each worked long hours and were never home. So, when this guy walked up to me one day, he didn't start with ideology, but with offering me a group and a cause and purpose to belong to." Hate groups offer often isolated people a new "community" or tribe to join. If life feels meaningless, you can be drawn to a group that offers you both a purpose and a community, a group to be part of.

And that is exactly what faith groups have to offer as well—meaning, purpose, and community. But in our church worlds today, even that Christian identity is weak. Kleinfeld also points out how both the right and the left each have their own "condemnatory cancel cultures"— where people are defined out rather than brought in. Who is to blame, who is most at fault, and where do we point our fingers becomes more important than a positive and inviting view of inclusion and change. And we now see that cancel culture even in some of our churches. Condemning has replaced inviting, sometimes on both sides of the political aisle, and it is time to turn that around—and the churches would be a great place to start.

Imagine if faith communities were offering that sense of a community that seeks to heal our fears, overcome our divisions, give us something to live for and not just against—and other people to live that vision with. Diversity is something we can come to know if we haven't before, and learning about other people can be a benefit, even a gift. I've had other former hate-group members tell me what finally changed them was when people from the very groups that they were taught to hate reached out personally to them to offer love in tough situations. The old phase "love wins" is actually true in most people's experience. The kid smoking weed alone in the ally can be brought into something hateful or something loving; and that's where faith communities have so much to offer. Pastors, take this to heart when people despair of all our polarized divisions: what your faith community has to offer may be just what is needed—helping to put diverse people in relationship to one another.

Faith in God, and mutual relationship between those who have been reconciled together, may be one of the few things strong enough now to counter and overcome our dangerous and increasingly violent divisions. Second Corinthians 5:20–21 is a text for divided societies: "So we are ambassadors for Christ, since God is making his appeal through us, we entreat you on behalf of Christ, be reconciled to God."

Will Campbell, a Baptist minister and preacher, born in Mississippi, where he ministered (among other places in the South), was one of the first white southern clergy to strongly come out in support of racial justice and integration. He joined the Civil Rights Movement in the 1960s, but also continued to pastor and care for the families of his bigoted white southern neighbors—even some members of the Ku Klux Klan. Campbell became the director of the Committee of Southern Churchmen and, with a few others, published a journal called *Katallagete*, derived from the New Testament Greek for the Pauline phrase in second Corinthians 5:20, which they put in capital letters: "BE RECONCILED!"

THE COST OF DRAINING THE POOL

In 1933, President Franklin D. Roosevelt's New Deal included an extraordinary rollout of economic reforms intended to revitalize the economy in response to the Great Depression. The New Deal initiated an unprecedented proliferation of federally sponsored public works and jobs, including major investments in public spaces, parks, and recreation areas. One result of this government spending was the construction of nearly two thousand public swimming pools.

On very hot days, especially in the South, communities often gathered at these massive pools, which were often attached to ornate, architecturally impressive, mansion-like buildings. But it wasn't until the 1950s and 1960s that Black communities began to find success in arguing that they too should be allowed to swim in pools paid for with their tax dollars. After the Civil Rights Law of 1964, it became illegal to deny Black people entry to public pools. Suddenly, Black and white children had proximity to one another in a safe and equitable space.

Predictably, there was swift backlash from white parents who believed that Blacks and whites swimming together in various levels of undress was an abomination. In some cities, public officials prohibited use despite the law. In 1960, Charlotte, North Carolina's chairman of the Parks and Recreation Commission, for example, admitted that "all people have a right under law to use all public facilities including swimming pools." But he said, "Of all public facilities, swimming pools put the tolerance of the white people to the test."[23] Accordingly, he declared that no Blacks would be allowed if managers feared that disorder could ensue. "Public order is more important than the rights of Negroes to use public facilities," the commission chairman concluded.

But with the passage of civil rights legislation, most public pools were simply shut down, and many were drained and even cemented over. The result, of course, was that now *no one* could enjoy a refreshing dip aside from wealthy white families who built pools in their own backyards and/or gained entrance to country clubs and other private, whites-only facilities. The drained pools became a symbol of our deep divisions.

That revealing example comes from Heather McGhee's powerful book *The Sum of Us*. McGhee sat down with me to discuss the symbolism of this series of events as it relates to the systemic and covert racism that exists today.[24] For one, the unraveling of legal desegregation reflected the fact that the change in policy outpaced the change in public narrative. "There was a massive shift in white support for the idea that the public has a role in investing in the public good, and in guaranteeing a high quality of life," said McGhee. "White supporters of the New Deal didn't bargain for the way these investments would collide with their racial prejudices and benefit black Americans. Basically, put briefly, the white opinion was, 'Public goods are good, but only for the public that we perceive to be good.'"

In other words, when public policy evolves without a reckoning in the narratives of white people about racial equity, then political backlash will undermine the good intentions of that policy—even when it works in the best interest of all parties.

This is what McGhee refers to as "the zero-sum world view at the heart of racism, the idea that something good for my ingroup must not benefit the outgroup. That is, efforts made to advance the social standing of Black people must not happen at white people's expense, a perspective perfectly illustrated by the knee-jerk, infantile reaction of those who respond to the assertion of 'Black lives matter' with 'What about *white* lives?'"

Those who hold this world view "end up cheering the destruction of benefits and goods and investments and policies that would potentially help them and their own community simply because it might also help the people that they've seen as being on the other side," says McGhee. "And that vulnerability has been absolutely exploited by the ruling elite to convince white voters to choose the politics of their perceived racial interest over their class interest."

Despite the flourishing middle class that resulted from social reform and shared prosperity from the New Deal era, white voters ultimately rejected such benefits because of racism. After signing the Civil Rights Law and Voting Rights Act, Lyndon Johnson became the last Democrat to win the majority of the white vote, ushering in an economic era of inequality and a shrinking middle class.

"Most white parents don't think, I'd rather go into debt and have my kid go into debt to go to college," said McGhee. "But they also don't make the connection between saying they're socially liberal but fiscally conservative, or make the connection between voting for Republicans who continue to pay more to incarcerate than to educate or give tax handouts to the wealthy and corporations rather than fund basic education and public college."

"Draining the pool" is a powerful metaphor for explaining the tragic consequences of much of our social divisions and public policies today. As McGhee graphically points out, racism costs everyone. Pastors should preach that.

"When we think about the cost of racism to our economic lives, we really do have to recognize that the fundamental belief in a hierarchy of human value is the rule for our economy," said McGhee. "We conduct our economy as if it's great for wealthy people to have more money in terms of tax cuts, but it's bad for poor people to have more money in terms of government assistance." This is the hidden arm of racism that is strengthened by a zero-sum world view that, in fact, makes fools of us all, save those in the extreme upper class.

All this, of course, stands in direct moral and spiritual opposition of Galatians 3:28. McGhee suggests we consider whether we truly are practicing what we preach when it comes to the fiscal policies we choose to support. "What if we ask, 'Does this policy that keeps white school districts funded at $23 billion more a year than the majority of color school districts truly see the image of God in children of color?' Or does it really express a belief in white superiority?"

Galatians 3:28 confronts our sinful tendencies to dominate on the basis of class, sex, and race. No matter the issue at hand—education, housing, jobs, unions—our policy positions reflect either that we believe in our unity in Christ and creation in the image of God—or we don't. And if we claim the former, then there is no other compatible option than to vote in ways that benefit the whole over the few.

Preach.

McGhee hopes that we are approaching the point at which our collective conscience unites to form a flourishing multicultural democracy. After the killing of George Floyd, "We are at a tipping point of mass mobilization among and of white people for the first time—and this was not the case of the Civil Rights Movements," she said hopefully. "And the majority of white people are saying, 'Alright, let's do this.'" More times than before, public polls and the conversations that are happening in schools, churches, the media, and corporate culture suggest a more widespread recognition of the extent of racism as part of the DNA among white Americans—especially by a new generation. And these changes are exactly what white Christian nationalism wants to push back on.

What does this all mean, systemically?

"Before we can bring the nation together, we need to come together as communities, get on the same page around the truth of how race has so shaped and racism has held the pen as we've written our laws and policies in our society," McGhee told me. "And then envision a world where we jettison this belief in a hierarchy of human value and [establish] a new moral infrastructure with policies that flow from that. But I think we have to do both in tandem."

That is really a restoration of Galatians 3:28, which is a pastoral and preaching task for pastors and other leaders. That's also where the hope and joy of freedom emerges, when it's not a zero-sum game of win-lose. When we face racism as the root issue of so many of our other problems—it is then that we can, in fact, repair this from the bottom up. That's what it means to be gospel radical, to create a new way forward, where a new generation can meet one another in the pool and build lifelong relationships that will drain these illusory lines of difference and renew this country in a spirit of solidarity.

A WAY FORWARD

Between the global pandemic that killed more than a million Americans and locked down communities for months on end to unprecedented political divisiveness and vitriol, we live in a time where many are afraid. In such a state of upheaval, it is only natural that we seek comfort in the familiar. This is very human. But when that natural fear turns to condemnation and even aggression, our lives and spirits begin to diverge from the vision that Paul proclaimed in Galatians 3:28.

Certainly, there are some who can be reached and invited to something different, and some who must be politically defeated—or sometimes, just ignored. These are those with the most extreme and explicitly bigoted views. They are the ones Ruth Braunstein described as living in a "far right fantasy" that continues to view this country as the rightful and sole domain of the white European American.[25] "We have a finite amount of civic energy," Eddie Glaude told me. "I don't want to spend my energy trying to convince those who hold noxious views that they ought not to have them."[26]

But for many who sympathize with Christian nationalism viewpoints yet stop short of fully avowing them, there may be a chance to change some hearts and minds. Certainly, many of their preexisting beliefs are shortsighted—belief in the power only of individual effort and in the illusion of a fair and colorblind system—but that is primarily because they were taught the rules of a game that was rigged in their favor. And who wants to think they did not succeed entirely fairly? But your own merits will help you succeed even in a system that is not fully meritorious. And to succeed, you don't have to ignore or undermine the experience of people not like you.

Where we go wrong with this group is when we just deprecate them for their ignorance of the problems of groups outside their gender, race, or class. "If you immediately label them an extremist who is promoting theocracy, they will tend to double down and actually move farther to the right in their ideas because the people that aren't yelling at them, who are welcoming them into their fold are going to be on the far right," said Braunstein.

Eddie Glaude suggests that conversations and education might be most successful among *those people who happen to be white* compared to those he calls *white people*. "Those people who happen to be white are engaged in the ongoing interrogation of how whiteness has distorted their characters and how it now forms the way in which we live our lives," he said. "And white people are the folk who are invested in the structures as they are—they find it the natural order of things that advantages and disadvantages are distributed in the way that they are along the lines of who's valued and who's not valued." In other words, some of those belonging to the former group could remain open enough to consider the possibility that there may be something to learn in terms of implicit and systemic racism, and those in the latter see no reason for critique so long as the system continues to serve their interests.

As Heather McGhee observed, some white Americans seem to have reached a tipping point where the covert and systemic racism that has been hidden in the corners of our consciences and society are coming to light. She believes this represents a real opportunity for change. Eddie Glaude agrees: "We have a chance to radically change how this country understands itself, how we live our lives together. . . . We cannot turn our backs on this moment and tinker around the edges. If we do, I am convinced that we will seal our fate." Professor Glaude calls for the *re-founding* of America—deeper than mere slow, incremental reform but without the unpredictable and costly violence of *revolution*. That's exactly what my students and many in their generation want to do.

Eddie Glaude believes we need to "Begin Again," the title of his 2020 book.[27] An excerpt in the *Atlantic* on July 18, 2020, was titled, "In the midst of a moral reckoning, America needs a third founding." The subtitle of this book suggests "Re-founding Democracy." Here is what Eddie Glaude says about what that re-founding must mean:

> The United States has confronted two crucial moments of moral reckoning where we faced the daunting challenge of beginning again; both times we failed. The first was during the Civil War and Reconstruction, which constituted a second founding for the country. The second was the Black-freedom struggle of the mid-twentieth century. What we need now is a third American founding. We need an America where "becoming white" is no longer the price of the ticket. Instead, we should set out to imagine the country in the full light of its diversity and with an honest recognition of our sins. . . .
>
> Now we find ourselves facing a moral reckoning of the same magni-

tude. By now, we should have learned the lesson that changing laws or putting our faith in politicians to do the right thing is not enough. We have to rid ourselves, once and for all, of this belief that white people matter more than others, or we're doomed to repeat the cycles of our ugly history over and over again. . . .

This will demand of us a new American story, different symbols, and robust policies to repair what we have done. I don't yet know what this will look like in its details—and my understanding of our history suggests that we will probably fail trying—but I do know that each element is important to any effort toward beginning again. As Samuel Beckett wrote in his 1983 novella, "Worstward Ho," "Try again. Fail again. Fail better."

A new story doesn't mean that we discard all the elements of the old story, nor does it mean that we dwell only on our sins. Instead, we narrate our national beginnings in light of our contradictions and our aspirations. Innocence is left aside. Who we aspire to be, without the safety of the lie, should always organize the stories we tell ourselves about who we are. I say this because our stories carry moral weight. Who and what we choose to exclude exposes the limits of our ideas of justice. Our stories can make some people the center of the plot and make others latecomers and objects of charity and goodwill or of scorn and derision. America's should be a story that begins with those who sought to make real the promise of this democracy. Put aside the fairy tale of America as "the shining city on the hill" or "the redeemer nation," and cast the idea of perfecting the union not as a guarantee of our goodness, but as a declaration of the ongoing work to address injustice in our midst. . . .

This story requires a different symbolic landscape. In moments of profound national transition, the symbols of the old order have to be removed. In our case, the statues of the Confederacy have to be torn down and some placed in museums. They do not represent who we are and who we aspire to be. Our built environment should reflect the brilliant diversity of the people who make up this country. But the shift in our symbolic landscape must go beyond statues. The value gap is experienced and lived as we move about in this country. It is evident in the spatial organization of towns, villages, and cities. The monuments of ghettos, housing projects, and highways that cut off and isolate communities all reflect an age shaped by the lie. We have to build a different America.[28]

According to Glaude, joining protests is not enough. He told me that painting "Black Lives Matter" on Fifth Avenue and tearing down Confederate monuments are not enough. "We have a penchant in this country to rush to self-congratulate," he says. "In fact, we know that there are structural realities that we have to address."

McGhee agrees. "In conversations with white people about Jim Crow and about slavery, they act as if, 'Of course I would have been one of the good guys back then,'" she said. "What we forget when we embrace that logic is how much the justifications of white supremacy morph and change, and how they were always the justifications for the status quo."

So instead, we must deeply educate ourselves and finally reckon with our history; and talk frankly with our white children.

We must finally replace idealistic, whitewashed notions of our American exceptionalism and our country as the city on the hill; with determination to do something *truly exceptional in becoming the first real, multiracial democracy in the world.* We need to be in conversations that cross the barriers of gender, class, and race, open now to the reality that the system designed for the shrinking majority is not equipped to work for the new demographic of minority majorities.

"We needed to knit together a sense of common purpose and common culture," McGhee told me. "And the question is, can we do that, again, in the modern era . . . but can we do it in a way that is not an assimilationist project into whiteness?"

When we cross these lines, we don't just give lip service to our shared humanity, we experience it. And when we do, says McGhee, "We discover the peace that transcends the lies, that transcends the fear, and we find a conviction and a fire for creating a better world."

THE RECKONING

In January 1838, a twenty-eight-year-old Abraham Lincoln saw the warning signs of a nation coming apart at the seams. "At what point then is the approach of danger to be expected?" Lincoln asked a group gathered in Springfield, Illinois. "I answer, if it ever reaches us, it must spring up amongst us. It cannot come from abroad. As a nation of freemen, we must live through all time, or die by suicide."[29]

Lincoln's words followed two murders at the hands of proslavery mobs—the burning of Black freedman Francis McIntosh and the shooting of Elijah Parish Lovejoy, a newspaper editor, Presbyterian minister, and abolitionist.[30] Lincoln recognized the depravity of these acts and understood that they represented a dire threat to the soul of the nation. Twenty-three years later, just over a month after he was sworn in as president, war was declared between the North and the South. Four years later, the war was over and 620,000 Americans were dead, and four days after that, Lincoln was murdered by a Confederate sympathizer, in large part because Lincoln now believed in the importance of giving the formerly enslaved the right to vote. After Emancipation, the period of Reconstruction was our first re-founding in America; the Civil Rights Movement in the mid-twentieth century was our second; and the time has come for a third re-founding, according to Eddie Glaude.

"We're at that moment where everything is about to collapse and everything is possible, all at once," Glaude says. "All of the contradictions are in view—a global power endemic, racial unrest, economic devastation—everything about the last forty years, all the problems that we've experienced over the last few generations in this country are all in view. We know that this place is broken, and there's a desire for something different."

Heather McGhee senses it too: "I am feeling like we have the wind at our backs," she said to me. "There is obviously a fire ahead. There's a burning white-supremacist, conspiracy-theorist, anti-democratic fascist movement. . . . But they are the reaction to and the *dying gasps* [emphasis added] of a force in politics that's always been there since the founding of our country."

In other words, we now see our sins. And "sin" is the right word to use for racism and sexism and classism in all their forms, because they undermine the very image of God. There is no Jew or Greek, slave or free, male or female because all are the children of God.

Galatians 3:28 essentially asks: Will we seek the unity and diversity of the kingdom of God? Or will we reinforce social barriers of race, religion, gender, and tribalism? This appeal to oneness remains a creed to those who claim the name of Jesus and an invitation to *all* those desiring to mend the toxic divides of the country. It also remains a source of encouragement to build new relationships, and to forge new understanding that crosses boundaries, and creates the foundation and fabric of the common good.

We have an opportunity to fulfill the vision shared by the fathers and mothers of our churches and our nation, to build a society where *all* are, indeed, treated in accordance with the self-evident truth of their equality. The white Christian nationalists must not be allowed to take the unity Christ extends and cut it out of the Bible. We are doing nothing less than restoring the Word of God. I believe that Eddie Glaude's words capture the signs of the times for right now: "We're at that moment where everything is about to collapse and everything is possible, all at once."

8

A REMNANT CHURCH

I LOVE THE STORIES OF CHARLES FINNEY, THE PREMIER AMERICAN REVIVAL preacher of the 1830s—the Billy Graham of his day. Finney was a different kind of evangelical than those who have submitted to the idolatry of white Christian nationalism. A committed abolitionist, Finney preached an antislavery message that came directly from his Christian faith. He trained runaway enslaved people and women to become ministers in his Oberlin College seminary, was active in the Underground Railroad, and questioned whether slave owners should be allowed to receive communion.

"Neither slave nor free" was core to the gospel he preached, in ways that drew hundreds of thousands to Christ in his huge public meetings—and changed the narrative of faith and justice in America. People responded to his altar calls by coming to Christ and committing to abolishing slavery on the same night! The two were vitally connected for Finney's evangelicalism. Why aren't evangelicals like they used to be?

Today, we are in a unique historical moment, one that will determine the future of both faith and democracy in America. We are past the scenario of mere incremental progress where we take two steps forward and one step back. We face moments and milestones in the days ahead that will determine our future. Critical choices are upon us at every level—from national politics to our local communities.

We are becoming a different demographic country—that much is apparent. And what remains to be seen is whether we will choose to ascend to a greater unity than we have ever known before or descend into a divisive battle characterized by political violence not seen since our last Civil War.

It is time for the renewal of an old practice in the Christian tradition: the altar call. The altar call, historically speaking, was a summons for people to rise from the comfort of their seats in a religious or revival service and make their way down the aisle to commit their lives to Jesus in view of all those gathered. It was public, and it signaled a change in the direction of one's life.

This moment in our country requires us all to make a fresh public commitment with diverse people coming together to help save the soul of our nation. At its core, it will still call many people to the way of Jesus and, indeed, call many Christians to *come back to Jesus.* "The Way" was actually the term the earliest disciples of Jesus used for what they were called to follow, even before the word "church" came to be used. Jesus offered a new way, which was the path they had chosen to take after their encounter with him. Even today, I am often struck by the growing number of people who certainly don't want to be called "evangelicals," or even "Christians," for that matter; but rather be known as "followers of Jesus." And that is most true of younger people. That term, *the way,* points to the One you follow, but not to all the things people have done to distort and abuse religious language; most especially now in white Christian nationalism. And a new altar call could also create a fresh meaning in the traditional ritual for people of different faiths or even no faith at all. A new altar call could also mean "civic discipleship." We now face a false civic religion grounded in fear and racial grievance, promoting a hate that leads to violence; and we all must respond— calling people to a true civic faith that invokes our nation's better angels against our worst demons. And, as we have seen in these book chapters, the true spirit of Jesus and other key biblical teachings can be directly applied to the crisis of democracy that we now face today.

A new civic discipleship will express itself in loving our neighbors, finding the truth that can set us free, acknowledging the image of God in every member of humanity, accepting practices of conflict resolution, reversing the structures of our dramatic inequities, and including all of our tribes in a genuine multiracial democracy.

Democracy is in peril all over the planet, including the United States, which fashions itself as a democratic model for the world. Many of my international students at Georgetown, who believed in that model before they arrived, are quite surprised to see a revival of nationalistic fervor rising up in America, zealously appealing to race, religion, and tribal identity. And that, as many friends around the world tell me, has very dangerous implications for the battles for democracy in their own countries. A growing minority of Americans are willing to accept the violent attacking of the government in order to seize political power without the legitimacy of elections. There is a name for that and it is fascism—racialized authoritarianism—which is now growing again in America. And the false white gospel of Christian nationalism is at the heart of it.

The only adequate response is to move from bad religion to true faith, to restore the authentic meaning of our best faith traditions and a call for a civic faith in democracy that could bring many of us together. A new "altar call."

We are all watching a national town meeting playing out in media, politics, and even churches that religiously mimics the rise of autocracy. But we are also hearing more and more sermons calling for the "beloved community" based on the recovery of true faith in our many religious traditions. That *beloved community* vision can provide the spiritual undergirding for multiracial democracy.

The question before all of us is, "What will I do? What will we do?" Having read this book and reexamined these core Scriptures, are you ready to walk down the aisle for true faith and genuine democracy? America is in critical need of a new public mindfulness, one that leads to direct action. We all can do that, no matter who we are, where we

live, what faith we have or don't have, or what positions we have in society. It is really up to all of us right now—up to you.

"WHY DO YOU CALL ME 'LORD, LORD,' AND DO NOT DO WHAT I TELL YOU?"

Much of the American church is infected with the disease and heresy of
white supremacy. Whiteness itself, making one skin color normative,
definitional, and controlling is a *sin*. There is no "white" Christianity;
there is only Christian faith for all and every race. *White Christianity
is nothing less than an idolatry, the worship of a false God.* Whiteness,
deliberately or unconsciously, becomes the real god to whom we offer
allegiance. And we have seen in this book how that false white gospel
is such a great threat to democracy today.

Depending on which side churches and congregations land, this crisis will also determine whether a new generation will ever set foot in
our faith communities again. Therefore, the call to *discipleship out of
whiteness* is necessary for the salvation of the church in our time, *and*
essential for the survival of democracy.

Many won't be familiar with the label "white Christian nationalist"
or recognize themselves as part of the problem. Leaders of this dangerous movement must be revealed and defeated, albeit with dignity,
humanity, and humility. And for those who are open to considering
how they have unwittingly accepted the false white gospel, we have
an opportunity to help people find a new and better sense of identity
and *belonging*.

Revealing that one need not be an ardent supporter of white Christian
nationalism to be influenced by it—and therefore tacitly letting both
faith and democracy atrophy—is still a significant step in saving both.

Will most white Christians come back to Jesus from their enmeshment with white idolatrous politics? Perhaps not; because too many
white Christians have never been close to the teachings of Jesus. But

my hope is that there will be a *remnant* of faithful white Christians who are persuadable, particularly a new generation decisively breaking away from white Christianity and coming alongside the leadership of Black and brown Christians. This could be the beginning of a *remnant church.*

Jesus says, "Why do you call me 'Lord, Lord,' and do not do what I tell you?" (Luke 6:46). This could be a founding text for a new church comprised as a remnant of people of faith. The Lukan text goes on to compare a man who builds his house on a rock to one who builds his house on the sand, a very familiar story for me from my childhood. Says Jesus, "I will show you what someone is like who comes to me, hears my words, and acts upon them. That one is like a man building a house, who dug deeply and laid the foundation on rock; when a flood arose, the river burst against that house, but could not shake it, because it had been well built. But the one who hears and does not act is like a man who built a house on the ground without a foundation. When the river burst against it, immediately it fell, and great was the ruin of that house" (Luke 6:47–49).

That is precisely our situation today. White Christian nationalism is clearly a house built on sand. But those who listen to the words of Jesus, and hear him, are building a house with solid foundations that will survive the floods of hate, fear, and violence; and may help democracy survive in the process.

The American churches, of course, were divided over slavery and the Civil War, and white Southern churches tried to use the Bible to justify slavery; but the vanguard of the abolitionist movement *was Christian,* led by the likes of Frederick Douglass, William Lloyd Garrison, Harriet Tubman, Lydia Maria Child, Thaddeus Stevens, Sojourner Truth, and evangelical revivalists like Charles Finney and the Grimké sisters. Those separations remain today in white and Black churches in the same southern and northern cities—but some of us are now coming together again.

If only slow incremental change will not be enough, then nothing but repentance, in the biblical meaning of the word—of turning around and going in a different direction—will suffice now and for the future of the church and the nation. Always today—and every day forward, we seek to understand the signs of the times, and discern how to be agents of the kingdom of God for believers, and for the surviving and fulfilling of democracy for all of us—and not to be *complicit participants* in the hateful violence and injustice of the kingdoms of this world. Those battles will continue to be with us, and will resurface in unexpected ways, for many years to come.

Another New Testament text that could be very helpful at this historical moment is one that forged our emerging new Christian faith when a number of us were seminarians. It is Romans 12:1–2: "I appeal to you therefore, brothers and sisters, by the mercies of God, to present your bodies as a living sacrifice, holy and acceptable to God, which is your spiritual worship. Do not be conformed to this world, but be transformed by the renewal of your minds, so that you may discern what is the will of God—what is good and acceptable and perfect."

The issue here is *conformity to the world*, and all its social, cultural, and spiritual values—or lack therof—and instead be *transformed by the renewal of your minds*. The call in the passage to resist cultural conformity is, in the text and context, literally part of our *spiritual worship* to God. We seminarians discovered this to be an extraordinary text— telling followers of Jesus how to live and not live. Don't just *conform* to everything around you with its materialistic, militaristic, individualistic, ideological, racial, ethnic, or tribal values, but rather be *renewed* in ways that you become *transformed*. If there was ever a text that is a clear call not to conform to the false messages of something like white Christian nationalism—this is it. The biblical interpreter, J. B. Phillips, paraphrases this text to say, "Don't let the world around you squeeze you into its mold, but let God re-mold your minds from within, so that you may prove in practice that the plan of God for you is good, meets all his demands and moves toward the goal of true maturity." This Romans text is a deep call and challenge, to not be socially conformed but spiritually transformed—which is literally an ongoing process of faith and discipleship. It is the substance of continual reflection and meditation. But while white Christian nationalism is a message of the moment, with a long history dating back to our nation's founding, *I believe that a new American church could be a divinely inspired result.* And that new American church could help point the way to democracy, with a faith community that looks like the global body of Christ—the most diverse human community on the planet.

Where do we turn for help?

FAITH AND JUSTICE ARE INSEPARABLE

In a new remnant church, faith and justice will be inseparable. I have spent my whole life relating to both church and state, seeking how one can and should impact the other. How do we shape the formation of a "faith that does justice" in the Jesuit tradition of Catholic social teaching? How do we create the kind of personal and public conversion that comes from the best of the evangelical revivalist abolishionist tradition? How do we cultivate a love of neighbor that is called for by the best of the mainline Protestant tradition? How can we adopt the peacemaking power of the Anabaptist, Mennonite, and Quaker heritages? How do we reflect upon the powerful creation modes of Celtic Christianity now being renewed, and perhaps linked to the environmental spirituality of indigenous peoples? How do we incorporate the faith of the Hebrew prophets that made righteousness and justice into the same word, and delivered God's truth to those in power, as the next generation rabbinical movement wants to do? How can the renewal forces of Islam help bring us back to a religion of peace as many younger imams now are committed to do?

Perhaps, most important to me, how can we engage the transformational vision of the Black church in America (which took me in when I was kicked out of my home white evangelical church as a teenager, and still today is my spiritual home)? In 1960s America,

214 THE FALSE WHITE GOSPEL

we saw a second Reconstruction with the Civil Rights Movement, led by the Black church, almost a century after the first attempt at Reconstruction after slavery was blocked after the death of Lincoln, and Black votes and hopes were ended with Jim Crow and the violence of lynchings. But from slavery through the Civil Rights Movement, and ever since, there has always been a spiritual battle underneath the political one. And, the American church that has most impacted the world today is clearly the American Black church—the church that emerged from the marginalized enslaved and the Black "spirituals" that spoke of both the here and the hereafter, often in a musical code language that only Black believers understood.

The Black churches have their origins in the "hush harbors," where enslaved people went to secretly worship away from white people. Here they learned to read, and read the Bible in which they found a source for their liberation. Here they developed leaders and a community who cared for itself. Here they built the networks and underground railroads to carry them to freedom. Here they created the visions, music, and preaching that would change their lives and, eventually, their new country. Often outside under trees, these communities became the safe places where a new church in America was being born. And most significant for me is how the Black church that was created there in the hush harbors of the enslaved did indeed become the Black church in America that has undoubtedly had the greatest impact and most powerful influence than any other American church on the rest of the world. Think about that. That historical fact for me is such a deep reminder of a God who creates the believing community of faith from the margins and the edges of society, rather than from the top.

The Black church has become a faith-saving model for many of us from America's white churches. In our pilgrimages away from the white churches that have raised us, we have found a Black church that holistically combines the personal and the social gospel, changing people's lives, impacting their communities, and prophetically calling for the nation to change as well. That consistent prophetic voice in the Black churches has drawn us in and has helped many of us to "keep the faith." To be honest, there are also ways that Black churches can still become conformed to the worst values of American culture as well—perhaps the best example is the ways that too many Black preachers and churches have also promoted the "prosperity gospel," which is literally an unbiblical heresy. But, for me and many others, "true faith" has been found in Black churches more than in most white churches. The preaching of the Word in Black churches is unparalleled in the white churches, the music of Black choirs and congregational singing brings deep spiritual life to many of us that we haven't found elsewhere, their pastoral care for people *and* communities brings integral ministry together, and the Black churches' prophetic calls for justice regularly hold the nation accountable, which is a critical role for Christian faith in the world. On Sunday mornings in America, the Black churches are the places that the gospel is most plainly and powerfully heard, offering personal salvation and calling for public justice. "Souls to the Polls," gets Black church people out to register and vote, Black churches become the meeting and organizing centers to confront key issues in the community and the nation, while at the same time caring for people's personal and pastoral lives—for the hungry and hungry of spirit—which Black churches offer to both.

Now we have all those rich resources, from all of the above, to help take us to a new and different place of faith in America. And more and more people, young and old, want to go there. We want personal faith *and* public discipleship, evangelism *and* social justice, contemplation *and* action, prayer *and* peacemaking, worship *and* politics. In seminary, and later at *Sojourners,* we sometimes called ourselves the *AND* movement.

Each chapter in this book has offered a new way forward for the prodigals who are repenting and returning from the far country of failed political dreams. The remnant church is characterized by the pillars of *repentance, return, and restoration*—all of which flow from Jesus' call to "repent, for the kingdom is at hand." Together, we can repent of seeking idols or saviors other than God. And together, we can return to the living God.

My wife, Joy Carroll, and I led a retreat in the summer of 2023 at Ring Lake Ranch in the Wyoming mountains. It was entitled "Vocation and Calling." There were pastors there from Episcopal, Lutheran, Methodist, Baptist, and more traditions from very "red" rural states. Also present were new-generation Christians like our twenty-year-old son Jack and the young volunteers on the retreat and ranch center's staff. The older pastors spoke of being in the midst of white Christian nationalist cultures as dissenting voices, and intuitively felt themselves to be part of a remnant church holding on to the core of Jesus' teaching amidst a culture of right-wing polarization. Jamie Anderson, an Episcopal priest, wanted us all to be "Bible believing churches," including all the biblical passages on justice. Her husband, John, an academic in Wyoming, spoke of joining with others from diverse political communities to build community projects in their hometown as a way of coming and being together. The younger people in the room spoke of the love, grace, and forgiveness they found in the gospel of Jesus, but which alienated them from many churches; some even with stories of personal hurt from hypocritical and even bullying Christians. But the week together provided new refection on faith for old and young alike; and we were all feeling called to deeper places. A lunch conversation became a "focus group" for me on what we hoped a remnant church could and should be for each of us and for the world now. That lunch discussion turned into another larger voluntary time together where everybody showed up! It was almost like a "mini-church," someone said.

I was reminded of a dear friend who was one of the original megachurch pastors but had to leave when the board of his now huge church asked him to stop asking hard questions, bringing new voices into the church, and taking stands on issues of justice. He decided to leave the big megachurch he founded, his life was changed and he now found himself becoming the "elder" that people would go to from countless little "mini-churches" in schools, workplaces, and homes. A megachurch pastor became a mini-church bishop! He now convenes regular forums for conversation and prayer around the issues people are afraid to discuss and with the real people who are most impacted by those tough questions.

The younger people at Ring Lake Ranch spoke of how they were drawn not so much to church services but to expressions of the church that were focused on serving communities, caring for people in need, and lifting up issues of social justice. All were enthusiastically and passionately attracted to the idea of a remnant church and were eager to discuss what it might look like—for them and their young peers. They were very drawn to the Jesus that they were getting to know and understand through the passages that we were looking into on retreat and that we have examined in this book.

FREEDOM

If we believe the gospel of John that we delved into in chapter 4, we know that the lack of truth results in captivity not just for our own political adversaries, but also the loss of freedom for people we love who have come to believe the lies. We know that a lying society easily leads to fear, hate, violence; and ultimately to the replacement of democracy with autocracy. So, let's not just blame the political liars but reach out to family, friends, and people around us who we want to help set free. Let's use our imaginations to find the things we have in common— like our personal and faith values, like the importance of our children, like our shared commitments—that could help us find some common ground. Standing up for truth, in both our inside circles and outside spaces, is now more critical than ever.

So, whoever you are, wherever you are, speaking up for what is right and true whenever you are with your family, friends, neighbors, and fellow congregants who live in another world of disinformation is absolutely essential for all of our freedom now. Finding the courage to speak up and out, both in close spaces and in the public square is part of the new altar call. And the people who know us and love us will be more likely to listen—so don't stop talking about certain subjects as many have decided to do.

White people, in particular, must speak to other white people and tell the truth—of the good *and* bad about American history and the promise of a new American future.

We, and white people in particular, must make it absolutely clear that we believe diversity to be a gift and not a threat; and we will live that way. Crossing the tribal lines of class, race, religion, and gender and sexual identity is essential and we can all be creative and courageous to discover what that means.

Speaking up from our diverse congregations will be a determining factor for the future of both our faith communities and our democracy. We are a multicultural, multiethnic, multiracial world and country; and religion is one thing that is supposed to bring us together, to promote unity that crosses all our human boundaries—because, *in the beginning,* God created us all. Keep going back to the beginning, to enable us to go forward.

It has never been more important for all of our religions to coexist and find common principles for the common ground of everyone. In particular, most systems of religious belief share in common a commitment to the pursuit of peace, not the stoking of violence. We are not looking for a new *interfaith* religion, one that waters down the things that each of us believes. Instead, we need a *multifaith* commitment to principles and practices that come out of our own traditions where we can find common ground at an important time like this.

Political freedom is a faith matter too. Fascism will live and die at the ballot box. The political and religious right understand that. We must understand and believe that the forces of white Christian nationalism are actively seeking to minimize, suppress, and silence the voices of their opposition—especially the voters of color in America. That is now a political fact that needs a spiritual response.

Therefore, voting in all elections, including local contests, is also a calling and even a personal and spiritual discipline—more than it's ever been. Voting rights must be seen as a moral and religious issue, in protection of the image of God in every person. "The vote is a kind of prayer for the world we desire for ourselves and for our children," says Senator Raphael Warnock. He continues, "I believe that it is sacred. Because at root, the vote is about your voice. And your voice is about your human dignity." And on every social issue this book has raised and discussed, your voice needs to be heard, as do other voices that you can clearly help to be heard.

STEWARDSHIP

I often tell my students that every generation must decide what is no longer acceptable and what can no longer be assumed to be unchangeable. Racialized policing, mass incarceration along color lines, and the acceptance of guns as a way of life and death—these are all issues that many young people are ready to call out as no longer acceptable and are ready to take on as their generational callings. Climate change is another, one they recognize will impact their children and grandchildren and, most of all, the poorest of the world. The commitment to reversing this damage to our planet unites many young people even across philosophical and political differences. And when these critical issues are brought into a remnant church—not as partisan matters but as moral convictions and commitments—it will attract a new generation and many older people who do not feel at home in white Christian nationalist churches.

One hopeful example of that is a young man I met named Reverend Kyle Meyaard-Schapp, an ordained evangelical minister in the Christian Reformed Church *and* a leading activist in the climate justice movement—something that would surprise some. We were put together in a published conversation moderated by Ruth Graham of *The*

New York Times in a series called "Taking The Lead," with elder-younger leaders in discussion. This conversation was called "Two Evangelical Leaders on Radical Faith." Kyle and I connected easily and quickly and both agreed that only "radical faith" could survive and take us forward from both the polarities of a church that is no longer growing and the secularization which is a natural response but is finally not the answer. In preparing for the discussion with a young leader new to me, I found what he had said in a CNN op-ed.

Kyle wrote:

> Young evangelicals across the U.S. are harnessing the tradition of testimony in their communities to tell the story of how God is empowering them to address climate change as an act of love toward God's world and toward their neighbors. They are grabbing microphones in front of their churches, leading Bible studies, navigating fraught holiday conversations and going out for coffee with their grandfather and his skeptical friends. And it is changing hearts and minds.

That such perspective and practice is now going on would stun some and perhaps encourage others whose cynicism had them give up on evangelicals and perhaps Christians and religion altogether. A committed activism is coming out of all this which is bringing new life and new constituencies to the environmental justice movement—which is much needed. Kyle went on to say:

> This "in-house" work is matched by young evangelicals' burgeoning climate activism in wider society. Young Christians are writing op-eds, marching in the streets, and meeting with their elected officials. Students are starting clubs on their Christian college campuses to educate and organize their peers, even transitioning to digital organizing and video group meetings in the era of Covid-induced distance-learning.

And this year, they are getting registered and making plans to vote. Republicans have been able to comfortably rely on evangelical votes for decades, largely by claiming the moral high ground on abortion. Abortion still factors significantly in the electoral calculations of many young evangelicals. Yet more and more, it is being incorporated into a more holistic ethic of life that recognizes climate change and the inhumane treatment of refugees—among others—as threats to the sacredness of life too.[1]

When's the last time you heard white Christian nationalists raise concerns about climate change? And what will they do with a younger generation of Christians, even new generation evangelicals who now say that the stewardship of the creation and all life that God created is a central matter of faith for them.

In our *New York Times* conversation, Kyle Meyaard-Schapp said:

> There's so much hand-wringing happening in the churches. Why are the young people leaving our churches? If you want your young people to stick around, start talking about the questions that they are talking about with their friends on Friday and Saturday night, the existential crises that they are grappling with. Give them a Jesus-shaped answer to the things that matter most to them, like climate action. And then watch them not only stick around but lead. Watch them reignite your church in a way you never imagined.

I agreed with Kyle and said, "Change never comes by majorities, countercultural minorities change majorities." Stewarship of the planet and all of the people on it is becoming a core faith issue that will help define the meaning of a remnant church now in early formation. And it will always take a critical minority to change the hearts and minds—and policies—of the majority culture.[2]

TEN COMMITMENTS: A NEW ALTAR CALL

Here are ten commitments we all can make. Consider the following a modern-day public discipleship altar call:

1. Pastoral Education. White Americans must start by earnestly reading, studying, and listening to learn the true history of America and then talk openly to other white people about the legacy of racism in America. "Repentance" goes beyond just being sorry for the past to understanding what "turning around" means from the moral errors of our previous ways. That is a pastoral task for clergy.

2. Solidarity. Black people, and other Americans of color, and those "who happen to be white" can reach out to each other as people they can trust and find solidarity with. And white people must unlearn their need to control and learn solidarity and the sharing of leadership. It's time to commit to working together for a new American future.

3. Truth-telling. All of us must actively oppose the selective erasing of our shared American history and culture—and especially the Black history which is our American history. We must defend all of our children's right to know all of their country's past—both the good and the bad—so that we can work toward a better American future.

4. Proximity. We have been deliberately separated from one another and must make the deliberate choice of proximity to one another, across all our boundaries—again and again. That is the only way we can authentically demonstrate that we believe diversity is a gift and not a threat. We especially need proximity to people who have been left behind and separated from us. And in those new relationships we will find the grace and hope to go forward together. Mistakes are allowed; but not continued segregation from one another.

5. Show Up. We all must show up and be present at local gatherings, school boards, town meetings, and both elected official and candidate forums to debate and decide fundamental issues of education and

equity and safety for our children and the nation's future. It is time
to expand and widen the tables that decide our public life, and make
sure all our voices are being heard. And, centrally, it's time to lift up
our voices in our own congregations for peacemaking and justice.

6. Citizenship. We should regard voting as a spiritual discipline,
and that includes becoming informed and involved in local elections
as well as national ones. And all of us who comprise this American
democracy—Democrats, Republicans, and Independents—must
commit to protect every vote in free and fair elections. Some of us
might be called to be "poll chaplains" who will be deployed at our
most vulnerable polling places during elections. And voting is only
the beginning of citizenship. Civic discipleship will lead us in many
local and national involvements to serve the common good in our
communities and our nation.

7. Safety. The commitment to public safety and security for all our
children and our families must become a faith issue. It is time for
all Americans—white, Black, Hispanic, and Asian Americans—to
make a personal and public declaration that racialized policing is
no longer acceptable to us and will be stopped. We must commit to
reimagining and renovating a public safety that allows Black and
brown and Asian parents to feel the same security for their children
as white parents do.

8. Security. We, as citizens and parents, must create a bipartisan
movement that reflects the national majority opinion and advocates for sensible gun violence legislation and control. The focus
should be ending the senseless violence, from both mass and individual shootings, and, in particular, removing the lethality of military weapons aimed at civilian society. Serious and sensible gun
accountability, safety, and regulation, is called for with the majority of the American people now in support of that. We must decide
to worship God and not guns.

9. Stewardship. All of God's creation, with all human beings made
in the image and likeness of God, require our respect, care, dignity,

protection, and love. And seeing God in all His children and in the beautiful environments around us should be the foundation for both our faith and our politics. A faith community call for environmental justice is crucial, focusing on those least responsible but most impacted by climate change.

10. Prophetic. Don't be afraid to be prophetic, even or especially in your congregations. The prophetic role of faith communities, calling for justice, must be restored in all of America's faith communities. Social and economic justice are direct outgrowths of faith and, as the biblical prophets show us, "righteousness" and "justice" are often the same word in our Scriptures. We can and must commit to replace racially and economically unjust systems with restorative justice in our criminal, legal, health, housing, and job sectors of our national life. Addressing the conditions of where and how people live, work, and flourish with others must become a faith priority. A nation of laws must be applied equally, and especially to those for whom this has not been the case before.

These are all commitments that will help create the *common good.* They don't require that people be of one religion or even any, but the commitments of faith can help inspire, motivate, and sustain them. They will draw the support of others and will help show the country how to build a diverse human community, while committing ourselves, unequivocally, to multiracial democracy. *A remnant church must not only be known for what it is against, but what it is for and starting to build.*

WHERE DO WE GO FROM HERE?

"Where do we go from here?" Rev. Dr. Martin Luther King, Jr., asked as the title of his final book. One of my favorite quotes from MLK is most relevant to our present moment: "*The church must be reminded that it is not the master of the state, not the servant of the state; but the con-*

science of the state." That is the course correction to white Christian nationalism that we most need now. Faith communities don't try to take over the state and impose their religious will. Neither do they accept oppressive systems or be satisfied just to take care of the victims of society. Instead, they provide the conscience of the state, the watchful eye, the moral accountability to government. They have the independent ability to challenge the systems because they are based outside of them and meant to live an alternative reality in community. And they are always supposed to be the advocates for justice.

I believe in the separation of church and state, but *the separation of church and state does not require the segregation of moral and religious values from public life.* Those clear moral values are crucial to challenge political and economic power and shape movements for social change.

And the most successful social movements have combined both personal and social responsibility, with spiritual values at their core.

I have said throughout this book that I believe movements must always decide who they can persuade and invite, and who they must defeat. We must reach out to those who are still persuadable, while at the same time providing the resources to nonviolently but politically defeat those who are dangerous to democracy. The white Christian nationalism that I call a *heresy* is now being acted upon by church leaders, with some using the word "excommunication" as a response to these false ideologies and idolatries of racism and white supremacy. In describing white Christian nationalism, I deliberately use the word "idolatry," along with "ideology," because that's what this is: the worship of the false gods of whiteness and nationalism over the true God who creates and unites all of us all over the world. That theological challenge to white Christian nationalism, deeper than just the political, is beginning to be taken on by Christian denominations. One of the first churches to address the issue of these "alt-right" false teachings was the Lutheran Church–Missouri Synod, the most conservative Lutheran church. A reading of the explicit letter from the denominational head Matthew Harrison and his fellow leaders to all of their churches, with promise of "excommunication" over such racist views, shows how these issues are indeed theological and not just political.[3] My hope is for other denominations to follow suit. The battle for the soul of the nation will be fought on many fronts and should be focused on in the theological deliberations of our ecclesiastical gatherings.

The forces of violent division need an even more powerful counterforce of love and justice—which faith communities can and should provide. As I have said, many young people fill out religious affiliation surveys with "none of the above." A majority of the "nones" still believe in God or at least something beyond themselves. And more than anything else, they are looking for courage and commitment and, too often, they look at religion and see mostly hypocrisy and inauthenticity. But I believe that can change.

"The church is an institution that has a lot of privilege in this country," says Black activist Brittany Packnett. "Anybody with privilege has to be willing to risk some of it in order to create equity."[4] Young people like Brittany are interested in faith that makes a difference. And they know that faith that does not produce justice and peace in the world is simply not the faith of Jesus. It is in the uncertainty and risk of social movements that many young activists are finding their way back to faith, as Brittany told me she had found God again in the violence, rubber bullets, and tear gas of the streets of Ferguson where she sometimes didn't know if she would live through the night.

If we want to be authentic and successful, we must come to see that if we are conforming to the same kind of rhetoric of division so prevalent in the world today, then we ourselves are driving people away. And *how* we fight these dangerous ideologies and idolatries is also very important. Author and television journalist Kirsten Powers reminded me of a quote from Nietzsche: "Beware that, when fighting monsters, you yourself do not become a monster."[5] She urges us to view our adversaries with grace, which, she says, "gives other people the space to not be you." Referring to her book *Saving Grace*,[6] Kirsten said:

If all you're doing is spending all your time in a rage, exhausted and miserable, because you're so wrapped up in what other people are doing, figure out what you're a "no" to, and the bigger ideas that you're a "yes" to. And so rather than going down the rabbit hole, berating other people and hating other people and all these very unproductive things, go do something—start an organization, volunteer, donate money, write a letter to the editor or a column, amplify voices that are actually being productive.

Skepticism and even pessimism some days is a natural response to continuing injustice, which sometimes seems never ready to change. But it is cynicism that is the greatest danger to change. I understand that temptation among the young students that I teach and try to help them sort those things out. But I teach these young people because I believe in them. And I have learned that the generation that I both teach and work with for justice does not want to become another "jaded generation." They are learning that cynicism is the biggest enemy to hope, while action is hope's best friend.

STOPPING THE TRAINS

In response to my book *The Soul of Politics,* some of the inmates at the infamous Sing Sing prison in New York wrote to me: "A number of us have carefully read your latest book and would like to invite you to come and unpack it with us and discuss how we can apply the things you say." I wrote back and asked when they would like me to come. "Well," came the reply, "we are free most nights and are quite a captive audience here."

Through the New York Theological Seminary's master's program, I was able to spend several hours together with about fifty prisoners within the walls of Sing Sing. It was my first contact with this unique clergy training program in a prison, and it would not be my last.

The same young brother who had invited me to come said at the outset of our discussion, "Jim, you need to understand that most of us here
at Sing Sing—a very large number of us—come from just four or five
neighborhoods in New York City. It's like a train that comes through the
places where we live; we get on those trains by the time we are about
nine or ten years old, and the trains end up here."

That powerful metaphor of an urban train, only passing through
certain zip codes and ending up at places like Sing Sing, all over the
country, has stayed with me ever since that day. I listened to their many
stories of those fast-moving pipelines and trains—in failing education,
systematic economic inequity and the lack of living wages, unafford-
able housing, the violence of poverty and what results from it, deeply
biased policing and criminal justice systems, the hopelessness of ad-
diction, and the wars on drugs meant to imprison and disenfranchise
only certain people; and endless racism everywhere you look. "But I
have had a conversion inside these walls," my new friend told me, "and
when I get out, I am going to stop those trains."

*Stopping those trains is now essentially the cause of saving humanity,
reclaiming faith, and achieving democracy.* Sometime later I gave the
commencement address for the graduates of the Sing Sing master's
program—both for prisoners whose sentences would one day be over;
and for those whose sentences would never end. I spoke about those
trains and how absolutely crucial it is to stop them, as my new friend
had promised to do. And he has—as the Reverend and now Bishop Dar-
ren Ferguson is stopping trains on the streets, from the pulpit and in
the pews, and in the institutions of criminal injustice along with some
of his former prison colleagues whom I am blessed to know.

I have told the Sing Sing story at every commencement address I have
ever given since that day—at seminaries and universities all over the
country. And the question I always ask the graduates about to go out
into the world is this: "What trains are you going to stop?" It's a kind
of altar call offered to believers and nonbelievers alike. And it is the
question I am leaving with all of you—the readers of this book—some

of you pastors, faith leaders, local activists, teachers, and, yes, students. People of faith and no faith at all. What trains that are derailing both people's lives and democracy are you willing to try to stop?

MY ENEMY TO MY FRIEND

There was a national white evangelical leader who became one of my biggest "enemies." Bill Bright was the founder and president of Campus Crusade for Christ, which created the "four spiritual laws" to bring salvation to college students. Bright, a former politically conservative businessman from Southern California, got involved in one of the first efforts to create what would become the "religious right." They developed a plan with a curriculum for infiltrating prayer groups to infuse right-wing politics and even conservative political candidates into Christian circles. He worked with politicians like John Conlan, a right-wing congressman from Arizona, who had hoped to become president one day.

At *Sojourners* magazine, we had heard rumors about this plan, and eventually found sources to investigate the story. One of them was a former FBI agent then attending Fuller Theological Seminary (we called him our "deep throat" after the famous Watergate source for the *Washington Post*!). Bill Bright was very hard to track down to talk to about this clandestine effort, but I finally reached him and gave him the chance to refute the evidence we had found, and even to offer a response in our upcoming story. Bright only said, "If you publish this, I will destroy you!" I understood then why so many people we spoke to about this emerging plan were afraid of Bill Bright.

Despite the threats, we published a cover story in 1976 called "The Plan to Save America" detailing what was indeed the first attempt to manipulate evangelical Christians into right-wing conservative politics and candidates. Wes Granberg-Michaelson and I wrote that story together. That initial attempt at manipulation failed. Our *Sojourners* story got picked up by national media around the country, Conlan lost his next election, and Bill Bright was very embarrassed.

Soon after I attended an evangelical prayer breakfast meeting and Bill Bright happened to be there as well. When it came time to make self-introductions around the room, he said, "I am Bill Bright, founder and president of Campus Crusade for Christ, and I am not a liar like Jim Wallis!" Immediately, Black evangelical leader Tom Skinner jumped out of his seat to confront Bright and said something like, "Finally we have a white evangelical leader who tells the truth about race, speaks up for social justice, and all people like you can do is attack him!" They were now face to face, and others had to intervene to break up a potential fistfight between these two evangelical leaders.

Vitriol against me and *Sojourners* continued to emanate from Bill Bright over the years. But we had a mutual friend, Mary Ann Richardson, the owner of the El Caribe Motel in Daytona Beach, Florida, who provided the Campus Crusade summer staff a base for their beach outreach, and often offered me and others a restful place to write. Mary Ann was always worried that when Bill and I were there at the same time, we might bump into each other—maybe in the laundry room!

Once when she told me that Bill was also in the motel, I decided to reach out to him. I called his room and said, "Bill, you and I have had some difficult times in the past, but I wondered if you might come for a walk with me on the beach?" Bill said yes, and we went for a long walk and talk. "Tell me how you came to Christ," he asked. I told him my story and then asked for his—those stories are always bonding for Christians. Then he said something that completely surprised me. "Jim, as you know, I am a Great Commission person" (the final instruction from Jesus to his disciples to go into all the world with the gospel of Jesus). Yes, I know, I told him. "Well," said Bill, "in my older years, I have noticed what Jesus said at the end of that Great Commission scripture. . . . Jesus told his disciples to 'teach them to observe everything that I have commanded you.'" Then Bill shared, "I have come to see that Jesus told us to care for the poor, and I had never understood that before. Jim, you have been saying and doing that for a long time. Please tell me how the poor in America are doing today." So, we talked for an even longer time, sitting at the beach after our walk was over. Bill asked me at the end of our time together if we could pray together—and we did.

Not too long after that, I got word that Bill Bright had died. And I was handed a letter that had just come in to me at *Sojourners*. It was from Bill Bright. His letter told me that he had been given some money and decided to divide it up and give it to people and ministries that he believed were calling people to follow Jesus; and he wanted to give some of that to *Sojourners*. With Bill's letter, that he had apparently written just days before he died, was a check made out to *Sojourners*. It was the most dramatic story in my life of an enemy turned into a friend. And that came from our discussing the Scriptures together, reexamining the words of Jesus, in this case the broader meaning of the Great Commission given by Jesus; and telling each other our own faith stories.

BACK TO THE TEXTS

So I would like to return to our Genesis text and to Jesus' words—one more time. And I want to invite both the religious and nonreligious to find the wisdom today in a reframing and refreshing of these ancient texts:

- Genesis 1:26: "Then God said, Let us make humankind in our own image, according to our own likeness." Do we believe that all of us were created after God's own image and likeness—or not?
- Luke 10:25–37: "You shall love the Lord your God with all your heart, and with all your strength, and with all your mind, and your neighbor as yourself." Do we believe that our love for our neighbors who are different from us determines our love for God—or not?

- John 8:32: "You will know the truth and the truth will make you free." Do we believe that not knowing the truth and submitting to lies will take away our freedom—or not?
- Mathew 25:31–46: "As you have done to the least of these, you have done to me." Do we believe these words in this last teaching of Jesus, before he went into Jerusalem; that how we treat the poor and vulnerable is literally how we treat Christ himself—or not?
- Matthew 5:9: "Blessed are the peacemakers, for they shall be called the children of God." Do we believe that the peacemakers, not the dividers, are God's real children—or not?
- Galatians 3:28: "There is no longer Jew or Gentile, there is no longer slave or free, there is no longer male or female, for all of you are one in Christ." Do we believe these words of the apostle Paul; that we are not just old tribes but meant to become a new community—or not?

"Jesus is not partisan," said Michael Curry, the presiding bishop of the Episcopal Church, at one of our recent Georgetown University forums on white Christian nationalism. "He can speak to more folk than I can just on my own. That's true for you and for all of us. Go to the text—let Jesus do the talking!"

I believe we are in a great position to resource and inspire many people in many places and on many levels to become new kinds of evangelists, pastors, preachers, and ambassadors, bringing prodigals back home to reconcile faith and justice and to bond diverse believers together in finding the path forward to fulfilling the promise of both faithfulness and democracy. Many of us are already creating collaborative networks and expanding our own constituencies.

I have asserted throughout this book that the best answer to bad religion is always true faith. The complete secularization of this debate is a big mistake, because we lose an essential vision of justice and peace that comes from faith. The political right must no longer get away with hijacking religion for the purposes of advancing their own narrow ideology. On the contrary, it will take honest and courageous good faith to help take our nation to a better place—for both believers and nonbelievers.

FAITH DOES JUSTICE

The banner reads: *Faith Does Justice* and you see them on lamp posts all across the Georgetown campus. I pass by that Jesuit statement on my way to my office and to my classes, and so do my students. That's the altar call right now. It is time for that faith to come back, come out, stand up, speak out, revive, renew, and put the faith that does justice into action—now. If the best of our faith traditions are not raised up and put into practice we could lose the genuineness of belief and true power of faith altogether in the United States of America, as our present crisis deepens.

Unprecedented is now our most overused word politically. Our public life keeps getting worse and the dangerous perils to our democracy grow every day. Never before has a president of the United States lied and conspired to block the results of a free and fair election and then incite mob violence to overturn that election's certification—for which Donald J. Trump was indicted as I wrote this, and then three more, amounting to ninety-one indictments and four trials to come for a former president—unprecedented. The peaceful transfer of power is at the heart of democracy, by the votes of the people, and for the first time since the founding of the republic a sitting president tried to prevent that peaceful and lawful transfer of power, seeking to corrupt the democratic process and break the laws to remain in power himself.

And now that former president is running again to return to the White House. He and his campaign have already stated unequivocally that his new administration would concentrate executive power with direct control over all other departments and agencies, with the power to decide which businesses are rewarded or punished, which media outlets are allowed to be open and which censored, and, perhaps most centrally, how the rule of law is decided and carried out with executive control over a formerly independent Department of Justice. Greatly expanded executive power would even decide when to defy the Congress in its bills and spending. When those plans and policy agendas for a next administration were revealed and released in the early summer of 2023, the former president and his 2024 campaign affirmed their reality. And Trump is clearly implying that he would pardon himself for all his criminal offenses, and even most of those who stormed the Congress.

Such seizure of executive power over other branches and institutions of government has been a strategy of authoritarian regimes throughout history and around the world, most recent examples being the autocratic takeovers in countries like Hungary and Turkey. The privatization of power with little or no restraints, with the enrichment of the leaders and their loyal enablers is a strategy of fascism—and that word must honestly and morally be used. The love and loyalty of those leaders for one another around the world is something we had already seen in the Trump administration and that would now certainly increase in an international movement to replace democracy with autocracy.

Therefore, the time has come for an *unprecedented exercise of faith* to resist and combat autocracy over democracy. *The importance of the faith factor in this battle for the soul of the nation cannot be underestimated.* When religion is in fact being used to support the rise of totalitarian rule, as it has also been in past history, true faith must rise over bad religion. That bad and dangerous religion is now put forward as white Christian nationalism and it is the single greatest threat to democracy today. And when such autocracy is racialized as this one is, and as most are, what is at stake is nothing less than the beginning of our sacred Scriptures, which teach us to treat every other human being as created in the image of God—*imago dei* remains our moral foundation and touchstone.

Indeed Jesus has suffered identity theft in America, and it is also time for Christians to come back to the real Jesus. His clear texts and teachings about loving our neighbor—especially those different from us, welcoming "the other," and finding the truth that will set us free from our ideological captivities—must all be believed and, if not, to no longer call Jesus Lord.

I am convinced this must and can be done. There is a deep hunger for reclaiming true faith against false religion, especially among a new generation. And Christians who show the courage to follow Jesus, no matter what the cost, will bring young people back to faith communities instead of turning them away. Democracy will not be saved or fulfilled by just politics and especially not by partisan agendas. We do need a theology of democracy and the spirituality of a new civic discipleship. The moral movement we now need is not just for Christians, but for those of many faiths and those with no faith at all.

We can make our voices heard from our many faith communities. And we must make them heard everywhere, in our own congregations and also moving out into our communities, where public debates are being had and decisions are being made. We must all be in fervent prayer for the repentance and restoration of both faith and democracy in America, which are now in an interlocking test together. And, as John Lewis and other Christian activists have taught us, we must also pray with our feet and go to the places where this national debate and battle is being had. From school boards to city councils to local and national legislative bodies, to media platforms social and otherwise in newspaper letters and op-eds, to candidate forums, to community events and gatherings on all political sides with different people; let the Faith Factor be heard! March for faith and justice with prayerful feet. It's time to take our faith communities into the streets where faith and freedom are literally at stake. And, if and when necessary, there may come a time for prayerful, reflective, nonviolent civil disobedience against powers that would subvert both faith and democracy.

The greatest threat to faith is not disbelief but cynicism. And hope is the greatest contribution that faith communities can make to the spiritual and political battles now before us. We can be the emissaries of hope, the carriers of grace to build bridges across divided lines, the ambassadors of justice and reconciliation that commit to keep the two together.

It's also time for each of us to focus on our vocations and not just our careers. Ask yourself about your gifts and not your assets. Reflect upon your callings and not your societal niche. Stop looking only inward but also look outward. Indeed, go deeper inward to find the courage to move outward. Where your calling meets the critical needs of the world, and in this moment—that is your vocation now. Find it, join with others who are finding their vocations now in this crisis. Everyone has influence, don't believe those who say you don't, and use that influence where it may most be influential—with family and loved ones, with friends, with fellow congregational members, with mutual school and team parents, at our workplaces, and in our local communities, and among our political representatives' constituents—all pressing and seeking common ground for the common good.

"Be still and know that I am God," says the Psalmist. Politics is not God. Politicians are not gods. Dictators are not gods—even when they act like they think they are. God made us for each other and for the stewardship of creation. Let's get on with that. It's God's work however we name it for ourselves. We will all be needed for this work that loves and protects our children, which might be the one thing that can bring us together. Just know that you are not alone.

HOPE

Let me end this book with the voice of someone who taught me my theology of hope. He is also the mentor and friend that my new chair at Georgetown University was named after: the Archbishop Desmond Tutu Chair in Faith and Justice.

In 1985, I was invited to come to South Africa by church leaders there who wanted to forge stronger bonds between their churches and the American churches in their life-and-death battle with apartheid, a system that was the literal antithesis of Genesis 1:26 and Galatians 3:28. I deeply wanted to come, but knew I would not get past the security checkpoints in South Africa because I had helped organize many protests against their apartheid government. We were in Washington, DC, where South African church leader Beyers Naudé had just been given the Robert F. Kennedy Human Rights Award. In a private conversation circle afterward, Beyers invited me to come. When I expressed my frustration over security concerns, another voice in the circle, Tom Getman from World Vision, made a courageous offer: he could invite me under the auspices of World Vision, whose visiting pastors were never checked by South African security. But everyone knew that Pretoria would eventually find out who had brought me in once I was in the country.

I arrived, with great trepidation going through security at the Cape Town airport, and headed directly to meet my South African colleagues who could not be seen with me at the airport. As instructed, I headed to St. George's Cathedral in Cape Town, where Archbishop Desmond Tutu would be presiding that day. A rally had been called, but abruptly canceled by the government, so a service of worship was convened instead. To get into the cathedral, I had to pass through countless numbers of South African police and military who now surrounded the small Anglican sanctuary in the heart of this beautiful South African city overlooking the South Atlantic Ocean. I finally made it inside and found a seat with some friends, just as Bishop Tutu was about to preach.

Suddenly, South African Security Police burst through the main door of St. George's Cathedral. They proceeded to enter the church and line its walls on both sides—glaring at the archbishop in the pulpit. I saw them take out notepads and even tape recorders as if to say, "We are watching you and recording whatever you say!" Tutu had just come out of prison and the message of the invading police was clearly, "Go ahead. Be prophetic. And we will just put you back in prison again!" I was brand new to South Africa; this was my first of many visits to come. But I really *felt* them saying, "We own this country. We own this cathedral. We own you. And we own your God!" These huge white South African policemen looked like thugs—and I would later learn more about that in my own first interrogation with a gun to my head.

What was the great leader Desmond Tutu going to do? We all wondered in that very dramatic moment.

The archbishop stopped speaking and bowed his head, seeming to pray. There he was, a short man standing in that tall pulpit surrounded by so many large, threatening policemen. Some have humorously compared Tutu to the *Star Wars* character Yoda, a little person in long, flowing robes with great authority and a twinkle in his eye! After what felt to be a long silence while the bishop was in prayer, he suddenly looked up and flashed his eyes at the greatly feared South African Security Police. "You are indeed powerful, very powerful," Tutu said, but then he turned to both sides, looking right at them, and proclaimed, "But you are not gods, and I serve a God who cannot be mocked!" Then, after smiling at them for a moment, he began to jump up and down like a good Black Baptist preacher, announcing with great boldness, "So, since you have already lost, I invite you today to come, and join the winning side!" The South African Security Police didn't know what to do or say, and we didn't either. All at once, young people in the cathedral began to jump to their feet and chant in joyful and happy voices, in a dance called the *toyi-toyi*—lifting their legs high in a prancing movement often used during protests in South Africa. They danced right out the front door to embrace the hundreds of police standing outside, and we all followed. The police had no idea what to do with all these dancing worshipers who showed no fear!

I was blessed to be with Desmond Tutu and many other South African church leaders and ordinary people for the next six weeks, over the season of Lent, to plan joint strategies between our churches for overcoming apartheid, including the economic sanctions that would eventually cripple the apartheid regime. And it was there, in South Africa, that I learned my theology of hope.

Ten years later, on May 10, 1994, I was back for the historic global gathering of the inauguration of former prisoner and new president, Nelson Mandela, and the beginning of the first real democracy in South Africa. Guess who was the master of ceremony? Of course, it was Archbishop Desmond Tutu! When I first saw him, I asked, "Bishop, do you remember that day at St. George's?" With a big smile, he nodded. He remembered. I smiled back and said to him, "Bishop, today they have all joined the winning side!" Because on that almost unbelievable inaugural day, everybody would have said that they had all always been against apartheid!

What I learned in South Africa is the vital spiritual sequence of social change. It's almost a liturgy for historical change. First there is the *faith,* which inspires the *hope,* which creates the *action* that leads to the *change.* And that's often, if not always, the path to real transformation. Ironically, the faith community is *least needed* at the parties or celebrations like in Pretoria that day—which was absolutely wonderful with 150,000 jubilant South Africans, and with tears in all our eyes. But where we are *most needed* is at the places like St. George's, where you can only see and imagine the future party, the coming celebration, and the victories we long for; *through the eyes of faith.*

Desmond Tutu also taught me that optimism and hope are not the same thing. Optimism, he said, is based on a *feeling or a mood*—even a personality type—about how things look today with people's emotional cups half full or half empty. But different and deeper than optimism, hope is *a choice, a decision,* and one based on what we call faith. There were not too many days of optimism in the South African struggle against apartheid, especially for a church leader who dealt with suffering, pain, and heartache every day. But Archbishop Desmond Tutu's signature smile grew from making hope the choice and the decision he *had* to make each and every day, which is what gave him such a deep sense of *joy.*

There is a favorite text of mine in the New Testament book of Hebrews which says it well: "Now faith is the substance of things hoped for, the evidence of things not seen" (Hebrews 11:1). My best personal paraphrase of that is "Hope means believing in spite of the evidence, then watching the evidence change."

This book is a call to action, a manifesto for a moment of crisis and opportunity. There is much ahead that we cannot either predict or control. We will face great challenges and many dangers, and with sighs of deep discouragement and encouragement all along the way. Our optimism will go up and down, but hope must remain our *choice*. The path to fulfilling the promise of democracy must be walked by all of us now. And through the actions of believers and nonbelievers alike, I believe that God, and we, can bless America.

ACKNOWLEDGMENTS

First, I want to thank Georgetown University and President Jack De-Gioia for the kind invitation and warm welcome. To be the inaugural holder of the Archbishop Desmond Tutu Chair in Faith and Justice at the McCourt School of Public Policy is a deeply humbling, great blessing for me, as this extraordinary faith leader was such a dear mentor and friend. I often say that I got my theology of hope from South Africa and Desmond Tutu. I am also grateful to be named the director of the new Center on Faith and Justice at Georgetown University. I want to thank my dean at the McCourt School of Public Policy, Maria Cancian, and close colleagues at Georgetown including Joe Ferrara and Tom Banchoff. I am thankful to sometimes collaborate with the Initiative on Catholic Social Thought and Public Life, led by John Carr and Kim Daniels. And I want to acknowledge my deep gratitude to the students with whom I have continuing dialogue, and whose voices and visions and conversations are featured throughout this book. They continue to be the best part of my weeks at Georgetown.

As to the people who have influenced and helped to inspire the writing of this book, let me start with my team at the new Center on Faith and Justice at Georgetown University. Jim Simpson, Executive Director of the center, makes everything work, oversees the vision, and skillfully manages all the center's work, and he generously prioritized my book writing. Daniel Burke, our highly experienced and strategic Director of Communications, coordinates my *Soul of the Nation* podcast, which was essential to the book; and also manages my Substack column called "God's Politics." Steven Harris, our Senior Director of Academic Programs, leads what I call our "underground seminary" each summer, connects with students all year, and helped shape the book's message—as did my whole team, including Kathleen Bonnette, Assistant and Events Coordinator, and Ernesto Godinez, our former Graduate Assistant and my teaching assistant.

I especially want to thank my book agent, Roger Freet, deeply for helping me to put this book into practice. Roger's enormously helpful experience and expertise were invaluable. No one is better at helping an author think through a book, format and rearrange it for clarity, and hone the message for the widest audience. This book agent really works for the readers of a book. And Roger's commitment to this book was evident throughout the process, long after we had a great publishing house for it.

And speaking of St. Martin's, I am so very grateful for the deep wisdom, great language skills, detailed editorial work, and fresh insights of my wonderful editor, Elisabeth Dyssegaard. To have a great editor is necessary for a great book—and I did. After our very first conversation, I knew that she believed in the message of this book and wanted to help spread it far and wide. I also want to thank all the enthusiastic work to get that message out by so many, including Joel Fotinos, Anne Marie Tallberg, Eric Meyer, Jamilah Lewis-Horton, Sophia Lauriello, and Martin Quinn.

I also want to thank Jeff Goins and Zack Williamson at Fresh Complaint for their extraordinary help in researching and collecting critical resources and material for the book—two very competent editors and both such a delight to work with.

The list of those whose work, lives, insights, and conversations have influenced this book are so many and too many to name, but they include Claude Alexander, Margaret Atwood, William Barber, David Beckmann, Steven Bland, Ruth Braunstein, Kelly Brown Douglas, Walter Brueggemann, T Bone Burnett, Diana Butler Bass, Galen Carey, Jimmy Carter, Raymond Chang, Shane Claiborne, Chris Coons, Tim Costello,

Michael Curry, Julian DeShazier, E. J. Dionne, Tim Dixon, Joshua Du-
Bois, Mohamed Elsanousi, Robert Franklin, the late Michael Gerson,
Eddie Glaude, Aaron Graham, David Gushee, Cynthia Hale, Lisa Sha-
ron Harper, Freddie Haynes, Obery Hendricks, Alvin Herring, David
Hollenbach, Joel Hunter, Hyepin Im, Robert Jones, Walter Kim, Rachel
Kleinfeld, Kristin Kobes Du Mez, Mark Labberton, Steven Levitsky,
Jo Anne Lyon, Carlos Malave, James Martin, Michael-Ray Mathews,
Heather McGhee, Vashti McKenzie, Brian McLaren, Jon Meacham, Ken
Medema, Russell Moore, Otis Moss Jr., Otis Moss III, Bill Moyers, Con-
stance Newman, Brittany Packnett, Parker Palmer, Eboo Patel, Samuel
Perry, Jonah Pesner, Dwight Radcliff, Jamie Raskin, Reggie Williams,
Bob Roberts, Gabe Salguero, David Saperstein, Rob Schenk, Bryan Ste-
venson, Jemar Tisby, Nikki Toyama-Szeto, Amanda Tyler, Beverly Van-
dermullen, Raphael Warnock, Peter Wehner, Barbara Williams-Skinner,
Garry Wills, Starsky Wilson, Jonathan Wilson-Hartgrove, N. T. Wright,
Marian Wright Edelman, Jenny Yang; and my siblings with whom I
discuss these issues: Barb Tamialis, Bill Weld-Wallis, Marcie Rahill,
and Teri Bailey.

A special shout-out to my brother-in-law, Jim Tamialis, who filled
in with support in the aftermath of my hip replacement surgery to free
up my wife, Joy Carroll, so she could go to her beloved Wild Goose Fes-
tival where she is chair of the board—while I finished up my final ed-
its in recovery!

I also want to thank Sojourners, where I was for fifty years after
founding it together with others in 1971. Those five decades and the relationships with countless people in the Sojourners community, staff,
and fellows, and the much wider Sojourners' circle and extended community across this country and around the world, are all part of who
I am today and what I believe. I want to thank, in particular, Adam
Taylor, the new president; Wes Granberg-Michaelson, longtime friend
and former chair of the Sojourners board; Joe Roos and Bob and Jackie
Sabbath, some of my cofounders and copastors at Sojourners. Jim Rice,
the longtime editor of *Sojourners,* Ed Spivey, our art director, who still

makes me laugh more than anyone else, and Karen Lattea, vice president and chief human resources officer; and original and early Sojourners board members, like Reverend Yvonne Delk, Marie Dennis, Peter Borgdorff, Colin Watson, Soong-Chan Rah, Bill Wylie Kellermann, and current board cochairs Kevin Carnahan and Alexia Salvatierra, who have all been vision sharers over the years.

So many longtime friends have been regular dialogue partners over many years, like Karl Gaspar, Peggy Flanagan, John O'Neil, Peter Price, Bob and Patty Lane, Tony Campolo, John Perkins, Joan Chittister, Sharon Watkins, William Pannell, Richard Rohr, and the late Ron Sider, Vincent Harding, Gordon Cosby, Gustavo Parajón, Henri Nouwen, William Stringfellow, and Daniel Berrigan.

Last, but most important, is my family. Joy Carroll, my wife, who is so committed to this message, and was always completely supportive of all the time it took to write this book. My parents, James and Phyllis Wallis, who laid foundations for me. And especially to my sons, Luke and Jack, who are continual dialogue partners on the message and mission of what became this book, and what is needed on faith and justice for the next generation. And now also to my new daughter-in-law, Anna-Sophia, who has joined in.

Words do not suffice, but gratitude is a constant refrain for me.

WHAT'S NEXT?

Reading can change us, reflection can carry us deeper, and acting can transform us and the world. Here are several questions to ask yourself and your friends—maybe even together in a small book group, Bible study, prayer fellowship, or a community group. If you don't belong to a group, consider starting one with *The False White Gospel*, and continuing with one of the books included in the bibliography.

FOR INDIVIDUAL QUESTIONERS

Where do you get your news and what other sources might prove helpful when trying to navigate these challenging issues? How and where can we find more truthful information and perspectives on things? Instead of going further right or left, how might you go deeper and what would that look like for you?

Consider identifying someone in your friend group with whom you disagree and offer to only listen to their views as a way to build equity and establish trust. As the old adage goes, love well and look for an opening.

Always start by looking for common ground. What do we agree upon? What personal and faith values do we share?

What did you find most disturbing and most encouraging while reading *The False White Gospel*? Did you come to new conclusions about these six biblical texts that gave you hope about the way forward for your faith community and for this country?

Who is your neighbor?

Are voting rights safe and secure in your community and state? Perhaps you might like to become involved in voter education or protection work like Faiths United to Save Democracy (turnoutsun day.com).

How do the book's questions relate to the issues at stake in your own communities—local, state, and national political debates now going on?

FOR FAMILIES AND CHILDREN

Instead of making hard questions off-limits within our families, try to create a loving environment to discuss what a politics of love and hope, instead of hate and fear, might look like.

How could you have conversations about these issues of faith and democracy in your family? Which family members tend to dominate the conversation when it comes to social and faith issues and how do you respond? What information, tools, or approaches in this book might present a fresh opportunity for communication and change? Again, what do we have in common? What does our faith mean to both of us or all of us?

Is there an older child (high school or college age) in your family that you could give this book to and perhaps invite them to discuss it with you? This could be a powerful invitation for them to reflect on how their own family and social circles have shaped their views on race, faith, and politics. Applying the same "listen first" approach, as I suggested above, might be a transformative and empowering way to engage with a younger generation.

FOR CONGREGATIONS AND FAITH FRIENDS

Leadership groups at churches, synagogues, mosques, or other faith communities will have much to offer as we all seek to preserve and extend democracy in America.

How could you take these urgent matters to your congregation, and which people in your faith community could be allies and advocates for exploring the themes raised in *The False White Gospel*? Start a small group to explore and go deeper.

Within the Christian tradition, talk to your pastor about the issues raised in this book and ask if they might like to read it with some of your fellow parishioners. Ask what a preaching and discussion series might look like around each of these chapters.

Beyond just study and reflection, ask the members of your congregation how we might be able to live out the spiritual values and public policy commitments in the community. Members of your congregation can be engaging in town meetings about

- diversity, inclusion, and equity
- books being used in classrooms
- how well and honestly Black history is being taught to our children

You can be the ones to ask the sometimes hard questions and to offer the resources we will all need to build a better country. And, of course, always ask how these faith and justice issues are coming up in your own denominations at the local, regional, and national levels.

GOVERNMENT AND DECISION-MAKING

Take the lessons you've learned from this book and those in the bibliography to your own elected officials, city council members, mayors, governors, and all the way to your members of Congress and senators.

Reach out to them; ask them the basic questions being raised in the book.

Go see them in your city and state, or when your national elected officials come home from Washington, DC, or when you go to the nation's capital. If they know what is on the minds and hearts of their representatives and voters, it will make a difference. Some of the examples of policies and decisions lifted up in the book are actually happening in legislative bodies now and your participation can make a difference. Make your voice and presence known to your political leaders. Help them know who you are.

Be ready to join and help organize and mobilize for crucial campaigns around the issues raised in the book. Be alert to those efforts in your community and engage with them.

HERE IS A SEQUENCE OF STEPS

1. Read the book carefully, even in reflection, meditation, and prayer. Take the time for in-depth conversation and dialogue with others about the issues raised in the chapters and around those core biblical texts.

2. Identify points of action around those questions being discussed in your communities and even with decisions being made.

3. Show up for those meetings to make yourself present, make sure all voices are being heard, and help support and facilitate the kind of rich, fair, and deep dialogues our local communities desperately need to have. Ask how we can be peacemakers, not conflict makers in our divided society and churches.

4. Make yourselves known—and the questions you want the country to answer—in your local media, letters to the editor, opinion pieces. Raise the issues in the book that resonated with you on all your social media platforms. Meet your member of Congress or their staff; your state legislators, and people at the governor's

office; city council members, and mayor's office; even your school board members making important decisions. Share the questions raised out of this book; and *ask them for answers.*

PASTORS

How about us pastors? That's a question I always hear so I tried to answer that throughout the book. Parishioners and members of congregations also ask me what their pastors can do, and tell me what they would like them to do!

TEN THINGS PASTORS CAN DO

1. Read *The False White Gospel.* In every chapter, ask how the questions raised impact you as a pastor—you and your crucial roles are raised throughout the book. How does the work of both faith and democracy apply to your situation, your congregation, your community, your own vocation and calling?
2. Share the book with other pastors, rabbis, imams, and other faith leaders in your community. Maybe even read it together and ask what it means for all of you in the environments you find yourselves in.
3. Preach it. There are six chapters that examine six key biblical texts. Consider preaching one Sunday on each chapter. Perhaps a series on faith and democracy—and the integral connection between them.
4. Encourage some small groups in your church for Bible study and prayer around the book. A free, robust online study guide for the book is available at www.jimwallis.org.
5. Go to the biblical texts—again and again—and ask how they can be refreshed and reframed for our contemporary context

and crisis today. Consult commentaries and leading scholars, as I did, to gain new insights about how to faithfully exegete and interpret these texts.

6. Let Jesus do the talking. What did he say, what did he do, and how can that be applied to our situations today?

7. At the end of each sermon on Sunday, and in your small groups, ask yourself, your brothers and sisters, and your family: "Do we believe this or not?" If we claim to believe what these six biblical texts are teaching us, then our lives and our congregations need to reflect that conviction in word and deed.

8. Lift up the hard questions where the truth must be told in your communities—because only the truth can set us free. What are the key issues from the book that need to be addressed and applied to the discussions, and debates, and decisions going on right now in your own communities, schools, workplaces, and political forums?

9. Decide, as a local pastor, to get to know some of those political and public decision makers from school boards to Washington, DC. Tell them who you are and why you are so concerned about the choices and decisions they are making. Impress upon them that these issues are matters of morality and faith that you would like to discuss with them.

10. For the longer term, ask what it would mean to begin a process, a way forward, with goals and timelines, to help develop a *civic discipleship* that would move us away from our current political trajectory of lies, fear, and violence and toward a public faith of truth, trust, and love. Let's find out what a practical politics of love might look like, and how a theology and spirituality of democracy could take us deeper than just partisan ideologies.

ADDITIONAL RESOURCES

God's Politics with Jim Wallis, on Substack: https://jimwallis.substack .com/.

My podcast, *Soul of the Nation,* available on iTunes or wherever you get your podcasts.

My website, www.jimwallis.org.

The Center on Faith and Justice at Georgetown University, https:// faithandjustice.georgetown.edu/.

The center focuses on four missions: uprooting systemic racism, building multiracial democracy, alleviating poverty, and peacemaking in the US and around the world. The center engages in direct advocacy, hosts public events, coordinates strategy sessions, convenes a weeklong Faith + Justice summer academy for seminarians and other academic programs throughout the year, while publishing regular opinion pieces, commentaries, and interviews for national media. Please sign up for the newsletter.

BIBLIOGRAPHY

Albright, Madeleine. *Fascism: A Warning.* New York: Harper, 2018.

Applebaum, Anne. *Twilight of Democracy: The Seductive Lure of Authoritarianism.* New York: Knopf Doubleday, 2021.

"A White Christian Nationalist Hotbed" with Jack Jenkins. *The Soul of the Nation with Jim Wallis* (podcast), March 29, 2023. https://www.audacy.com/podcast/the-soul-of-the-nation-with-jim-wallis-866b1/episodes/a-white-christian-nationalist-hotbed-f618a.

Balmer, Randall. *Bad Faith: Race and the Rise of the Religious Right.* Eerdmans, 2021.

Bonhoeffer, Dietrich. *Letters and Papers from Prison.* Minneapolis, MN: Fortress Press, 2015.

Bonhoeffer, Dietrich. *Life Together: The Classic Exploration of Christian Community.* New York: HarperOne, 1978.

Bonhoeffer, Dietrich. *The Cost of Discipleship.* New York: Touchstone, 1995.

Braunstein, Ruth. "The 'Right' History: Religion, Race, and Nostalgic Stories of Christian America." *Religions*, 2021, 12 (2), 95: https://doi.org/10.3390/rel12020095.

Desmond, Matthew. *Poverty, by America.* New York: Crown, 2023.

Douglass, Frederick. *Narrative of the Life of Frederick Douglass: The Original 1845 Edition.*

Dunkel, Tom. *White Knights in the Black Orchestra: The Extraordinary Story of the Germans Who Resisted Hitler.* New York: Hachette, 2022.

Emerson, Michael O. and Christian Smith. *Divided By Faith: Evangelical Religion and the Problem of Race in America.* New York: Oxford University Press, 2001.

Glaude, Eddie. *Begin Again: James Baldwin's America and Its Urgent Lessons for Our Own.* New York: Crown, 2021.

Gorski, Philip and Samuel Perry. *The Flag and the Cross: White Christian Nationalism and the Threat to American Democracy.* New York: Oxford University Press, 2022.

Gushee, David P. *Defending Democracy from Its Christian Enemies.* New York: Eerdmans, 2023.

Hedges, Chris. *American Fascists: The Christian Right and the War on America.* New York: Simon and Schuster, 2008.

"How to Talk to Kids About Race" featuring Jemar Tisby. *The Atlantic* (video), October 16, 2018. https://www.theatlantic.com/video/index/573184/talk-kids-race/.

"How White Christian Nationalism Threatens Democracy." Center on Faith and Justice, YouTube, November 3, 2022. https://www.youtube.com/watch?v=NH5LHQMVfH8.

Jenkins, Jack. "How Big Christian Nationalism Has Come Courting in North Idaho." Religion News Service. (February 2023): https://religionnews.com/2023/02/22/how-big-christian-nationalism-has-come-courting-in-north-idaho/.

Jones, Robert P. *The Hidden Roots of White Supremacy and the Path to a Shared American Future.* New York: Simon & Schuster, 2023.

Jones, Robert P. *White Too Long: The Legacy of White Supremacy in American Christianity.* New York: Simon & Schuster, 2020.

Kleinfeld, Rachel. "The Rise of Political Violence in the United States." *Journal of Democracy,* 32, no. 4, (October 2021): https://www.journalofdemocracy.org/articles/the-rise-of-political-violence-in-the-united-states/.

Kobes Du Mez, Kristin. *Jesus and John Wayne: How White Evangelicals Corrupted a Faith and Fractured a Nation.* New York: Liveright, 2020.

Levitsky, Steven and Daniel Ziblatt. *How Democracies Die.* New York: Crown, 2018.

Levitsky, Steven and Daniel Ziblatt. *Tyranny of the Minority: Why American Democracy Reached the Breaking Point.* New York: Crown, 2023.

McGhee, Heather. *The Sum of Us: What Racism Costs Everyone and How We Can Prosper Together.* New York: One World, 2021.

Miller, Paul D. *The Religion of American Greatness: What's Wrong with Christian Nationalism.* Westmont, IL: IVP Academic, 2022.

Nelson, Anne. *Shadow Network: Media, Money, and the Secret Hub of the Radical Right.* New York: Bloomsbury, 2019.

Paine, Thomas. *Common Sense.* Philadelphia, 1776.

Powers, Kirsten. *Saving Grace: Speak Your Truth, Stay Centered, and Learn to Coexist with People Who Drive You Nuts.* New York: Convergent Books, 2021.

Raskin, Jamie. *Unthinkable: Trauma, Truth, and the Trials of American Democracy.* New York: Harper, 2022.

Tisby, Jemar. *The Color of Change: The Truth About the American Church's Complicity in Racism.* Grand Rapids, MI: Zondervan, 2019.

Wallis, Jim. *America's Original Sin: Racism, White Privilege, and the Bridge to a New America.* Ada, MI: Brazos Press, 2016.

Warnock, Raphael. *A Way Out Of No Way: A Memoir of Truth, Transformation, and the New American Story.* New York: Penguin, 2022.

Whitehead, Andrew and Samuel Perry. *Taking America Back for God: Christian Nationalism in the United States.* New York: Oxford University Press, 2022.

Williams, Reggie L. *Bonhoeffer's Black Jesus: Harlem Renaissance Theology and an Ethic of Resistance.* Waco, TX: Baylor University Press, 2021.

Wills, Garry. *What Jesus Meant.* New York: Viking, 2006.

Wills, Garry. *What the Gospels Meant.* New York: Viking, 2008.

Tisby, Jemar. "Footnotes by Jemar Tisby." https://jemartisby.substack.com/.

PODCASTS

The Soul of the Nation with Jim Wallis:

The Historical Roots of White Christian Nationalism with Philip Gorski

Four Orientations Toward White Christian Nationalism with Andrew Whitehead

What a New Survey Reveals about White Christian Nationalism with Robert Jones

Evangelicals' Dangerous Amnesia with Ruth Braunstein

The Looming Threat of White Nationalist Political Violence with Rachel Kleinfeld

NOTES

INTRODUCTION: CROSSING THE COLOR LINE

1. Reggie L. Williams and Ferdinand Schlingensiepen, *Bonhoeffer's Black Jesus: Harlem Renaissance Theology and an Ethic of Resistance* (Waco, TX: Baylor University Press, 2021).

2. Bryan Stevenson, "Ep. 9: Bryan Stevenson," *Jim Wallis in Conversation*, July 6, 2018, https://podcasts.apple.com/us/podcast/jim-wallis-in-conversation/id1383855740.

1. THE FALSE WHITE GOSPEL

1. Samuel L. Perry, "Violence Isn't the Only Way Christian Nationalism Endangers Democracy," *Religion News Service*, January 5, 2022, https://religionnews.com/2022/01/05/violence-isnt-the-only-way-christian-nationalism-endangers-democracy/?fbclid=IwAR1OpCM9hZyuUiaGXrOrcEgfSyc4ayytGNUJ9d7iEvurBsw45P-HTGtEfnQ.

2. Cotton Mather and Increase Mather, *The Wonders of the Invisible World* (Scott's Valley, CA: CreateSpace Independent Publishing Platform, July 23, 2015).

3. Iveson Lewis Brookes, *A Defence of the South Against the Reproaches and Incroachments of the North* (Marrickville: Wentworth Press, 2016).

4. Jim Wallis, "The Historical Roots of White Christian Nationalism," *The Soul of the Nation*, November 23, 2022, https://podcasts.apple.com/us/podcast/the-historical-roots-of-white-christian-nationalism/id1282035947?i=1000587233003.

5. Jim Wallis, "How White Christian Nationalism Threatens Democracy," *The Soul of the Nation*, November 8, 2022, https://podcasts.apple.com/it/podcast/how-white-christian-nationalism-threatens-democracy/id1282035947?i=1000585588194.

6. Jim Wallis, "Four Orientations Toward White Christian Nationalism," *The Soul of the Nation*, December 7, 2022, https://podcasts.apple.com/us/podcast/four-orientations-toward-white-christian-nationalism/id1282035947?i=1000589189509.

7. Jemar Tisby, https://m.facebook.com/videos/critical-race-theory-part -2/1603177293376072/.

8. Jemar Tisby, religionnews.com/2019/05/01/why-white-nationalism -tempts-white-christians/.

9. Michael Gerson, "Opinion | 'Gaffes' Aside, I Once Assumed GOP Goodwill on Race. I Was Wrong," *The Washington Post,* October 20, 2022, https://www .washingtonpost.com/opinions/2022/10/20/gop-maga-trump-racism-white -grievance-strategy/.

10. Megan Trimble, "Trump White House Has Highest Turnover in 40 Years," *US and World Report News,* December 28, 2017, https://www.usnews.com/news /national-news/articles/2017–12–28/trumps-white-house-has-highest-turnover -rate-in-40-years.

11. David Brooks, "The Dissenters Trying to Save Evangelicalism From It-self," *The New York Times,* February 4, 2022, https://www.nytimes.com/2022 /02/04/opinion/evangelicalism-division-renewal.html.

12. Richard Quebedeaux, *The Young Evangelicals* (New York: Harper & Row, 1974).

13. "Chicago Declaration of Evangelical Social Concern," (Chicago, Illinois, November 25, 1973) https://canvas.dartmouth.edu/files/5264567/download ?download_frd=1.

14. Joel A. Carpenter, "Compassionate Evangelicalism," *Christianity Today,* December 1, 2003, https://www.christianitytoday.com/ct/2003/december/2 .40.html.

15. Randall Balmer, *Bad Faith: Race and the Rise of the Religious Right* (Grand Rapids, MI: Eerdmans, 2021).

16. C-SPAN, "Robert Jones on *The End of White Christian America,*" Wash-ington Journal (series), December 24, 2016, https://www.c-span.org/video /?419684–4/washington-journal-robert-jones-the-end-white-christian -america.

17. Tom Gjelten, "2020 Faith Vote Reflects 2016 Patterns," NPR, November 8, 2020, https://www.npr.org/2020/11/08/932263516/2020-faith-vote-reflects -2016-patterns.

18. Kristen Kobes Du Mez, https://www.goodreads.com/quotes/10425926 -for-conservative-white-evangelicals-the-good-news-of-the-christian.

19. Jim Wallis, "American Evangelism Is Destroying the Good News of Jesus," *Sojourners,* https://sojo.net/media/american-evangelism-destroying -good-news-jesus.

20. Jessica Taylor, "Trump Calls For 'Total and Complete Shutdown of Muslims Entering' U.S.," NPR, December 7, 2015, https://www.npr.org/2015 /12/07/458836388/trump-calls-for-total-and-complete-shutdown-of-muslims -entering-u-s.

21. Jim Wallis, "Why White Evangelicals Fell Hard for Donald Trump," *The Soul of the Nation,* July 6, 2022, https://podcasts.apple.com/us/podcast/why -white-evangelicals-fell-hard-for-donald-trump/id1282035947?i=1000571288299.

22. Frontline, "Lies, Politics and Democracy," September 6, 2022, https:// www.pbs.org/wgbh/frontline/documentary/lies-politics-and-democracy/.

23. U2 (@U2). 2021. "Bono: "As an Irishman, I've always believed America isn't just a country, it's an idea, one the whole world has a stake in. Lady Liberty's been bruised and battered these past four years . . ." Twitter, January 20, 2021, 1:50. https://twitter.com/U2/status/1351980461422211081.

24. Frederick Douglass, *Narrative of the Life of Frederick Douglass: An American Slave* (Boston, MA: Anti-Slavery Office, 1845).

2. YOUR NEIGHBOR DOESN'T LIVE NEXT DOOR

1. Diana Butler Bass, "Sunday Musings: View From the Ditch," Substack, July 10, 2022, https://dianabutlerbass.substack.com/p/sunday-musings-840.

2. Martin Luther King, Jr., "The Jericho Road" (speech, Atlanta, GA, July 1, 1962), Stanford University, https://kinginstitute.stanford.edu/king-papers /documents/draft-chapter-iii-being-good-neighbor.

3. Lee Smithey, "Martin Luther King, Jr. Day and Fixing the Jericho Road," Department of Peace and Conflict Studies at Swarthmore College, January 15, 2018, https://blogs.swarthmore.edu/academics/pcs/2018/01/15/martin-luther -king-jr-day-and-fixing-the-jericho-road/.

4. N. T. Wright, *Luke for Everyone* (Louisville, KY: Westminster John Knox Press, 2004), 128–129.

5. John Dominic Crossan, *The Power of Parable: How Fiction by Jesus Became Fiction about Jesus* (San Francisco, CA: HarperOne, 2013).

6. Howard Thurman and Vincent Harding, *Jesus and the Disinherited* (Boston, MA: Beacon Press, 1996).

7. David B. Growler and Kipton E. Jensen, *Sermons on the Parables* (Ossining, NY: Orbis Books, 2001), 47–56.

8. Michael Gerson, "Trump Should Fill Christians With Rage. How Come He Doesn't?" *The Washington Post,* September 1, 2022, https://www.washingtonpost .com/opinions/2022/09/01/michael-gerson-evangelical-christian-maga -democracy/.

9. Michael Gerson, "Opinion | 'Gaffes' Aside, I Once Assumed GOP Goodwill on Race. I Was Wrong," *The Washington Post,* October 20, 2022, https://www .washingtonpost.com/opinions/2022/10/20/gop-maga-trump-racism-white -grievance-strategy/.

10. Daniel Cox, Juhem Navarro-Rivera, Robert P. Jones, "Race, Religion, and Political Affiliation of Americans' Core Social Networks," PRRI, August

3, 2016, https://www.prri.org/research/poll-race-religion-politics-americans-social-networks/.

11.   Gustavo Gutierrez, *Seeds Of the Spirit: Wisdom of the Twentieth Century,* ed. Richard H. Bell and Barbara Battin (Louisville, KY: Westminster John Knox, 1995), 160.

12.   Lesley Kennedy, "How the 2000 Election Came Down to a Supreme Court Decision," History, November 4, 2020, https://www.history.com/news/2000-election-bush-gore-votes-supreme-court.

13.   Joe Biden, "Statement from President Joe Biden on the 20th Anniversary of the U.S. President's Emergency Plan for AIDS Relief (PEPFAR)," The White House, January 28, 2022, https://www.whitehouse.gov/briefing-room/statements-releases/2023/01/28/statement-from-president-joe-biden-on-the-20th-anniversary-of-the-u-s-presidents-emergency-plan-for-aids-relief-pepfar/.

14.   Adam B. Ellick, Jonah M. Kessel, and Nicholas Kristof, "In This Story, George W. Bush Is the Hero," *The New York Times,* March 21, 2023, https://www.nytimes.com/2023/03/21/opinion/george-bush-iraq-pepfar.html.

15.   Thurman and Harding, *Jesus and the Disinherited.*

3. MADE IN GOD'S IMAGE—OR NOT?

1. Jim Wallis, "How White Christian Nationalism Threatens Democracy," *The Soul of the Nation,* November 8, 2022, https://podcasts.apple.com/us/podcast/the-house-is-on-fire-democracy-under-attack/id1282035947?i=1000562295886.

2. Philip S. Gorski and Samuel L. Perry, *The Flag and the Cross: White Christian Nationalism and the Threat to American Democracy* (Oxford: Oxford University Press, 2022).

3. Kathleen Malloy, "Understanding Barriers to Voter Registration—And How to Fix Them," The Leadership Conference of Civil and Human Rights, September 28, 2021, https://civilrights.org/blog/understanding-barriers-to-voter-registration-and-how-to-fix-them/.

4. Samuel L. Perry, "Violence Isn't the Only Way Christian Nationalism Endangers Democracy," *Religion News Service,* January 5, 2022, https://religionnews.com/2022/01/05/violence-isnt-the-only-way-christian-nationalism-endangers-democracy/.

5. Walter Brueggeman, *Genesis: Interpretation: A Bible Commentary for Teaching and Preaching* (Atlanta: John Knox Press, 1982), 32–33.

6. Brueggemann, *Genesis,* 32.

7. John Blake, "An 'Imposter Christianity' Is Threatening American Democracy," CNN, July 24, 2022, https://www.cnn.com/2022/07/24/us/white-christian-nationalism-blake-cec/index.html.

8. Jacob Fabina, "Despite Pandemic Challenges, 2020 Election Had Largest Increase in Voting Between Presidential Elections on Record," United States Census Bureau, April 29, 2021, https://www.census.gov/library/stories/2021/04/record-high-turnout-in-2020-general-election.html.

9. Aaron Blake, "The Most Remarkable Rebukes of Trump's Legal Case: From the Judges He Hand-Picked," *The Washington Post,* December 14, 2020, https://www.washingtonpost.com/politics/2020/12/14/most-remarkable-rebukes-trumps-legal-case-judges-he-hand-picked/.

10. Amy Gardner, "A Majority of GOP Nominees Deny or Question the 2020 Election Results," *The Washington Post,* October 12, 2022, https://www.washingtonpost.com/nation/2022/10/06/elections-deniers-midterm-elections-2022/.

11. Jane C. Timm, "19 States Enacted Voting Restrictions in 2021. What's Next?" NBC News, December 21, 2021, https://www.nbcnews.com/politics/elections/19-states-enacted-voting-restrictions-2021-rcna8342.

12. The Associated Press, "N.C. Judges Strike Down A Voter ID Law They Say Discriminates Against Black Voters," NPR, September 17, https://www.npr.org/2021/09/17/1038354159/n-c-judges-strike-down-a-voter-id-law-they-say-discriminates-against-black-voter.

13. Stacey Abrams, "We've Got to Talk About Power," *Sojourners,* September/October 2020, https://sojo.net/magazine/septemberoctober-2020/stacey-abrams-we-ve-got-talk-about-power.

14. Brennan Center for Justice, "Voting Laws Roundup: December 2021," December 21, 2021, https://www.brennancenter.org/our-work/research-reports/voting-laws-roundup-december-2021.

15. Heidi Przybyla, "'It's Going to Be an Army': Tapes Reveal GOP Plan to Contest Elections," Politico, June 1, 2022, https://www.politico.com/news/2022/06/01/gop-contest-elections-tapes-00035758.

16. CNN, "4 Most Powerful Words in a Democracy Are 'The People Have Spoken,'" November 8, 2020, https://www.cnn.com/videos/politics/2020/11/08/raphael-warnock-georgia-runoff-senate-2020-race-kelly-loeffler-postelex-vpx.cnn.

4. LIES THAT DEMAND OUR LOYALTY

1. Kevin M. Kruse and Julian Zelizer, "How Policy Decisions Spawned Today's Hyperpolarized Media," *The Washington Post,* January 17, 2019, https://www.washingtonpost.com/outlook/2019/01/17/how-policy-decisions-spawned-todays-hyperpolarized-media/.

2. Tom Wright, *John for Everyone: Part 2* (Louisville, KY: Westminster John Knox Press, 2004), 122–123.

3. Tom Wright, *John for Everyone, Part 1* (Louisville, KY: Westminster John Knox Press, 2004), 123.

4. Tom Wright and Kristie Berglund, *John: 26 Studies for Individuals and Groups* (Westmont, IL: InterVarsity Press, 2009).

5. Amy Henderson, "That's The Way It Was: Remembering Walter Cronkite," *Smithsonian Magazine,* August 27, 2012, https://www.smithsonianmag.com /smithsonian-institution/thats-the-way-it-was-remembering-walter-cronkite -16465625/.

6. Sara Fischer, "Trust in News Collapses to Historic Low," Axios, July 8, 2022, https://www.axios.com/2022/07/08/news-republicans-democrats-trust -partisanship.

7. Jeffrey Gottfried, "Republicans Less Likely to Trust Their Main News Source if They See It as 'Mainstream'; Democrats More Likely," Pew Research Center, July 1, 2021, https://www.pewresearch.org/fact-tank/2021/07/01/republicans -less-likely-to-trust-their-main-news-source-if-they-see-it-as-mainstream -democrats-more-likely/.

8. Jeffrey Jones, "Trump Third Year Sets New Standard for Party Polarization," Gallup, January 21, 2020, https://news.gallup.com/poll/283910/trump -third-year-sets-new-standard-party-polarization.aspx.

9. Pew Research Center, "Partisan Antipathy: More Intense, More Personal," October 10, 2019, https://www.pewresearch.org/politics/2019/10/10/partisan -antipathy-more-intense-more-personal/.

10. Matthew Stanley et al., "Resistance to Position Change, Motivated Reasoning, and Polarization," *Political Behavior* 42, (2020): 891–913, https://link .springer.com/article/10.1007/s11109-019-09526-z.

11. Cass Sunstein, *#Republic: Divided Democracy in the Age of Social Media* (Princeton, NJ: Princeton University Press, 2018).

12. Karen Yourish et al., "Over 370 Republican Candidates Have Cast Doubt on the 2020 Election," *The New York Times,* October 13, 2022. https://www.nytimes .com/interactive/2022/10/13/us/politics/republican-candidates-2020-election -misinformation.html.

13. Jim Wallis, "Rep. Jamie Raskin: The Jan. 6 Investigation Will 'Blow the Roof Off the House,'" *The Soul of the Nation,* June 8, 2022, https://podcasts .apple.com/us/podcast/rep-jamie-raskin-the-jan-6-investigation-will-blow /id1282035947?i=1000565659536.

14. Thomas Paine, *Common Sense* (Carlisle, MA: Applewood Books, 2002).

15. Glenn Kessler, Salvador Rizzo, and Meg Kelly, "Trump's False or Misleading Claims Total 30,573 Over 4 Years," *The Washington Post,* January 4, 2021, https://www.washingtonpost.com/politics/2021/01/24/trumps-false-or -misleading-claims-total-30573-over-four-years/.

16. Steven Levitsky and Daniel Ziblatt, *How Democracies Die* (New York: Crown, 2018).

17. Nicole Gaudiano and Oma Seddiq, "Cassidy Hutchinson Testified That

Trump Told Mark Meadows 'I Don't Want People to Know That We Lost' 2020 Election Court Case," October 13, 2022, https://www.businessinsider .com/trump-cassidy-hutchinson-meadows-january-6-supreme-court-2020 -election-2022–10.

18.   Amanda Holpuch, "US Capitol's Last Breach Was More Than 200 Years Ago," *The Guardian,* January 6, 2021, https://www.theguardian.com/us-news /2021/jan/06/us-capitol-building-washington-history-breach.

19.   Charles Homans, "Out of the Barrel of a Gun," *The New York Times,* January 26, 2021, https://www.nytimes.com/interactive/2021/01/26/magazine /armed-militia-movement-gun-laws.html.

20.   Yvonne Wingett Sanchez, "Alone in Washington, Rusty Bowers Tells World What Happened in Arizona," *The Washington Post,* June 21, 2022, https:// www.washingtonpost.com/national-security/2022/06/21/rusty-bowers-jan-6/.

21.   Catie Edmonson, "'There Is Nowhere I Feel Safe': Election Officials Describe Threats Fueled by Trump," *The New York Times,* June 21, 2022, https:// www.nytimes.com/2022/06/21/us/politics/jan-6-trump-threats.html.

22.   David Graham, "January 6 Never Ended," *The Atlantic,* October 28, 2022, https://www.theatlantic.com/ideas/archive/2022/10/paul-pelosi-attack-nancy -pelosi-husband-january-6/671918/.

23.   Hannah Arendt, *The Origins of Totalitarianism* (San Diego, CA: Harcourt Brace Jovanovich, 1973).

24.   Brad Braxton, "Emancipation Proclamation Day and Juneteenth," The African American Lectionary, June 19, 2008, http://www.theafricanamericanlectionary .org/PopupLectionaryReading.asp?LRID=2.

25.   Federal Bureau of Investigation, "Statement on the FBI Response to the Shooting in Buffalo, New York," May 16, 2022, https://www.fbi.gov/news /press-releases/press-releases/statement-on-the-fbi-response-to-the-shooting -in-buffalo-new-york.

26.   Fox News, "Tucker: Why Would Biden Do This to His Own Country?" September 22, 2021, https://www.youtube.com/watch?v=Z_0iFBJPWoY&t=156s.

27.   Nancy Egan, "The Turner Diaries," Britannica, January 8, 2020, https:// www.britannica.com/topic/The-Turner-Diaries.

28.   David Folkenflik and Mary Yang, "Fox News Settles Blockbuster Defamation Lawsuit With Dominion Voting Systems," NPR, April 18, 2023, https:// www.npr.org/2023/04/18/1170339114/fox-news-settles-blockbuster-defamation -lawsuit-with-dominion-voting-systems.

29.   Donald Trump, "Executive Order on Combating Race and Sex Stereotyping," Trump White House, September 22, 2020, https://trumpwhitehouse.archives .gov/presidential-actions/executive-order-combating-race-sex-stereotyping/.

30.   PEN America 100, "Educational Gag Orders," https://pen.org/report /educational-gag-orders/.

31. Florida Government, "Governor DeSantis Announces Legislative Proposal to Stop W.O.K.E. Activism and Critical Race Theory in Schools and Corporations," December 15, 2021, https://www.flgov.com/2021/12/15/governor -desantis-announces-legislative-proposal-to-stop-w-o-k-e-activism-and-critical -race-theory-in-schools-and-corporations/.

32. Taiyler Simone Mitchell, "Gov. Glenn Youngkin Opposes Teaching Critical Race Theory Because 'We Shouldn't Play Privilege Bingo with Children,'" Business Insider, July 10, 2022, https://www.businessinsider.com/gov-glenn -youngkin-critical-race-theory-play-privilege-bingo-children-2022-7.

33. "DoSomething Banned Books List: Black History," https://www.dosomething .org/us/articles/banned-books-list.

34. Toria Barnhart, "Martin Luther King, Jr., Rosa Parks Books Among Those Banned in Penn. School District," Newsweek, September 20, 2021, https:// www.newsweek.com/martin-luther-king-jr-rosa-parks-books-among-those -banned-penn-school-district-1630953.

35. PEN America, "New Report: 2,500+ Book Bans Across 32 States During 2021–22 School Year," September 19, 2022, https://pen.org/press-release/new -report-2500-book-bans-across-32-states-during-2021–22-school-year/.

36. Elizabeth A. Harris and Alexandra Alter, "A Fast-Growing Network of Conservative Groups Is Fueling a Surge in Book Bans," The New York Times, January 10, 2023, https://www.nytimes.com/2022/12/12/books/book-bans -libraries.html.

37. Jon Meacham, "Can the Country Come to Terms With Its Original Sin?" The New York Times, January, 17, 2023, https://www.nytimes.com/2023/01/17 /books/review/american-inheritance-edward-larson.html.

38. Bryan Stevenson, "Ep. 9: Bryan Stevenson," Jim Wallis in Conversation.

39. Anders Anglesey, "Pastor Who Called Democrats 'Demons' Claims He Gave Up Tax-Exempt Status," Newsweek, May 24, 2022, https://www.newsweek .com/pastor-greg-locke-claims-he-gave-tax-exempt-status-church-1709615.

5. JESUS' FINAL TEST OF DISCIPLESHIP

1. https://www.youtube.com/watch?v=FgEtzEqppMw.

2. https://www.amazon.com/CEV-Poverty-Justice-Bible-American/dp /1585169730.

3. Donald Kraybill, The Upside-Down Kingdom (Harrisburg, PA: Herald Press, 2018).

4. Tom Wright, John for Everyone, Part 2: Chapters 11–21 (Louisville, KY: Westminster John Knox Press, 2004), 141.

5. Wright, John for Everyone, 143.

6. Albert Raboteau, "'The Least of These'—Martin Luther King's Advocacy

for the Poor," Huffington Post, January 16, 2011, https://www.huffpost.com/entry/roboteau-on-mlk_b_809347.

7. Albert Raboteau, "The Least of These," In Communion, Winter 2011, https://incommunion.org/2011/02/20/the-least-of-these/.

8. Albert Raboteau, "The Least of These," In Communion.

9. David B. Gowler and Kipton E. Jensen, *Sermons on the Parables* (Ossining, NY: Orbis Books, 2001).

10. David B. Gowler and Kipton E. Jensen, *Sermons*, 141.

11. https://oll.libertyfund.org/quote/st-augustine-states-that-kingdoms-without-justice-are-mere-robberies-and-robberies-are-like-small-kingdoms-but-large-empires-are-piracy-writ-large-5th-c.

12. Center on Poverty and Social Policy, "3.7 Million More Children in Poverty in Jan 2022 Without Monthly Child Tax Credit," February 17, 2022, https://www.povertycenter.columbia.edu/news-internal/monthly-poverty-january-2022.

13. Robin Cohen, Amy Cha, Emily Terlizzi, and Michael Martinez, "Health Insurance Coverage: Early Release of Estimates From the National Health Interview Survey, 2021," National Center for Health Statistics, https://www.cdc.gov/nchs/data/nhis/earlyrelease/insur202205.pdf.

14. National Low Income Housing Coalition, "The Problem," https://nlihc.org/explore-issues/why-we-care/problem.

15. CPI Inflation Calculator, "Value of $1 from 2009 to 2023," https://www.in2013dollars.com/us/inflation/2009?amount=1.

16. The National Association for the Advancement of Colored People, "Criminal Justice Fact Sheet," https://naacp.org/resources/criminal-justice-fact-sheet.

17. American Civil Liberties Union, "Mass Incarceration," https://www.aclu.org/issues/smart-justice/mass-incarceration/mass-incarceration-animated-series.

18. Wendy McMahan, "The Poor You Will Always Have With You—What Did Jesus Mean?" Food for the Hungry, https://www.fh.org/blog/poor-you-will-always-have-with-you-meaning/.

19. René Girard, *Deceit, Desire, and the Novel: Self and Other in Literary Structure*, trans. Yvonne Freccero (Baltimore, MD: Johns Hopkins University Press, 1965).

20. FBI National Press Office, "FBI Releases 2019 Hate Crime Statistics," Federal Bureau of Investigation, November 16, 2020, https://www.fbi.gov/news/press-releases/fbi-releases-2019-hate-crime-statistics.

21. Daniel Villarreal, "Hate Crimes Under Trump Surged Nearly 20 Percent Says FBI Report," *Newsweek*, November 16, 2020, https://www.newsweek.com/hate-crimes-under-trump-surged-nearly-20-percent-says-fbi-report-1547870.

22. Faiza Patel, "The Islamophobic Administration," Brennan Center for

Justice, April 19, 2017, https://www.brennancenter.org/our-work/research-reports/islamophobic-administration.

23. Michael Wines, "'Looting' Comment From Trump Dates Back to Racial Unrest of the 1960s," *The New York Times,* May 29, 2020, https://www.nytimes.com/2020/05/29/us/looting-starts-shooting-starts.html.

24. Arecelli Crew, "FBI: Hate Crimes Against Latinos Increased More Than 8% in 2019," The Americano, November 19, 2020, https://theamericanonews.com/2020/11/18/hate-crimes-latinos/.

25. "Sen. Booker on 'Radical' Faith and Its Role in Civic Spaces," *Sojourners,* November 20, 2019, https://sojo.net/articles/sen-cory-booker-radical-faith-and-its-role-civic-spaces.

26. Jeff Stein, Josh Dawsey, and Isaac Arnsdorf, "The Former Trump Aide Crafting the House GOP's Debt Ceiling Playbook," *The Washington Post,* February 19, 2023, https://www.washingtonpost.com/us-policy/2023/02/19/russ-vought-republican-debt-ceiling-strategy/.

27. Zach Schonfeld, "Child Poverty Fell by 46 Percent in 2021 Amid Tax Credit Expansion," *The Hill,* September 13, 2022, https://thehill.com/policy/finance/3641094-child-poverty-fell-by-46-percent-in-2021-amid-tax-credit-expansion/.

28. Kalee Burns, Liana Fox, and Danielle Wilson, "Child Poverty Fell to Record Low 5.2% in 2021," United States Census Bureau, September 13, 2022, https://www.census.gov/library/stories/2022/09/record-drop-in-child-poverty.html

29. Center on Poverty and Social Policy, "December Child Tax Credit Kept 3.7 Million Children From Poverty," January 20, 2022, https://www.povertycenter.columbia.edu/news-internal/monthly-poverty-december-2021.

30. Matthew Desmond, *Poverty, by America* (New York: Crown, 2023).

31. Dave Davies, "Private Opulence, Public Squalor: How the U.S. Helps the Rich and Hurts the Poor," NPR, March 21, 2023, https://www.npr.org/sections/health-shots/2023/03/21/1164275807/poverty-by-america-matthew-desmond-inequality

32. Feeding America, "Hunger and Poverty in America," https://www.feedingamerica.org/hunger-in-america/poverty.

33. National Center for Homeless Education, "Student Homelessness in America," https://nche.ed.gov/wp-content/uploads/2021/12/Student-Homelessness-in-America-2021.pdf.

34. "Matthew Desmond on America's 'Sinful' Treatment of Poor People," *The Soul of the Nation with Jim Wallis,* May 10, 2023, https://podcasts.apple.com/dk/podcast/matthew-desmond-on-americas-sinful-treatment-of-poor/id1282035947?i=1000612456723.

6. PEACEMAKERS, NOT CONFLICT MAKERS

1. Rachel Treisman, "Many Midterm Races Focus on Rising Crime. Here's What the Data Does and Doesn't Show," NPR, October 28, 2022, https://www.npr.org/2022/10/27/1131825858/us-crime-data-midterm-elections.

2. Alan Feuer, "As Right-Wing Rhetoric Escalates, So Do Threats and Violence," *The New York Times,* August 13, 2022, https://www.nytimes.com/2022/08/13/nyregion/right-wing-rhetoric-threats-violence.html.

3. Cornelius Plantinga Jr., *Not the Way It's Supposed to Be: A Breviary of Sin* (Grand Rapids, MI: Eerdmans, 1996), 9–10.

4. Jim Wallis, "The Peacemaker Question: The Difference in Loving and Making Peace," *Sojourners,* November 14, 2019, https://sojo.net/articles/peacemaker-question-difference-loving-and-making-peace.

5. Daniel Berrigan, *No Bars to Manhood: A Powerful, Personal Statement on Radical Confrontation with Contemporary Society* (Eugene, Oregon: Wipf and Stock, 2007).

6. The United States Department of Justice, "Justice Department Announces Closing of Investigation into 2014 Officer Involved Shooting in Cleveland, Ohio," December 29, 2020, https://www.justice.gov/opa/pr/justice-department-announces-closing-investigation-2014-officer-involved-shooting-cleveland.

7. James Bouie, "Where American Democracy Isn't Very Democratic," *The New York Times,* February, 3, 2023, https://www.nytimes.com/2023/02/03/opinion/police-violence-democracy.html.

8. Drew Desilver, Michael Lipka, and Dalia Fahmy, "10 Things We Know About Race and Policing in the U.S.," Pew Research Center, June 3, 2020, https://www.pewresearch.org/fact-tank/2020/06/03/10-things-we-know-about-race-and-policing-in-the-u-s/.

9. Emma Pierson et al., "A Large-Scale Analysis of Racial Disparities in Police Stops Across the United States," *Nature* 4, no. 7 (2020): 736–745.

10. Craig Palosky, "Poll: 7 in 10 Black Americans Say They Have Experienced Incidents of Discrimination or Police Mistreatment in Their Lifetime, Including Nearly Half Who Felt Their Lives Were in Danger," Kaiser Family Foundation, June 18, 2020, https://www.kff.org/racial-equity-and-health-policy/press-release/poll-7-in-10-black-americans-say-they-have-experienced-incidents-of-discrimination-or-police-mistreatment-in-lifetime-including-nearly-half-who-felt-lives-were-in-danger/.

11. "Fatal Force," *The Washington Post,* October 3, 2021, https://www.washingtonpost.com/graphics/investigations/police-shootings-database/.

12. Ella Baker, https://www.goodreads.com/quotes/1329988-until-the-killing-of-black-men-black-mothers-sons-becomes.

13. United States Sentencing Commission, "Demographic Differences

in Sentencing," November 14, 2017, https://www.ussc.gov/research/research -reports/demographic-differences-sentencing.

14.   National Registry of Exonerations, "Race and Wrongful Convictions in the United States 2022," University of Michigan, September 2022, https:// www.law.umich.edu/special/exoneration/Documents/Race%20Report%20 Preview.pdf.

15.   Samuel Gross, Maurice Possley, and Klara Stephen, "Race and Wrongful Convictions in the United States," National Registry of Exonerations, March 7, 2017, https://www.law.umich.edu/special/exoneration/Documents/Race_and _Wrongful_Convictions.pdf.

16.   American Civil Liberties Union, "Race and the Death Penalty," https:// www.aclu.org/other/race-and-death-penalty.

17.   American Psychological Association, "Incarceration Nation," October 2014, https://www.apa.org/monitor/2014/10/incarceration.

18.   NAACP, "Criminal Justice Fact Sheet," https://naacp.org/resources /criminal-justice-fact-sheet.

19.   Evelyn J. Patterson, "The Dose–Response of Time Served in Prison on Mortality: New York State, 1989–2003," *American Journal of Public Health,* 103, no. 3 (2013): 523–528.

20.   "Ep. 9: Bryan Stevenson," *Jim Wallis in Conversation,* https://sojo.net /media/ep-9-bryan-stevenson.

21.   Tori Otten, "Nashville Rep. Andy Ogles Still Hasn't Taken Down This Horrific Instagram Post After School Shooting," *The New Republic,* March 29, 2023, https://newrepublic.com/post/171466/nashville-rep-andy-ogles-horrific -instagram-post-school-shooting.

22.   Steve Benen, "New Republican Bill Would Make the AR-15 the 'National Gun,'" MSNBC, February 23, 2023, https://www.msnbc.com/rachel-maddow -show/maddowblog/new-republican-bill-make-ar-15-national-gun-rcna72143.

23.   The Gun Violence Archive, "Mass Shootings in 2022," https://www .gunviolencearchive.org/reports/mass-shooting?year=2022.

24.   Michael Levenson, "Parents Were Asked for DNA Samples to Help Iden- tify Victims," *The New York Times,* May 25, 2022, https://www.nytimes.com /2022/05/25/us/texas-shooting-parents-dna-victims.html.

25.   Kate McGee and Jolie McCullough, "Confronted with Mass Shootings, Texas Republicans Have Repeatedly Loosened Gun Laws," *The Texas Tribune,* May 24, 2022, https://www.texastribune.org/2022/05/24/texas-gun-laws-uvalde -mass-shootings/.

26.   Mike Lillis, "Partisan Divide on Guns Just Grows Larger With Each Tragedy," *The Hill,* June 4, 2022, https://thehill.com/homenews/house/3511605 -partisan-divide-on-guns-just-grows-larger-with-each-tragedy/.

27. Monique Beals, "88 Percent in New Poll Support Background Checks on All Gun Sales," *The Hill*, April 26, 2022, https://thehill.com/homenews/state-watch/3502285–88-percent-in-new-poll-support-background-checks-on-all-gun-sales/.

28. Charles DiMaggio et al., "Changes in US Mass Shooting Deaths Associated With the 1994–2004 Federal Assault Weapons Ban: Analysis of Open-Source Data," *The Journal of Trauma and Acute Care Surgery*, 86, no. 1 (2019): 11–19.

29. Ahmed, Saeed, "It's 19 Weeks Into the Year and America Has Already Seen 198 Mass Shootings," NPR, November 20, 2022, https://www.npr.org/2022/05/15/1099008586/mass-shootings-us-2022-tally-number.

30. Don Beyer, "Gun Companies are Making Millions at the Expense of American Lives," Joint Economic Committee Democrats, https://www.jec.senate.gov/public/_cache/files/9bfdef03–67b9–49d3–8252–23f7b90a01d6/jec-gun-industry-profits-final.pdf.

31. George Wright and Matt Murphy, "Congress Passes First Gun Control Bill in Decades," BBC News, June 24, 2022, https://www.bbc.com/news/world-us-canada-61919752.

32. Jim Wallis, "The New Gun-Safety Law Is Good, but It's Just a Start. Here's What We Need to Do Now," Substack, July 14, 2022, https://jimwallis.substack.com/p/the-new-gun-safety-law-is-good-but.

33. District of Columbia v. Heller, 554 US 570 (2008).

34. Eric Levenson, Isabelle Chapman, Andy Rose, Shimon Prokupecz and Claire Colbert, "Uvalde School Shooting Suspect Was a Loner Who Bought Two Assault Rifles for His 18th Birthday," CNN, May 27, 2022, https://www.cnn.com/2022/05/25/us/uvalde-texas-school-shooting-salvador-ramos/index.html.

35. Glenn Thrush and Matt Richtel, "A Disturbing New Pattern in Mass Shootings: Young Assailants," *The New York Times*, June 2, 2022, https://www.nytimes.com/2022/06/02/us/politics/mass-shootings-young-men-guns.html.

36. John Gramlich, "What the Data Says About Gun Deaths in the U.S.," Pew Research Center, February 3, 2022, https://www.pewresearch.org/fact-tank/2022/02/03/what-the-data-says-about-gun-deaths-in-the-u-s/.

37. Glenn Kessler, "Biden's Startling Statistic on School-Age Gun Deaths," *The Washington Post,* June 7, 2022, https://www.washingtonpost.com/politics/2022/06/07/bidens-startling-statistic-school-age-gun-deaths/.

38. Garry Wills, "Our Moloch," *The New York Review of Books,* December 15, 2012, https://www.nybooks.com/online/2012/12/15/our-moloch/.

39. "Heeding God's Call to End Gun Violence," https://www.heedinggodscall.org/.

40. "Episode 5: Brittany Packnett," *Jim Wallis in Conversation,* June 8, 2018, https://podcasts.apple.com/sn/podcast/ep-5-brittany-packnett/id1383855740?i=1000413294339.

7. OUR COMMUNITY IS NOT A TRIBE

1. Michel Martin, "Slave Bible From The 1800s Omitted Key Passages That Could Incite Rebellion," NPR, December 9, 2018, https://www.npr.org/2018/12/09/674995075/slave-bible-from-the-1800s-omitted-key-passages-that-could-incite-rebellion.

2. Darius Jankiewicz, "Hermeneutics of Slavery: A 'Bible-Alone' Faith and the Problem of Human Enslavement," *Journal of Adventist Mission Studies,* 12 (1) (2016), 47–73.

3. Martin Luther King, Jr., "'For All . . . A Non-Segregated Society,' A Message for Race Relations Sunday," The Martin Luther King, Jr., Research and Education Institute, February 10, 1957, https://kinginstitute.stanford.edu/king-papers/documents/all-non-segregated-society-message-race-relations-sunday.

4. Jim Wallis, "Eddie Glaude Uncovers 'The Heart of the Rot' in America's White Supremacy," *The Soul of the Nation,* June 22, 2022, https://podcasts.apple.com/us/podcast/eddie-glaude-uncovers-the-heart-of-the-rot-in/id1282035947?i=1000567383668.

5. PRRI Staff, "A Christian Nation? Understanding the Threat of Christian Nationalism to American Democracy and Culture," PRRI, February 8, 2023, https://www.prri.org/research/a-christian-nation-understanding-the-threat-of-christian-nationalism-to-american-democracy-and-culture/.

6. Paul Jewett, *Man as Male and Female: A Study in Sexual Relationships from a Theological Point of View* (Grand Rapids, MI: William B. Eerdmans Publishing Company, 1990).

7. "Introduction to the Book of Galatians," *ESV Study Bible* (Wheaton, IL: Crossway, 2008).

8. Jakobus M. Vorster, (2019), "The Theological-Ethical Implications of Galatians 3:28 for a Christian Perspective on Equality as a Foundational Value in the Human Rights Discourse," In die Skriflig / In *Luce Verbi.* 53 (1): 8.

9. Stephen J. Patterson, *The Forgotten Creed: Christianity's Original Struggle against Bigotry, Slavery, and Sexism* (Oxford: Oxford University Press, 2018).

10. Jeffrey Jones, "U.S. Church Membership Falls Below Majority for First Time," Gallup, March 21, 2021, https://news.gallup.com/poll/341963/church-membership-falls-below-majority-first-time.aspx.

11. David Campbell, Geoffrey Layman, and John Green, *Secular Surge: A New Fault Line in American Politics* (Cambridge: Cambridge University Press, 2020).

12. Jim Wallis, "Evangelicals' Dangerous Amnesia," *The Soul of the Nation,* March 1, 2023, https://podcasts.apple.com/us/podcast/evangelicals-dangerous -amnesia/id1282035947?i=100060226907.

13. Bruce Hansen, *"All of You are One": The Social Vision of Gal 3.28, 1 Cor 12.13 and Col 3.11* (New York: T & T Clark, 2010).

14. Gabriella Borter, Joseph Ax, and Joseph Tanfani, "School Boards Get Death Threats Amid Rage Over Race, Gender, Mask Policies," Reuters, February 15, 2022, https://www.reuters.com/investigates/special-report/usa-education -threats/.

15. Dan Farmer, Nathan Lee, and Joel Day, "High Rates of Harassment and Threats May Deter Entry Into Local Politics," Civic Pulse, December 14, 2022, https://www.civicpulse.org/post/high-rates-of-harassment-and-threats-may -deter-entry-into-local-politics.

16. Moira Warburton and Jason Lange, "Exclusive: Two in Five U.S. Voters Worry About Intimidation at Polls-Reuters/Ipsos," October 26, 2022, https://www .reuters.com/world/us/exclusive-two-five-us-voters-worry-about-intimidation -polls-reutersipsos-2022–10–26/.

17. Rocio Fabbro, "Election Officials Combat Voter Intimidation Across U.S. as Extremist Groups Post Armed Militia at Some Polls," CNBC, November 6, 2022, https://www.cnbc.com/2022/11/06/election-officials-facing-armed -militia-presence-at-some-polls.html.

18. Isaac Arnsdorf, "Oath Keepers in the State House: How a Militia Movement Took Root in the Republican Mainstream," ProPublica, Oct. 20, 2021, https://www.propublica.org/article/oath-keepers-in-the-state-house-how-a -militia-movement-took-root-in-the-republican-mainstream.

19. Rachel Kleinfeld, "The Rise of Political Violence in the United States," *Journal of Democracy,* 32, no, 4, (2021): 160–176.

20. Jim Wallis, "The Looming Threat of White Nationalist Political Violence," *Soul of the Nation,* March 15, 2023, https://podcasts.apple.com/us/podcast/the -looming-threat-of-white-nationalist/id1282035947?i=1000604278640.

21. Press Release, "GW Politics Poll Shows Lack of Trust by Republicans in Biden Won States," George Washington School of Media & Public Affairs, July 26, 2021, https://smpa.gwu.edu/gw-politics-poll-shows-lack-trust-republicans -biden-won-states.

22. Rachel Kleinfeld, "American Democracy is Dodging Bullets," *The Hill,* January 20, 2023, https://thehill.com/opinion/campaign/3820637-american -democracy-is-dodging-bullets/.

23. Victoria Wolcott, "The Forgotten History of Segregated Swimming Pools and Amusement Parks," The Conversation, July 9, 2019, https://theconversation .com/the-forgotten-history-of-segregated-swimming-pools-and-amusement -parks-119586.

24. Jim Wallis, "Heather McGhee on the True Cost of Racism," *The Soul of the Nation,* July 15, 2021, https://podcasts.apple.com/us/podcast/the-soul-of-the-nation-with-jim-wallis/id1282035947.

25. Jim Wallis, "Evangelicals' Dangerous Amnesia," *The Soul of the Nation.*

26. Jim Wallis, "Eddie Glaude Uncovers 'The Heart of the Rot' in America's White Supremacy," *The Soul of the Nation.*

27. Eddie Glaude Jr., *Begin Again: James Baldwin's America and its Urgent Lessons for Our Own.* (New York: Random House, 2020).

28. Eddie S. Glaude, Jr., https://www.theatlantic.com/ideas/archive/2020/07/why-we-need-begin-again/614326/.

29. Abraham Lincoln Online, "Lyceum Address," https://www.abrahamlincolnonline.org/lincoln/speeches/lyceum.htm.

30. Eric Foner, *The Fiery Trial: Abraham Lincoln and American Slavery* (New York: W. W. Norton & Company, 2010), 27.

8. A REMNANT CHURCH

1. Kyle Meyaard-Schaap, https://www.cnn.com/2020/09/29/opinions/young-evangelicals-fight-climate-change-and-trump-meyaard-schaap/index.html.

2. Ruth Graham, https://www.nytimes.com/2023/02/20/us/evangelical-leaders-progressive-jim-wallis-kyle-meyaard-schaap.html.

3. Matthew Harrison, "President Harrison Denounces Disturbing Ideologies," Reporter, February 21, 2023, https://reporter.lcms.org/2023/president-harrison-denounces-disturbing-ideologies/.

4. Jim Wallis, "Episode 5: Brittany Packnett," *Jim Wallis in Conversation.*

5. Jim Wallis, "Kirsten Powers on Loving Your (Political) Enemies," *The Soul of the Nation,* July 6, 2022, https://podcasts.apple.com/us/podcast/kirsten-powers-on-loving-your-political-enemies/id1282035947?i=1000569043292.

6. Kirsten Powers, *Saving Grace: Speak Your Truth, Stay Centered, and Learn to Coexist with People Who Drive You Nuts* (Colorado Springs, CO: Convergent, 2021).

INDEX

Politico, 87

politics. *See also* authoritarianism/
    autocracy; fascism
  of love, 75–8
  separation of church and state in,
    37, 90, 225
  white Christian nationalism as
    tool of, 14, 18–9, 25–41, 44,
    58–62, 198, 229–31, 232–3
  white grievance as strategy in, 18,
    22, 25, 61, 107
poll chaplains, 88–91, 223
poverty, 2
  child tax credit and, 131, 145–6
  as Christianity focus, 6, 13, 28,
    33, 45–6, 54, 69–70, 85, 116–52,
    209, 231–2
  federal spending on, 143–7
  and income inequality, 135, 147–8
  scapegoating of, 136–9
  as violence factor, 163
  voter suppression and, 79
The Poverty and Justice Bible, 121
Poverty, by America (Desmond),
    147–8
Powers, Kirsten, 226–7
Presbyterian Church, 1, 89, 205
President's Emergency Plan for
    AIDS Relief (PEPFAR), 70–1
prosperity gospel, 124, 132, 215
Protestant Church, 77, 135, 143,
    213
Proud Boys, 102, 104
Proverbs 19:17, 119
proximity, as counter to "othering,"
    5–8, 62–5, 146, 148, 162, 222
Psalm 34, 157
public discipleship, 13–4, 27, 215,
    222
Public Religion Research Institute
    (PRRI), 62, 183

QAnon, 60, 192

Raboteau, Albert, 126–8
racism, 31
  by Christians, historic, xiii–xvi,
    1–12, 13, 19–24, 38, 46, 211
  by Christians, white Nationalist,
    xv, 2–5, 10–1, 15–8, 22–4, 25–7,
    34–5, 40–4, 46, 59, 61, 182, 186,
    196–200, 208–11, 225–6
  in Confederate symbols, 60, 91,
    154
  at core of fascism, 102–5
  in criminal justice system, 9, 10,
    85, 88, 134, 163, 169–71, 219
  in economic policy, 9
  education about, 24, 60, 109–14,
    192, 222, 247
  evangelical declaration on,
    28–30
  at expense of economic interests,
    196–200
  and hate crimes, 106, 136–7
  in immigration policy, 10, 22, 25,
    34–5, 61, 66, 124, 126, 137–41
  Jim Crow, xv, 8–12, 87, 204, 214
  via lynching, 113–4, 214
  Matthew 25 group against,
    139–43
  and path forward, 200–6
  in policing, 7–8, 9, 85, 141–2, 163,
    164–9, 219, 223, 226
  and scapegoating, 136–8
  via segregation, 17, 32, 56, 63, 77,
    182, 196–8, 222
  via slavery, xiii–xv, 10, 19, 20,
    21–4, 41–3, 60–2, 80–1, 96,
    105–6, 109–12, 192, 204–5, 211,
    222, 247
  systemic, 64, 110, 148, 163–4, 200,
    202